THE HISTORY OF PUERTO RICO IDENTITY FORMATION AND NATIONALISM

By Val Karanxha

HELIOS PUBLISHING
The History of Puerto Rico, Identity Formation and
Nationalism

ABOUT THE AUTHOR
Val Karanxha is an Adjunct Professor at Western
Connecticut State University and the author of *The
History of Puerto Rico, Identity Formation and
Nationalism. Colombia: Surviving the Failed State,
and Identity in Spirituality, the Book about Self.* She
is a contributing author with Rutledge Publications
and a five-time Yale New - Haven Teacher Institute
fellow.

Contents

INTRODUCTION

THE INTENSE CULTURAL NATIONALISM WITHOUT THE PRESENCE OF A NATION-STATE

When one reads the intense stream of news about Puerto Rico, it is easy to create the impression that people on the island are firmly opposed to its present status and the political relationship with the US. Formally, Puerto Rico is an Associated State (Estado Asociado), yet the constitutional rights of US citizens do not fully apply to the island. Unless they move to the mainland US, Puerto Rican people cannot vote in the general elections, nor do they have representation in the US Congress with voting power. A cursory evaluation of the latest political and electoral campaigns on the island shows that Puerto Rican people use conventional and democratic ways of political mobilization, explicitly advocating for the independence of Puerto Rico - through elections and political representation. Among such methods of political engagement was the campaign "Juntos por la Independencia" in 2016, led by the Puerto Rican Independence Party.

One remarkable, common thread of these periodical campaigns is the stagnancy of the defining rhetoric since the 1950's. Typical of these earlier nationalistic bursts was the incident that happened in April 1999. A US Navy bomb detonated on the island of Vieques, Puerto Rico. The bomb accidentally killed one and wounded four other people. The incident was widely covered by the Puerto Rican and US mainstream media, awakening a nationalist sentiment against the US. Various nationalist groups and activists immediately reacted, and in May 1999, a group of Puerto Rican protesters challenged the authorities by crossing the parameters of the US Naval Base. The activists made territorial claims against the US military presence and demanded that the base leave the island. Four years later, in 2003, after a prolonged anti-US campaign that was marked by many arrests, civil disobedience, anti-colonial protesting, and international pressure, the US Navy withdrew from Nena Island.[1] The independence and nationalist proponents were at the forefront of the protests, and several of them - not unknown to the public - were among those arrested.[2] Considering this angle, it seems that the nationalist and independence movement that was so intense in the 1950s is still alive and strong.

There is another side to the Puerto Rican identity that is firmly based on nationalism. Since 1995, the Puerto Rican diaspora in the mainland United States has celebrated the Puerto Rican Day Parade every second week in June. They do so with buoyancy, flags, dances, and nationalist symbols. The event is one of the most exuberant manifestations of Puerto Rican cultural nationalism of the diaspora in the US. Nowhere is the Puerto Rican nationalist sentiment more evident than in New York City. In short, Puerto Ricans remain fierce nationalists, acutely aware of and very proud of their own national identity.

This paradox is quite challenging to explain in the theories of nationalism. For instance, the most exuberant shows of cultural nationalism in the United States are the Puerto Rican Day Parades and el Dia de la Puertorriqueñidad in Puerto Rico. Yet, regardless of the nationalist flares and the enthusiasm of the parades, Puerto Rican people have always drifted away from the independence option on the ballot when it decides the political status. Whenever the opportunity arose to make Puerto Rico an independent country, the people of Puerto Rico have preferred the status quo. The startling evidence of this discrepancy is that less than three percent of the people vote pro-independence in referendums and elections. Instead, most Puerto Rican voters vote for a *free state associated with the United States*, preserving the status quo.

This collective behavior runs against everything that theories of the nation tell us and what a nation and nationalists should do when it comes to nation-state building. Nationalism is an ideology based on the assumption that a nation, culturally defined, would always search for a state. Hence, we face an essential paradox that becomes a challenging argument when considered by various theoretical frameworks. Why are the people of Puerto Rico fervent nationalists, yet they continue to vote against a Puerto Rican Republic or a Puerto Rican nation-state? Puerto Rico represents a critical case study and a puzzle that needs to be evaluated against the theories of nationalism.

The core and traditional theories of nation-formation and theories of identity formation do not offer convincing explanations for this paradox. I argue that the rationale lies in the history of Puerto Rico going back to the early establishment of the Spanish colonial administration. The paradigms downplay the specific path-dependent process of Puerto Rican identity formation. They downplay the strong effect of the institutional imperial legacy and the leading role of the insular elites in manipulating and morphing the identity of Puerto Ricans. The results of the policies pursued by the state and the elites become clearer at critical points and eras, such as, for example, the 1950's politics on the island. The failure to properly appreciate the historical confluences and the effort to make the Puerto Rican case fit the theoretical templates has led to an impasse.

The core and traditional theories of nation-formation only partially explain this dichotomy. I argue that the rationale lies in the history of Puerto

Rico, going back to the early establishment of the Spanish colonial administration. The paradigms downplay the specific path-dependent process of Puerto Rican identity formation. They downplay the institutional imperial legacy, its strong effect, and the insular elites' leading role in manipulating and morphing the identity of Puerto Ricans. The results of the policies pursued by the state and the elites become clearer at critical points and eras, such as the 1950's politics on the island.

The core claim of this book is that Puerto Rico is the outcome of distinct imperial policies that shaped its identity. The US takeover in 1898 became critical regarding preserving the imperial identity or embracing the North American identity and culture. In their effort to maintain their control over Puerto Rico, the local nationalist elites embraced the nation-state's idea to block assimilation attempts by promoting a Puerto Rican national identity. This political objective became divisive, clashing between the elite clusters competing for power. One cluster of Puerto Rican elites supported independence from the United States. The other cluster promoted cultural nationalism within the United States. Hence, in their political discourse, the other was the United States for both clusters. This power struggle leads to the fundamental premise of the book. The conflict between *self and others* becomes essential to preserving one's identity. The result, in this case, was prompted by the leadership in the diaspora, which sided with *the other* and became the existential threat to the presumed shared national Puerto Rican identity.

The Puerto Rican National Identity Formation: frameworks, theories, and arguments

All efforts to examine the evolution of the Puerto Rican national identity must consider at least two unique perspectives. First, it is the set of frameworks offered by the leading scholars of nationalism, such as Smith, Anderson, and Gellner. Their approaches provide various interpretations to conceptualize and analyze the theories of a nation. The other perspectives and explanations about Puerto Rican identity formation are offered more exclusively by Stuart Hall, Jorge Duany, and Jose Luis Gonzalez. Jorge Duany has carefully treated the identity path of the Puerto Rican people by creating a mental image of a nation on the move. He argues that Puerto Rico is indeed a nation, but a nation on the move. Paradoxically, nations on the move do not have a nation-state project, nor are they willing to establish an independent state. In this case, we have to look at the dichotomy. Is Puerto Rico a cultural nation or a political nation? This puzzle has been on the table for many years and is fraught with many complexities. Reiterating the same debate does not remove the importance of cultural nationalism and the strong sense of identity, au contraire. As long as the sense of identity exists, a nation will always be defined by its culture, tradition, shared historical territory, etc.

There is a coherence between the works of Jacqueline Guzman Font, Jorge Duany, Juan Manuel Carrion, and Arlene Davila in how Puerto Rican identity travels with nationalism, especially throughout the 20th century after the US takeover. These authors deal with identity, nationalism, national identity, and citizenship. Symbiotically, nationalism and identity are closely related, and the researchers who have dealt with nationalism in Puerto Rico seem to agree that at the foundation of Puerto Rican nationalism, there is a strong mindfulness of the Puerto Rican identity. Thus, in this book, I examine how these perspectives and views explain the evolution of Puerto Rican national identity.

The Perennialist Approach: Strong cultural nationalism but without an ethnicity and not searching for a state

Puerto Rico has a compelling case of cultural nationalism that seeks an independent state. Most primordialists, perennialists, or even ethno-symbolists would argue that ethnicity is necessary, as it is the desire to attain a nation-state. For example, Anthony D. Smith explains that there are three fundamental ideas at the core of nationalism as an ideological movement. These core beliefs are national autonomy, national unity, and national ideology.[3] Smith claims that for every nation to have its state, it must be able to express its autonomy fully in a multifaceted way. Primarily, autonomy means freedom to decide and regulate on behalf of oneself without any constraints from external sources, and this is a pre-condition for self-determination movements. More importantly, autonomy means political freedom and collective self-rule by the people.

Nationalism is tied to the state as well. Smith seems to use Weber's idea of the nation-state's emergence. Thus, the core belief of an etatist interpretation emphasizes the emergence of a state as an instrument to guarantee the nation's continuity. Without a country – a nation will assimilate or attach itself elsewhere. Weber cites, "A nation is a community of sentiment that would adequately manifest itself in a state of its own; hence, a nation is a community which normally intends to produce a state of its own." [4] Secondly, national unity is a broader term beyond a subtle or abstract understanding of national unification.

According to Smith, national unity is a concrete and inclusive term. It comprises ideological unity embedded in a unified culture and territorial, political, and economic unity. Among others, unity – not to be confused with homogeneity nor uniformity – is an essential social and cultural unification of the nation's members; a unison instead, more so than likeness. Thirdly, national identity is none other than the collective character that a nation or people in a nation must have.[5] More importantly, for Smith, the national identity cannot be limited to mere sociological constructs inherited by primordialism. Nations are a living concept; as such, they evolve by following their path and carving their past, traditions, and customs into the present.

Hence, defining Puerto Rican nationalism from the perennial perspective is somewhat tricky.[6] The distinct and presumably shared identity is a claim that Puerto Rican people put forth with great enthusiasm and pride. As Segal 1994 argues, not all myths about national identity emphasize homogeneity.[7] Due to the colonization process and the arrival of many transplanted populations, nationalism in the New World, particularly in the Caribbean, embraces ancestral diversity. This can be true for countries like Colombia, where clusters of indigenous people, African ancestry, and mixed races (mestizos) are still segregated in certain areas. Or even better, racial groups in Colombia are known as Euro-Colombianos or Afro-Colombianos. In Puerto Rico, diversity is melted in one concept, "La Puertorriqueñidad," where people embrace homogeneity more than their distinct cultures. Without romanticizing the subject and what has been sponsored and sold by the institutional culture, this is precisely how Puerto Ricans in the United States perceive themselves. They view themselves as part of *La Raza*, a homogenous group that emerged from three different races. Various studies show that Puerto Ricans see their ethnicity to be a sub-section of "La Raza." When defining the collective identity, Puerto Ricans point out cultural elements. Hence, cultural nationalism remains integral to the identifiable traits that each

Puerto Rican sees in himself concerning the North American identity. The Puerto Rican ethnicity and ethnogenesis - like most of Latin America is a result of the process of mestizaje. Can the Puerto Rican constructed identity be considered "ethnicity?" Proponents of ethnic nationalism restrict nation formation based on the drive to procreate within the same ethnicity through endogamy to maximize the gene pool.[8]

This interpretation, however, excludes the case of Puerto Rico. The desire to procreate after the establishment of the settlements did not occur based on preserving ethnicity but rather on the physiological need to engage in intimate relations in communities where the indigenous population was near extinction. Spaniard females were close to absent; the only interacting groups were Spaniard men, indigenous women, and African men and women. Thus, the sociobiological changes in the island after the Spanish conquest were dictated by the drastic decrease in the number of natives, the lack of European females on the island, and, later, the introduction of enslaved Africans. In the first one hundred years, the island had already gone through the process of mestizaje.[9]

Three centuries later, on the verge of the Spanish-American war, approximately 73% of the population lived in the countryside. They were called campesinos,[10] otherwise known as jibaros. El Jibaro or el Gibaro is perceived in many writings as the Puerto Rican socio-genetic identity; el jibaro is very particular to the island and incorporates the three races: Taíno Indian, European, and African. [11] Argimiro Ruano, in "La Identidad de los Puertorriqueños," explains that even one hundred years after Puerto Rico was ceded to the United States, it continues to be a lab of conflicted identities. The chronological evolution of the Puerto Rican identity traverses the first sociobiological stage from 1493 until 1898, where, despite

12

establishing the hierarchical order, it allowed interracial conjugal practices. Ruano mentions that the Spanish colonial laws enabled the peninsular to marry the natives, unlike the Anglo-Saxon counterparts up north, who prohibited marriages between the natives and the colonists. The second stage of identity shaping began after the island became a US territory. The dichotomy of Criollo vs. Gentleman, or el Jibaro vs. el Norteamericano, characterizes it. [12]

These ideological and cultural constructs reveal that the Puerto Ricans couldn't assimilate into another hegemonic culture after the change in the political status from "debated" autonomous (1897) Spain's colony to a US unincorporated territory to a Commonwealth of the United States. The ideology that characterized la puertorriqueñidad was embedded in the mentality of a former Spain colony, its traditions more so than socio-genetics, and it meant to preserve that identity at any cost. Argimiro Ruano writes, "Two differential and differentiated types of human race cannot give. As a result, a third one. Living together in confusion cannot be confused nor merged. There cannot be a second criollo." [13] Here, Ruano implies that a mixture between the Puerto Rican and the North American identities will never be possible. El Jibaro or el *Criollo* is a constructed identity and is widely accepted on the island as the Puerto Rican identity or the dominant group. Even though Ruano has a conservative view on the Puerto Rican identity, he agrees that no matter what angle people see the problem, the Puerto Rican identity is inherent in the standard historical past and a product of Colonial times. This new social construct will serve as a basis for non-institutionalized cultural and political nationalism in the quest for independence. The modern view of nationalism dismisses ethnicity and gives it a secondary role. Albeit, ideologically, there have been efforts to deconstruct the Puerto

Rican identity, as we have seen in the previous sections, as we will discuss in the Taino identity debate about *sangre pura*.

The Constructivist Approach to Nationalism: Can Creoles Form Their Nations?

Benedict Anderson offers a constructivist interpretation of nation formation in his book Imagined Communities. Acknowledging the complexity of defining the nation, Anderson states that nation, nationality, and nationalism have proved challenging to determine, let alone analyze.[14] Anderson sees the nation as a construct, a social relationship, a subconscious bond that ties the individual to the group. His theory implies that the individual establishes a silent understanding within a group or with other so-called nationals. Substantially, the group expands into a nation, and a nation is an imagined community or imagined communities held together by newspapers, maps, censi, literature, and a broad understanding of the culture. The members know about the existence of others without knowing who they are.

Yet Puerto Ricans see themselves as Puerto Ricans or Spanish-speaking US citizens. Puerto Rican scholars of nationalism agree with Anderson while describing the US civic nationalism as imaginary to Puerto Rican nationalism. Following Juan Manuel Carrion's argument, the relationship between these two types of nationalism has substantial incongruities.[15] This dichotomy rests on the belief that these two distinct national identities are irreconcilably different. As Anderson claims, linguistics is a crucial factor, yet not determinant to form a nation; Carrion sustains that the differences between these two imaginary nationalisms are not only linguistic but also cultural, political, and of a much larger scale.[16]

14

Anderson suggests that imagined communities are limited because even the most significant community has finite and elastic boundaries. This hypothesis sustains that nations need their territory to establish a state. Yet, his assumption can lead to conflicts between groups and or states since borders are a loose concept in Anderson's definition. The idea of the state and territory needed to preserve the nation and its sovereignty is challenged here. More importantly, Anderson suggested that nationalism has different historical origins, and that is primarily true based on primordial group formation or even in non-traditional settings such as group emergence in colonial systems. He emphasizes that there is always hope in building a nation as long as there is willingness. Anderson underlines that identity and country can be constructed ideologically like religion. Group identity and nation-forming happen constructively, and the development of the printed press defines the realm of vernacular languages used to bond people ideologically.[17]

Overall, Anderson defined the nation as an imagined political community and imagined as both inherently limited and sovereign. Anderson's definition is merely a group behavior theory that bases its assumption on the fact that people identify with one group, what they share and have in common, and how they see themselves no longer as individuals but as a group with the same traits and characteristics. Determining loyalties in Anderson's perspective is a loose concept as well. Since the community is imagined, adherence to the nation is malleable and hard to define. Thus, the individual can search for other identities since he is only bound to the nation by imagination. That means they can use the same vernacular language, have consistent patterns of group behavior, and inherit but "unsettled" culture, civic practices, and undefined artifacts and symbols. Nonetheless,

Anderson's perspective in this book is valuable in explaining how communities in Latin America have evolved.

A specific interpretation offered by Anderson is valuable to my argument. In the case of *Creole Pioneers*, Anderson raises the question of how new nations can be formed inside an empire that existed for four hundred years and flourished into roughly eighteen distinct nations. [18] The idea is that el Criollismo, more than an identity, was a distinguished group of people born in the colonies to parents from the Iberian Peninsula but as a (semi) rank-society. Creoles inherited their social position under the Spaniards. As a class, Creoles had unlimited access to wealth and land. In that case, the rank system became problematic for the Creoles because it did not allow them to hold positions in the metropolis or gubernatorial positions in the virreinatos (settlements).

Thus, the wars for independence in Latin America - per Anderson's postulations - attempted to detach the Creoles from Spain's rule and establish their nation-states. [19] The Creole pioneers had a few problems, especially in Latin America. The local communities became distinct only if local Creoles decided what group they had identified with. After Bolivar liberated *el Virreinato de la Nueva Granada*, it split into different nation-states. Nevertheless, the question remains: what made Colombians Colombian and Panamanians Panamanian after 1903, when Panama seceded?[20] What were the boundaries of their imagined community? As for Spanish as the vernacular language, it remains a unifier for the Latin American communities as a much larger imagined community. Anderson remains faithful to his Marxist roots. Criollismo is nothing less than a supranational unifying ideology against mercantile imperialism based on an invented historical past, territory, and language that later served to oppose the annexation of various Latin American countries to the territory of the United States. [21]

Cohesively, the independence movements in Latin America - especially in the *Virreinatos de la Plata* and *de la Nueva Granada* were a series of Pan-American revolutionary wars rather than nationalist movements.[22] The viceroyalties were not prototypes of identity or nationality but rather settlements under a strict, administrative colonial rule in which struggles for identity became secondary to the liberation from Spain. On the verge of the independence wars in Latin America, nationality and nations were forged, and the belligerent press at the time magnified the conflict between the Creoles and Peninsulares.[23] The Creole leaders wanted to preserve a supranational view of independence with a distinct particularity. The overarching idea of the supranational view unified mainly the Latin American Spanish-speaking countries. With this unifying ideology, the new states opposed any association with North America. However, the case of the Antilles was less complex than the viceroyalties of the South American continent. The Antilles, as administrative and political units, had well-defined territories. Cuba, Puerto Rico, and Haiti, with the Dominican Republic, offered fewer worries to establish nation-states since they had defined boundaries.

Modernization Theory: The failure to build a nation-state

Inherently, modern nationalism presumes the building of a current nation-state. *Puerto Rico is neither a modern nation nor a state within the Union. It continues to be an incorporated territory of the United States. The nationalist movement in Puerto Rico in the 1950s, being very political,* was primarily an effort to enlighten the people with the idea that they could have their own nation-state. Later on, and after pressure from the insular government, the Nationalist Party took a different direction and approach that vehemently demanded the Republic of Puerto Rico. This approach turned into a movement to secede using force from the United States, more so than cultivating the spirit of nationalism.[24]

Gellner's modern nationalism seems to follow a coherent, sequential timeline with phases that will lead to the rise of a nation with a national consciousness. Modern nationalism, as a theory, bases its assumption on the need of the state for nationalism to flourish. On the other hand, Gellner sustains that no matter how nationalist a group of people are, the state will not happen if there is no willingness but, foremost if there is no territory where this group of people feels empowered and endowed. Indeed, the metaphor of Ruritanians is perhaps the most illustrative allegory of Puerto Rico and Puerto Ricans inside of "Megalomania." [25] Let us suppose for a moment that Megalomania is the United States. It will serve as a theoretical framework to explain the role of Luis Muñoz Marin, his Popular Democratic Party (PPD), and the drifting from the independence cause. Suppose we continue to replace Puerto Rico with Ruritania and the US with Megalomania. In that case, we will see a perfect parallelism with Gellner's allegory in the relationship, attitudes, and expectations of Ruritanians as citizens inside Megalomania. Ruritanians – who reside in Megalomania – will succumb to assimilation, willingly or unwillingly.

Thus, Megalomania, a hegemon, offers a dignified life for Ruritanians where they can practice democracy and democratic values under the umbrella of the overarching constitution. Moreover, Ruritanians inside of Megalomania have the same opportunities under the dominant mainstream culture instead of their own culture. The Ruritanian culture no longer exists inside Megalomania unless celebrated in confined communities or cultural clusters entirely segregated from the mainstream culture. Regarding opportunities, as generations go by, Ruritanians will hold significant positions, sometimes as representatives in Megalomania's politics, but only if they are assimilated into mainstream politics. Unlike Gellners' fable, where Ruritanians attained independence, the Puerto Rican diaspora, who played a crucial role in Puerto Rico's politics, did away with it and no longer sought sovereignty. Gellner did not predict that the nation-state would not be possible in the case of a complex political association.[26]

In the case of Puerto Rico, Gellner's framework would not be able to explain the transfer of sovereignty from one imperial power to the other, which assumes that nations under colonial or protectorate systems become prone to legal and political hurdles that undermine self-determination efforts. In my view, the problem of using a framework based on the modern view of nationalism to define the case of Puerto Rico, just as the theory postulates, would leave out cultural and ethnic nationalism as a driving force to help establish collective identity, imperial for the self-determination movements. However, ethnic and cultural nationalism will argue for a solid interpretation as ancillaries of political nationalism. More importantly, in this study, cultural nationalism will be considered a factor in identity formation.

What Gellner's universality cannot explain in the case of Puerto Rico is the pre-conditions that omit other forms of political and modern nationalism. For example, Gellner's absolutism restrains modern nationalism from urbanization and industrialization of large communities or former metropolises, mercantile, and colonialist powers. Gellner sustains that modern nationalism can flourish with the rise of the proletariat. Yet Gellner had overlooked the competing ideologies of the 1800s that completely undermined the contemporary sense of the nation. In addition, Gellner does not explain the rise of the nations in the Creole communities after Spain, Portugal, and the imperialist powers of others granted independence. Most of these communities formed their nation-states in the peripheries and without passing through the stages of industrialization. Moreover, following Gellner's framework of low culture and high culture, the "low" culture of the jibaros became prevalent undermining the "high" culture of the peninsulares.

Problematizing the Case of Puerto Rico

As the previous discussion shows, Puerto Rico is a very paradoxical case for theories of nation and nationalism. The case of Puerto Rico nationalism is quite challenging to outline due to many changes in sociobiological transformation throughout the Spanish colonization of the island. There is another layer to it, though, that is connected to the specific relation that Puerto Rico has with the United States. Therefore, and interestingly enough, the challenge of defining nationalism in Puerto Rico comes from two different views and perspectives and, consequently, from two other sources. This is the dichotomy between how the islanders perceive themselves as Spanish-speaking citizens of the United States and how the Anglo-Saxon (North American) perspective has theoretically approached their case. Some research has been done in the field of cultural nationalism, and it shows a marked peculiarity between these identities. Seen through the lenses of nationalism, it is evident that the Anglo-Saxon perspective leaves out an essential part of the quest for self-determination: the national identity. In many studies, national identity is entirely mute as part of self-determination efforts, especially during the 1950s upheaval in search of independence.

When it comes to defining Puerto Rico's cultural nationalism, I agree with the argument made by Jacqueline Guzman Font. In congruency with Antony Smith's ethnonationalism, Guzman Font argues that Puertorriqueñidad, as the uniqueness of Puerto Rican identity, cannot be understood without the trajectory of the national symbols since El Grito de Lares until the Gag law of 1948. This is the period of the rise and fall of the nationalist movement in Puerto Rico. It started with the cry for independence in 1868 and continued until the outlawing of the nationalist movement in 1948.

From the same perspective, Juan Manuel Carrion discusses the same idea – the dichotomy between the collective identity and the presence of the institutionalized *other*. Manuel Carrion emphasizes that the war on symbols has left a sour taste of banal nationalism.[27] Thus, split loyalties have turned to existential threats and physical altercations at times between loyalists of the Puerto Rican identity and those in favor of a more inclusive identity under the commonwealth or statehood status. Overall, one can confidently say that the Puerto Rican case represents a significant puzzle for theories of the nation. Many core concepts that are assumed to be given, such as ethnicity, the drive for an independent state, and modernization theory claims, are perplexing or not even there. The matter becomes more complex when one adds the layer of interpretations, debates, and arguments specific to the Antilles, the Caribbean basin, or the former Spanish possessions. In the coming section, I discuss some of the most representative and influential approaches to Puerto Rican identity formation from a cultural perspective.

How do People Experience Nationalism in Puerto Rico? Culture, Oppression, and Distinctiveness

There is a widely accepted view that people in the Caribbean and Antilles share the same path to identity. Not surprisingly, the influence of Stuart Hall is noticed in the discussion of identity forming. While describing the path of identity forming in the Antilles, especially in his homeland, Jamaica, Hall makes the same argument as José Luis González about Puerto Rico's identity. They both emphasize the presence of the Afro-Caribbean factor. To have an identity, we need a shared collective identity and the presence of "the other."[28] Hall argues that cultural identity is a binary concept, a relationship between two distinct views. First, cultural identity is "what we are," and the other side is "what we are not." This is a distinctive perception of what we are as individuals, the "oneness" in each of us.[29] The other perception of cultural identity is the difference among us, thus, what we are not. Based on this definition, identity makes "us" unique and distinct. Hall assumes that the foundations of Antilles are Afro-Caribbean; hence, "the other" implies the colonizers and developed countries, and in the case of Puerto Rico, the other means the United States.

This thesis is not accepted by many scholars that emphasize the distinctiveness of the Puerto Rican identity *vis a vis* the Afro-Caribbean heritage. Scholars such as Jacqueline Font-Guzman and Juan Manuel Carrion argue that a shared identity pertains to Puerto Ricans. The shift that took place in 1898 catalyzed a new cultural oneness that has two sides.[30] However, various scholars agree that the distinction between *self and others* stands on firm grounds regarding the relationship between Puerto Rico and the United States. To illustrate the case of Puerto Rico's cultural identity and in agreement with Stuart Hall, Font-Guzman states, "Theories of difference highlight what is different or distinct from others."[31] Yet, while Stuart Hall juxtaposes the Afro-Caribbean identity to the Creoles and the colonizers, Jacqueline Font-Guzman uses the dichotomy (self-other) to contrast the Puerto Rican identity from the United States. She creates two distinct paths that Puerto Rican people keep completely separated when it comes to their identity: A cultural Puerto Rican identity and a legal status as a US Citizen of Puerto Rican background. This apparent duality is not that simple to explain. This peculiar relationship yields problems with loyalties, but more importantly, it is a counterargument to what Anthony D. Smith argues about the fundamental elements of national identity.[32] Hall's framework does not convincingly explain the evolution of the Puerto Rican identity because it frames it within a more significant Afro-Caribbean or Afro-Antillean identity. Hall's framework includes three contributing factors yet excludes the uniqueness of the Puerto Rican identity.

On the other hand, the widely known pro-independence philosopher Jose Luis González[33] points out many layers of Puerto Rican identity in his essay *El Pais de Cuatro Pisos*. According to Luis González, the Puerto Rican identity has four layers or pisos (floors), as he calls them. In his dialectic interpretation of the Puerto Rican identity, Jose Luis Gonzales explains two sides of the Puerto Rican culture: The national culture, as the island's dominant culture, and the culture of the dominating class. Luis Gonzalez assumes that this dichotomy - known as the class warfare between the exploited (the islanders) and the exploiter (colonizers) is the natural state of the Puerto Rican culture since its conception. Thus, the Puerto Rican national culture – continues to be dominated by the exploiting class. In the exploiting class, José Luis

González includes – politically - the imperial powers that had sovereignty over Puerto Rico – such as Spain and the US, and, secondly, the vassals - or the colonizers who enabled such a system of exploitation. From a Marxist point of view, José Luis González has extended the conflicted identity probe to class warfare, from the base to the superstructure.

In Luis González' identity framework, the Afro-Caribbean mestizo and the mulatto are at the very base of the socio-hierarchical taxonomy. On the second floor are the Spaniards, white Creoles, and peninsulas; the third layer consists of the North American influence and Anglo-Saxon culture, and the last layer is the fusion of contemporary cultures under the commonwealth status. The layers in his framework are a tad conflicting. José Luis González acknowledges that the "jibaro" is a conflicted figure that identifies with today's Puerto Rican. Yet the jibaro as a figure has been tamed and used for political purposes – implies Luis Gonzalez while referring to the conservative Creoles. As discussed in the following chapters, the jibaro is sometimes portrayed as white, indigenous, of a mixed race, a farmer, striking poor villager, etc. José Luis González claims that the jibaro is not a white Spaniard but a widely accepted Puerto Rican identity. Rooting for the Afro-Caribbean factor, Luis Gonzalez argues that conservatives have used the jibaro to whiten the Puerto Rican identity and reduce the Afro-Caribbean contributor.[34] The Puerto Rican cultural identity rests on an imaginary and broad interpretation of the idealized figure of the peasant, el jibaro, at least since 1849. The core argument around el jibaro, in which scholars seem to disagree, is the cultural, socio-genetic pertinence. More importantly, few have probed in depth about the jibaro identity, and it is still to be determined if the jibaro is a cultural construct and the widely accepted cultural identity or if it is a mere socio-genetic product of colonial times. During the 1930s, the jibaro shifted from a cultural construct to an exploited class Luis Muñoz Marin contacted while campaigning with the Puerto Rican Socialist Party.

José Luis González' perception of the Puerto Rican identity is of great importance to the Puerto Rican community, yet the taxonomy he has used is debatable. Many of the perplexities are related to the dialectic perspective he adopts. Luis González' sees the problem from a class struggle perspective. To fit the Marxist perceptions of the social structure, the social class of mestizos is defined as the oppressed class, and the whites (Peninsulares and North Americans) are the oppressors. Luis Gonzalez does not see el Jibaro as an ethno-cultural construct that emerged from the colonial period. In his view, the Puerto Rican identity is not inherent to the island and its history but is part of a larger framework, the Afro-Antillean identity. In agreement with Hall, Luis Gonzalez assumes that the overarching class identity is a product of the rule imposed by the common oppressors.

In short, to make a Marxist argument, Jose Luis Gonzalez ignores the foundations of Puerto Rico's mythomoteurs, symbols, ethnogenesis, and historical past. He relies on the assumption of a supranational ideology to define the Puerto Rican identity as a subset of a broader class identity. Jose Luis Gonzalez considers the Puerto Rican identity part of a larger unified, Pan-American context. His ideological interpretation enables him to shift from the mere sociobiological factor to a class stratification analysis. Still, for José Luis González, the base of Puerto Rican identity is the Afro-Antillean, which, as it stands, is broader than el jibarismo in Puerto Rico.

While he criticizes el jibaro as a forged cultural identity by the Creole elites, Luis González argues that the homogenization is also a forged claim promulgated by the nationalists in the 1930s and 1940s, such as Pedro Albizu Campos, whom he considered a conservative. As I have explained above, la puertorriqueñidad, the cultural blending with an Afro-Caribbean base, is the sole identity, and "the other" is the three layers: Spain, North America, and the contemporary culture. Luis González and Albizu Campos have two fundamentally different perceptions of the Puerto Rican identity. While Luis González excludes the Spanish factor and input in the Puerto Rican identity, he undermines the centrality of the Spanish language as the vernacular in Puerto Rico. Luis Gonzalez argues that the Pan-American society has many languages, and Puerto Rico is no exception. Such a claim is a blow to the Spanish heritage in the Puerto Rican identity and a mere denial of historical facts.

Albizu Campos, on the other hand, promulgates the identity that draws its foundations from the typical historical past, the Hispanic heritage, and the Spanish language, which is inherently different from the Anglo-Saxon culture and language. The class-stratification view, proposed by Luis González, also undermines cultural nationalism and the idea of "la puertorriqueñidad." As a Marxist, he considers nationalism a form of alienation and false consciousness. The "oneness" – according to Luis Gonzalez - expands to a much broader realm of Pan-American exploited proletarians and peasants. What will unify the Puerto Rican identity with the other Latin American countries in the Antilles is to overcome the identities sponsored by a commercial system imposed after the Spanish-American War.[35] Luis González' dialectic approach is congruent with many critics of the cultural nationalism emerging from neocolonialism after the 1950's. There are similarities in the interpretations of cultural identity in the Antilles between Hall and Luis González. The value of their argument relies on a post-modern interpretation of the origins of the Antillean mestizo.

Albizu Campos also embraces the idea of a larger Pan-American society not as an overarching identity but as a collective solidarity against the *other* – the North American presence in Latin America. The Puerto Rican collective identity strengthened during the nationalist upheaval of the fifties. Since then, there have been efforts in the quest for self-determination in democratic and "unconventional ways."[36] However, there are no significant changes to the fundamentals of the Puerto Rican identity. A self-determination movement usually bases its ideology on a solid and enduring sense of national identity. However, these efforts did not change the legislation or Puerto Rico's Constitution of 1952. The elites, on the other hand, seemed to be divided on the issue.[37] Despite the popularity of the independence cause, the people of Puerto Rico, by many referendums, have decided to keep the commonwealth status as a two-way relationship with benefits, but ideally, no strings attached; at least, this is a widespread perception. Nowadays, the debate between the political parties still revolves around the colonial vocabulary, and the pro-annexation politicians struggle to convince the electorate that the commonwealth does not imply a colony.

On the other side of the political spectrum, el Partido Independentista advocates for independence and full sovereignty from the United States. The political discourse is very heated on the island. The nationalist circles in Ponce[38] demand full economic and political sovereignty, whereas civil rights activists demand equal representation and a change in voting rights.

In the last twenty years, there have been studies on Puerto Rican nationalism from many approaches, such as legal, anthropology, and political science. Jacqueline Font Guzman has discussed the case of cultural nationalism in the trajectory of Puerto Rico as a self-governing, unincorporated territory. Font Guzman has dramatically improved our understanding of the impact of US citizenship in shaping Puerto Rican identity and the collective consciousness after the Spanish-American War of 1898. This perspective is precious to show how US citizenship substantially changed the self-perception of Puerto Ricans as a cultural nation. On the other hand, Nelson Denis (2015), in War Against All Puerto Ricans: Revolution and Terror in America's Colony,[39] treats indigenous Puerto Rican nationalism with much more interest. Yet, Nelson Denis remains in the framework of political nationalism and the struggle for self-determination in the 1950s. The lead figure Nelson Denis uses to define the problem is Pedro Albizu Campos, the most vital voice for independence and self-determination during the 1950s and 1960s. The book reveals the refusal to assimilate into North American society under the principle of hegemony and the lack of cultural and political compatibility between the island and the United States. According to Nelson Denis, other polities - opposite of the nationalist elite hushed to cover up and belittle the efforts of self-determination in exchange for either the commonwealth or the statehood option.

In her influential study, *Sponsored Identities: Cultural Politics in Puerto Rico,* Arlene Davila emphasizes that the quest for independence became a priority for the Nationalist Party under the leadership of Pedro Albizu Campos, who adopted a non-negotiable, anti-imperial, anticolonial stance.[40] Davila raises the problem of state-sponsored cultural nationalism, institutionalized under the auspices of the insular government, to create a distinct type of nationalism to drift away from the heated independence rhetoric. In the framework of modern nationalism, if the elites fail to unify the masses under the same ideology, the efforts for self-determination will not prevail. According to Nelson Denis, this hypothesis mirrored the lack of civil liberties on the island, drastically reducing the unification efforts under the cause of independence.

There is a discrepancy in treating Puerto Rico's nationalism and the many forms of its manifestation. The literature in the English language offers a comprehensive view of cultural nationalism but hardly mentions the 1950s – or it avoids the subject. Other literature sources in Spanish, while exploring the identity path and the impact of Spain on identity, focus more on ideology and legitimacy during the colonial period. The proponents of this view are conservative voices who see Spain as the cradle of the Puerto Rican identity. North American perspective romanticizes Puerto Rican cultural nationalism as a "novelty" inside the mainstream culture to diversify and create a sense of multicultural and multi-linguistic society. The nationalist discourse in Puerto Rico arose in the 1920s with the founding of the Nationalist Party. During the 1930's, the nationalists confronted the US-appointed officials on the island. [41] However, the equation had one missing variable: the role of the local elites and the diaspora; their impact either accepting the commonwealth status as the solution or advocating for independence. Hence, the elites' war culminated in the open conflict between Pedro Albizu Campos and Luis Muñoz Marin. 1948 marked –de facto- for years to come, the end of the political organizations that favored independence.[42] Amidst the political turmoil, collective identity, national identity, cultural nationalism, and political nationalism were no longer part of a glibly speech. Nationalists meant what they'd said and had done what they were meant to do. The conflict turned into an insurgency that lasted for many years. This is missing from these otherwise valuable discussions of the formation of national identity in Puerto Rico.

THE INSTITUTIONAL LEGACY, INDIGENOUS ELITES, AND NATIONAL IDENTITY FORMATION IN PUERTO RICO

While studying the case of Puerto Rico, the fundamental question seemed to be, *why does political nationalism fail?* In this book, I present an argument that many scholars have approached from different perspectives within the social sciences, particularly those that deal with nationalism, identity, and self-determination.

The book explains that under specific historical conditions, different groups would merge and embrace an overarching identity to seek their nation-state. They would do so to preserve their identity and, therefore, their existence. Yet, every group envisions the nation based on their own identity. There is a particular path one needs to follow to unravel this puzzle. To understand why Puerto Rico failed to build an independent and sovereign state, we must first understand their identity's evolution. Therefore, without clarifying how identity emerged in Puerto Rico and the most critical influences on its evolution are, we would not be able to understand how the various groups of people in Puerto Rico transformed their collective identities into a national identity.

This, of course, is tied to the explanation of identity formation. How was identity constructed in Puerto Rico? Puerto Rico, like Latin America, had gone through the same process of identity construction that we call mestizaje. Mestizaje, apart from a mix of two or three ethnic/racial groups, was more of a cultural construct that resulted in the identity we now see in Puerto Rico. Nevertheless, this very process made the identity more complex. Groups made identity claims based on ideologies and pragmatism. These ideologies matched each identity. I examine the path of Puerto Rican identities, looking at many forms and ideological shapes. First, there is a sociobiological identity, then a cultural identity, a political identity, an islander identity, a diaspora (Americanized Puerto Rican) identity, and so forth. Some of these identities are conflicting, and some are congruent. People created loyalties to their groups based on these identities, overlooking national identity. Hence, the book explains that ethnic/racial and cultural heterogeneity, homogenized during the colonial period through mestizaje,[43] became widely accepted as a new identity. While the Puerto Rican identity became the only identity inherent to the island, people rejected any other modifications or other cultural interferences from the North American culture and the English language. Ethnicity, as a form of ethnic identity, was also constructed and continues to be conflicted through the rise of ethnic/racial groups that once contributed to the process of mestizaje. Yet, these claims are only ideological. The groups became homogenized over the longue durée and formed a community through kinship (affinity, marriage, relations). Over time, they shared a common historical past, tradition, culture, and beliefs that went beyond racial generalizations.

In light of this historical trajectory, the awareness of ethnic identity led to political nationalism, independence, and collective self-determination efforts. Thus, political nationalism in Puerto Rico was unavoidable. Returning to the fundamental question of *why it did not prevail,* we must consider the case of the Philippines. *The* Philippines had attained independence under historically and politically similar conditions to Puerto Rico. Julian Go argued that what pushed the efforts of independence in the Philippines were the insurgencies and the role of the elites, who were entirely against the idea of any teaching or colonial relationship under the US. However, as I have mentioned before, the role of the populist elites in changing the course of history was paramount. By understanding how elites used their political power, we cannot exclude the idea that in the absence of a sovereign nation-state, the emerging political groups led by local elites will attach themselves to the new political or colonial power and seek economic and political security by eradicating other elites striving to form a sovereign nation-state.

In this exploratory identity path, I will argue that the Puerto Rican nationalist ideology – is an anticolonial sentiment within a community united by culture, tradition, common historical past, language, religion, and territory. This sentiment arose due to crucial historical events that led to the forming of Puerto Rican identity - that of constructing a unified distinctiveness based on the relationship among three races during the process of mestizaje. The historical trajectory and the need to be affirmed as a nation whose new identity was traversed through historical sacrifices and hardship dictated the use of national identity as a means of self-determination. I will argue that it is possible to experience political nationalism without a nation-state based on the awareness of national identity. The construction of national identity in a territorially defined community is inherent to a common historical past, tradition, and culture and will reject the idea of integration into a new, more prominent, overarching civic nationalism.

As noted above, several theories of nationalism can be used to frame and analyze the case of Puerto Rico. Yet, most of them would fall short of explaining the puzzle of identity formation. Most theories are formulated to explain other instances or straight jacket the Puerto Rican case to fit the grand theories of social sciences. This shortcoming becomes apparent when the Puerto Rican identity is problematized. The complex nature of Puerto Rican nationalism is significant for the identity debate. This is an excellent point to start with.

The test for any theory is to account for and explain the explosion of the Puerto Rican nationalism of the 1950s. Much of the literature notes that Puerto Rico in the 1950s was defined by intense and heated nationalist rhetoric activism. But many treat it as an unexpected event. Yet, this is the culmination of the process of identity formation in Puerto Rico itself. The evolution of Puerto Rico's nationalism and the upheaval of the 1950s is complex and delicate to define due to the timing, the heated political debate surrounding it, and the political actors involved.

The literature on nationalism offers a partial explanation for the nationalist wave of the 1950s, debates, and arguments. Since then, the independence movement has faded, but cultural nationalism has grown stronger.[44] As I've said before, every year, people gather in major cities of the United States to celebrate the Puerto Rican Day Parade or *la Puertorriqueñidad* with national symbols and a strong feeling of national pride and identity. The event remains within the frame of pop culture imagery and symbolism. Yet, the main question is how do we explain the declining political nationalism in Puerto Rico while cultural nationalism continues to be one of the most muscular heritage landmarks? This study will stop at the 1950s, but as an extension of the argument, one should ask why Puerto Rico's nationalism has not been produced insofar as a substantial independence movement since the 1950s. The only political party on the island that aligns with the nationalist rhetoric is the Independence Party, yet less than three percent of the island votes for it in Puerto Rico's elections. The views on nationalism are diverse and, for that matter, their interpretations. There is a general assumption that the ideology of nationalism stands on firm grounds. *Hence, how is the nation-state so crucial to nationalism? And how do Puerto Ricans understand it?*

The crushing of the nationalist movement in the 1950s revealed that the cause of independence had suffered a deadly blow. Public Law 53 had erased the nationalists from the political spectrum. The populist movement led by Luis Muñoz Marin gave the people the right to administer their territory but did not grant people sovereignty or independence. The difference is substantial: a commonwealth versus a modern state. Disintegrating the efforts of self-determination and shifting to sponsored identities had a much greater price beyond the PPD.[45] The populist elites using the US as a proxy established their political rule for years to come and architected a hybrid political system. The populists overlooked national autonomy, national unity, and national identity.[46] Thus, the system was halfhearted for many who were silenced during the decade of the Gag Law. It showed the inside conflict and the lack of democratic values, consensus, and the unequal representation of the island's politics. Elites struggled to seize power and dominate politics. It questioned the political culture and democratic values. People were divided on rhetoric, but most of all, people lost their confidence in self-government and never been *owners* of their own homes. Therefore, it became an existential dilemma. We must not forget that the dilemma of failed political nationalism starts with the question of identity.

What was distinct from the explosion of nationalist sentiment in Puerto Rico in the 1950s were the methods and models that political nationalists adopted. The nationalists, inspired by the decolonization movements in Asia and Africa, sought complete independence from the United States. Aligning themselves with the Zeitgeist of the time, the Puerto Rican nationalists adopted the rhetoric of anti-imperialism and self-determination.

They did not stop at the rhetoric. Some segments of Puerto Rican nationalist organizations promoted a Sinn Fein type of movement that was successful in the 20th century in gaining Ireland's independence.[47] Amidst the turmoil, which lasted for several decades, the insular authorities, controlled by the Puerto Rican elites, scrambled to control and contain the clashes with the nationalists so that their clash would not turn into a full-blown conflict.

After decades of contentious politics, including numerous incidents and the imprisonment of several nationalist leaders and activists, Puerto Rican political nationalism failed to achieve its goal of independence. Yet, cultural nationalism is alive and well. This is the paradox that we have to explain. Tied to this is the legitimate question of "Why did Puerto Rican political nationalism fail?" As I have noted above, scholars have pointed out numerous factors, such as intense political pressure, economic migration that served as a valve to release social tensions, and the corruption of the political elites. In this book, I argue that there is more than meets the eye.

I argue that the political nationalism in Puerto Rico failed for reasons rooted deep in history and the institutional legacy of the Spanish empire. The effect of these policies was that they shaped multiple and often irreconcilable identities that were contested at different levels. First, I argue that contested identities in Puerto Rico played a role in determining loyalties to the cause of independence. With contested identities, I understand the overlap of different and often incompatible identities threaded in the Puerto Rican identity. I show how several identities, such as Taino indigenous, Afro-Antillean, Spaniards, Creoles, jibaros, and class identities, were essential to the process. These ideological tropes fueled by political entities, organizations, and even influential individuals were used in their efforts to create an institutionalized counterbalance with the inherent Puerto Rican identity. More importantly, the Puerto Rican nationalist movement lacked a cohesive ideology of national unity embraced by everyone on the island, including the diaspora in the US. Instead, the unifying ideology was far-fetched.

Secondly, the early 20th-century politicians in the diaspora embraced international Marxist ideologies of class struggles and oppression as opposed to self-determination and pre-independent activism. Paramount among them is the towering figure of Luis Muñoz Marin. Politicians like Luis Muñoz Marin sought solutions to the Puerto Rican problem by integrating it into the more significant cause in their ideological framework of the fight against capitalism and exploitation. They sought to problematize the Puerto Rican issue by making it integral to the presumed international proletarian. Moreover, they focused on drawing support from the societies, organizations, and regimes that formally embraced such an agenda. Hence, it is essential to note that they did not search for the solution to the Puerto Rican cause within the island and thereby ignored the deep divisions and conflicting agendas pursued by other Puerto Rican politicians that advocated a rupture with the US and for independence. Instead, they had made all their calculations based on external factors, including Puerto Rico's economic dependence on the United States. Within Puerto Rico, influential political parties and entities adopted the outlook offered by these ideologies in their platforms and programs before and after establishing the Commonwealth status to solve the island's class struggle problem, as they understood it. This antecedent is essential to show that they were not addressing the real issues on the ground, as their people considered them.

Thirdly, the Puerto Rican diaspora in the United States relied on the US to assert its political position and power vis-a-vis the elites on the island. The Puerto Rican diaspora was immensely empowered by its active participation in the US economy and its relative well-being and wealth that made it independent of the ruling elite on the island. As a result, the diaspora no longer supported building a sovereign nation-state. Diaspora is made up mainly of people originally coming from the lower income strata, which was focused on improving the economic situation of the workers and the farmers. Later on, the diaspora pushed for the status of the commonwealth. This specific status, which designated Puerto Rico as an unincorporated territory and yet politically, legally, and economically dependent on the metropolis, was strongly supported by the diaspora and their supporters on the island.

Fourthly, the local elites were deeply divided and were fighting against one another. The segment of the elites against independence, including the substantial diaspora, engaged in a heated political battle with the pro-independence elites on the island. Using the United States presence on the island, the pro-annexation elites outlawed nationalist and independence activism. Their objective was to defeat all efforts based on the principle of self-determination that would lead to independence. As I've said above, the benefits they've drawn from the status quo were substantial. This unforgiving battle, which was quite intense and prolonged, resulted in intense political turmoil culminating with the clashes of the 1950's. The political elites in power used institutionalized coercion to crush the independence efforts and the political violence as a means exerted by the nationalists.

Thus, the point of clash between the elites and the diaspora was the issue of independence. As I noted, the nationalist elites and the pro-annexation proponents each assumed a political position opposed to the other. Moreover, these were firmly based on irreconcilable ideologies. In the process, both sides went to the extremes. Thus, the nationalist elites espoused a formative type of nationalism, which translated into anti-imperialist rhetoric, insurgency, violent protests, and refusing everything North American. The pro-annexation elites adopted a pragmatic position toward the United States to secure the island's economic development; their objective was to ensure their hold on political power. To make sure they'd accomplished their purpose. The ruling elites waived the option of territorial, economic, military, and judicial sovereignty.

The case had a broad significance that became immensely important to national-formation discussions. For example, the case leads me to explore the complex matter of the nation's homogeneity. Most theories assume substantial homogeneity. How does a homogenous or non-homogenous nation form? Using the case of Puerto Rico, I argue that the idea of the nation becomes prevalent, and the nation becomes at some level homogenous when the collective conscience becomes the underpinning of shared values, ideas, traditions, and morals of the unified *selves*. In this sense, the Puerto Rican identity and nation are new.

The structure of the book

The book is organized in the following manner. It traces the process of identity formation over four centuries. It shows what policies were essential to the process of identity formation. It highlights the contributing ethnogenetic factors and examines the cultures involved in mestizaje.

The first chapter examines the role assumed by one of the most critical players in Puerto Rico's history and identity formation, the Spanish Crown:

the state and the colonial institutions' role in identity-building set Puerto Rico on a path-dependent journey. Besides, I show how the state contributed to what Spaniards called the birth of an imperial race. I do so by analyzing the distinct groups that provide an essential and enduring influence on the Puerto Rican identity. I pay special attention to the Taíno population and identity in this chapter. I trace their trajectory from the pre-Columbian era until the modern day. I also show how the identity building in Puerto Rico cannot be understood without the presence of the Peninsulares. The role of the Spanish hidalgos in the social structure set the stage for the ideological debate, characteristic of Spanish America, an ideology that separated the self and the other in the Puerto Rican identity.

The second chapter covers the role of the Catholic Church and the clergy in the Caribbean Islands. Apart from establishing order and preaching Christian values in the colony, the clergy played an essential role in identity-shaping and preserving the native factor. The main point of the second chapter is the interpretation of mestizaje from a socio-genetic aspect. Understanding how the social cast worked in colonial Spain helps us understand why societies evolved the way they did. This chapter also covers the emergence of the mestizo as an essential part of society, although left out in the trenches for almost three hundred years. Understanding the classist mentality that Spaniards transferred into the New World will help the reader realize that the new political and economic elites to hold power and accumulate wealth became not only classist but also racist. The racially divided societies changed the social fabric of Latin America; they ostracized and dehumanized an entire "race" that emerged from the interactions of indigenous people and enslaved Africans, the Latin American mestizo.

40

Chapter three presents how cultural nationalism evolved from tradition to cultural identity. It shows how cultures were mixed and unified and what the mythos-moteurs that emerged in popular culture from colonial times to modern Puerto Rico were. Cultural nationalism in Puerto Rico became a political catalyst in 1868 when Ramon Emeterio Betances declared independence. During the twentieth century, it evolved as one of the most identifiable traits of Puerto Rico's institutionalized culture. Chapter three treats not only the early exhibition of cultural artifacts and practices but also various mytho-moteurs dating from colonial times to the present day with consideration. Such pop culture symbols are the figures of jibaro or the picaresque characters of Juan Bobo in children's literature.

Chapter four is an examination of the complex process of elite efforts to shape a unique Puerto Rican identity on the verge of the Spanish-American War. Throughout the 19th century, the elites in Puerto Rico, much like the other Latin American countries, had taken their political character. By the end of the 1800s, the elites struggled to maintain a political balance by dealing with loyalties, conflicts, and the presence of a new political power on the island. Faced with two imperialist powers, one in decline and the other on the rise, the elites in Puerto Rico found themselves between a moral decision to preserve their old ties with Spain or to embrace a new political relationship with the US.

Chapter five focuses on the subsequent change of the Puerto Rican national identity, this time vis the US. It defines Puerto Rican national identity and how Puerto Ricans experience US citizenship. The chapter focuses on the dichotomy between citizenship and nationality. I have chosen some specific cases, like the Mari Bras case. By analyzing the case of Mari Bras, I point out that the incongruent relationship between the two concepts (nationality and citizenship) has caused dissatisfaction with the status quo.

In chapter six, I describe the diaspora's role, the elites' influence on the island's politics, and the final blow to the independence cause. Here, I examine the efforts made by the Committee of the Interior and the Insular Affairs in the US Senate to grant independence to Puerto Rico. I explain that the independence bill proposed by Senator Millard Tydings, amidst the rise of social upheaval, the island, and the cultural incompatibility with the US, was an effort to end the conflict and to allow Puerto Rican people to gain independence and full sovereignty. More importantly, in this chapter, I focus on the battle regarding the island's political future between two political opponents, Luis Muñoz Marin and Pedro Albizu Campos. This is the chapter in which I examine in depth the failure of political nationalism and the 1950's.

In the conclusion, I summarize my findings. I describe the trajectory of the identity path formation. I also discuss the post-1950s dominance of cultural nationalism. Finally, I discuss the significance that this has for theories of nation-formation and identity formation.

HISTORICAL NARRATIVE

This chapter covers the trajectory of the Boricua[48] people and their transformations during the early years of Spanish colonization. I offer a historical narrative of the social order and changes upon the arrival of the Spaniards in the Greater Antilles. The narrative focuses on two particular islands, Puerto Rico and Hispaniola. I present a panoramic view of how indigenous communities became scattered, destroyed, and were rebuilt to suit the needs of the settlers. The main argument in this chapter covers the politics and the power of the Spanish monarchy, which was delegated to the hands of the first settlers and the hidalgos. Such unbalanced and misused power resulted in a complete change of the social order and caused the drastic decline of the indigenous people, but foremost accounted for the construction of new identities. More importantly, I will analyze two concepts, the Spanish Hidalgo and la hidalguía as the ruling ideology in the colonies and the state's role in the conquest of the Americas.

In this chapter, the role of the Taíno people and their contribution to their identity is essential. I will analyze the trends and the debate around their role in Puerto Rico's identity and nationalism. I retake Taino's identity and construct a narrative congruent with the assimilationist theories. At the same time, I use a dialectic method to analyze the reasons for the "deconstruction" of the Puerto Rican identity, the rise of the Neo-Taino movement, and the transplantation of the Taino factor at the expense of the Puerto Rican identity. Lastly, grounded on literature and historical resources, I reconstruct the first interactions between the natives and the peninsulares and the efforts to shape a community controlled by the laws and ordinances following the military model of the Reconquista.

Social Order Issues in the Old and the New World

A society strives to find a balance and to maintain the status quo, or at least to sustain continuity and security for its members. However, this is only realizable if men have entered a social contract where they collectively agree to protect themselves and their property. Secondly, they decide to subjugate to a higher authority, surrendering their rights in exchange for protection. Otherwise, men tend to behave like they live in a state of nature and anarchy. They are willing to fight for resources and justify the means of war. [49] The conquest of the Americas was a hazardous enterprise, and it required a well-thought process of institutionalizing the system of laws and ordinances inherent in the metropolis. What type of social order were Spaniards looking to establish in the Americas? The endeavor presented two significant challenges - the distance from the metropolis and the indigenous population. The *capitulations contract, a legal agreement that enabled the transplantation of the political and economic system from the metropolis to the periphery,* became the legal model of the conquest. Spain was an established society, and the question of the Americas was not to invent anything new but to transfer the power and the traditional authority through formal or informal institutions. Many of these institutions were pre-established during the Reconquista. New to this old social contract was the case of the natives, and this was more a question of morals and Christian values. The encomienda, or the "natural" enslavement of the indigenous people, explains the rationale beyond the social behavior of the Spaniards as a hegemonic group. Spaniards were in search of establishing "order" at any cost in indigenous societies, even when conflict and the bloody pacifications factorized entire communities. They sought a society to benefit their needs and secure the monarchy's legitimacy overseas. This order was frequently challenged because of the conflicts stemming from the natives' resistance to submit to a higher authority. The pacification of the natives sought to establish a legal authority, and it was a military practice used in the Reconquista. Economically, the model allowed the settlers to accrue wealth by prior agreements. In other words, the military style of the conquest of the West was justified neither by the Just War doctrine nor by reclaiming lost territories. The settlers and the Crown agreed that the endeavor was an imperialist ambition to strengthen the monarchy and exploit resources. The natives were out of the equation and served as property. There were no changes in the social order while conquering the West; the same legal and political system that functioned in the metropolis was transferred to the periphery.

The Rise of the Catholic King and Queen

The role of the Catholic Monarchs in the Conquest of the Americas is one of the most disputed arguments in modern history. One has to have an understanding of the evil European politics during the 15th and 16th centuries. Without a clear idea of how principalities arose, declined, made alliances, and expanded, it is impossible to explain the shrewdness of Isabella and Ferdinand. The success of their reign was mainly due to overcoming the most significant obstacles that would have weakened the union: First, instead of mixing their principalities, they each kept their administrative systems, and secondly, the hereditary monarchs dealt separately with the political problems that their principalities had inherited. [50] On October 19, 1479, Isabella, Castile's heiress, marries Ferdinand, King of Sicily and heir to the throne of Aragon, in a private ceremony. Many monarchs, rivals to the throne, and aspirants were opposed to the wedding, starting with Louis XI, who saw the union of the young heirs as a potential threat to his country. [51] J. H Elliott, in Imperial Spain 1469-1716, says there was a dynastic logic to whoever Isabella chose to marry. It was a well-thought-out judicial union of two (out of five) Crowns of the Iberian Peninsula, the Crown of Castile and the Crown of Aragon. John II of Aragon sought an alliance and ways to strengthen his principality in the Crown of Castile.

The assistance John II hoped to get from Castile would end the political turmoil in Catalonia and avoid all other internal threats in Aragon. John II faced external threats from the political situation with the neighboring principalities. The international situation was unfavorable for the Aragon Monarchs; the French were becoming an imminent threat alongside the Pyrenees. The end of the Hundred Years War marked a schism between the two countries (France and England) and the birth of strong national identities. At the same time, in the Iberian Peninsula, the word Hispania emerged in the social-political scene to distinguish Iberians from Frenchmen and Englishmen and push for the national identity. Mark Zuili writes.[52]

> *"This personal connection between the sovereigns, of two largest states (Crowns) of the Iberian Peninsula constituted one of the key phases of the process that will precede Spain's national unity."*

The author continues that although it was very early to discuss nationalism in Spain, the two monarchs were credited with building a solid state, consolidating the territory, and implementing many administrative reforms. [53] Hence, John II of Aragon had more pragmatic reasons for such a union. Using Castile's resources, he sought an alliance to help solve the need for stability inside the monarchy.[54] The Aragon monarchs backed this union using a powerful branch inside Castile's court - Archbishop of Toledo- along with the influence of prominent Jewish families.[55] Isabella, a stern woman of character, made the decision on her own for reasons that she sought fit politically and personally. [56] Both monarchs were motivated to work hand in hand. The union marked an alliance of two allies that boosted Spain's reputation as a world power.

> *John II of Aragon (1458–79) was facing not only the revolution in Catalonia but also the expansionist ambitions of Louis XI of France. With inadequate resources to meet the threat on his own, his best hope seemed to lie in the assistance of Castile, and a matrimonial alliance could best secure this. It was, therefore, primarily the international situation – the ending of the Hundred Years' War and the consequent renewal of French pressure along the Pyrenees – that made a Castilian alliance desirable and necessary to the King of Aragon. Securing this alliance became the principal object of John II's diplomacy. [57]*

They embarked on the most critical historical journey of the age of exploration - the Reconquista and the discovery. The empire established in the Iberian Peninsula and overseas will make Spain one of the most significant critical players in international politics in 1500s Europe. The success was due to the Crown of Castile's self-confidence and military experience. On the other hand, the Crown of Aragon had an excellent reputation in administration, diplomacy, and government matters. [58] In 1479, after a three-year conflict with Juana la Beltraneja, the illegitimate daughter of Henry the IV, Queen Isabella defeated the Portuguese troops and gained control over Castile's territory.[59] January of 1942 marked the triumph of Isabella and Ferdinand over the last Moorish hold, the city of

Granada. On January 6, 1492, the Catholic Queen and King entered victorious in Granada, and shortly after, they signed the agreement of the Reconquista. Thus, the ending of the Reconquista marked a new epoch in the modern history of Spain.

Consolidating the State

By the 1490's, the state treasury was in shambles. The expenditures from the wars of Granada and the Canary Islands have exhausted many financial resources. The monarchs found the higher stratum of nobility to be an economic burden but, more importantly, a threat. Isabella and Ferdinand would seize any opportunity to bring funds to the treasury. The Conquest presented ample challenges ahead, albeit it looked very promising. The existential threats from the internal and the external factors became eminent. Internal threats encompassed the high nobility (haute noblesse) and the legal-political power it had through voting. In addition, the rise of imperialist powers in Europe and the search for expansion would become an external threat if the Crown did not show interest in Columbus' proposal. Such an endeavor required readiness, funding, a clear action plan, and a unifying ideology that would bind the parties together. The Monarchs sought to consolidate the state by reforming the administration, unifying the country ideologically, restoring finances, and building a modern military power. They needed to reassert their absolutism to preserve their union and revamp the entire political caste. First, the Monarchs stripped the nobility of all voting powers. The "high nobility" took a big slice out of the treasury as an entitlement, which exhausted the public finances. The traditional authority granted their right to vote no longer suited the Crown's decision-making power. The Monarchs fathomed that if stripped of their political and economic power, the nobility could no longer be a threat. They handpicked the new administrative personnel and recruited state employees from two social milieus other than the Royal Court. First were – los letrados, – a group of competent, educated individuals in jurisprudence from Colegios Mayores (Salamanca and Valladolid), and in the second group were Los Caballeros. [60] Caballeros or (hidalgos) were military men of a lower nobility status yet faithful to the Crown. The new system ended the privilege abuse of the upper class that had left the treasury in a deplorable state. After restoring the finances, the Crown needed to rebuild and modernize the military. It needed to shift the tactics from old feudal orders and practices to a new modern organization with heterogeneous unities such as infantry, artillery, and chivalry divisions. Furthermore, the Crown would reattribute the mercenaries directly from the public treasury. Later that year, in the fall of 1492, Christopher Columbus, a shipbuilder from Genoa promoted to Admiral, made his first voyage in the New World, which he named the Indies. His first voyage did not mark the beginning of the Age of Exploration. Reducing the Conquest to the Age of Exploration undermined an entire historical process and the position of Spain in the first hundred years as an undefeatable imperialist power.

Hidalguía as the Ruling Ideology

The Spanish hidalguía ideology dominated the colonies for almost four hundred years. Many historians underestimate the role of the hidalgos or limit it only to the first period of the conquest. But when it comes to identity, the debate evolves more around Tainos, the Afro-Antillean, and the Creoles, leaving out the most potent stratum of Peninsulares, the hidalgos. Others portray hidalgos as scoundrels searching for glory, money, and power, which they might have well been.

Why is hidalguía so crucial to the mentality and ideology of the Indies and Latin American settlements? Who were the hidalgos beyond the Spanish lower nobility rank? La hidalguía is no longer limited to aristocracy but to an entire ideology and system of values stemming from Medieval Spain. What is very surprising is how hidalguía has impacted nationalism and identity in Puerto Rico. When the rhetoric evolves about Old Spain and its legacy, we see immediately how the nationalist feelings spark arduously. On the other hand, discussions about Tainos and the African heritage go as far as the identity debate. In other words, nationalism in Puerto Rico invokes ties with Spain as the imperial power. The "other"- North American nationalism can only be an imaginary nationalism to Puerto Ricans. In this case, the identity is the majority, the mix of Taino, African, Creole, and mestizos, but not the peninsular. To understand the conquest of the Americas, one must be able to fathom what hidalguía as ideology meant.

The Spanish hidalgo became one of the prominent key players in the colonial state and politics of the metropolis on the periphery. It would represent par excellence in the interests of the monarchy. Theoretically, the emergence of the "hidalguía" [61] is unclear. Hidalguía fits in the framework of social stratification and must be considered a social status. As such, it must use social resources as a power tool to legitimize the traditional authority that comes with the status of nobility. Unlike class, which is strictly determined by the individual's position in society, Spanish hidalguía stemmed in a feudal system where economic or social resources were pre-determined, and the traditional authority was legitimized only when it acquired wealth and power. Why did hidalgos in Medieval Spain obtain status but not power, wealth, or formal authority? Trincado González, Íñigo[62], says hidalguía dates before the Middle Ages,

> *"To be more precise, the majority of the theories that intend to illuminate these questions go as far as the epoch of the Germanic invasions of Roman Spain and the subsequent establishment of the Visigoth kingdom."*[63]

Among the theories that have traveled with time, two hypotheses stand out. Cited in Trincado González; Íñigo, Mayer, and Sanchez Albornoz have introduced two different views about the origin of the hidalguía. According to Mayer, the Germanic invasion of Roman Spain created a schism between the two elites, the Spanish Roman aristocracy and the Visigoths. Once the Visigoths asserted their rule, they established the governing elites around the 7th century. Visigoths regarded the Roman Spaniards with disdain and kept them out of political power. Hence, this class of Visigoth became - according to Mayer - the ruling elite and, subsequently, the nobility. [64] The Spanish historian Claudio Sanchez Alborno[65] defends the argument that leadership had become problematic after the Germanic invasion of Roman Spain because the Visigoth rule's population spoke a different language and had other traditions and religions. Hence, the Visigoths had many difficulties ruling the conquered territories. It is believed that the Visigoths extended their invitation to the Spanish-Roman elite to share power and control the population. On the other hand, the Spanish Roman elite used the Visigoths to assert their social status. The children of Roman Spaniard elite were called "Filii primatum, los primogénitos de la nobleza hispanogoda,"[66] the first-born of the Hispanogoda nobility. It meant that the entitlements applied only to the first-born, whereas hidalgos did not inherit the title nor wealth. This lack of access to wealth and power became the driving force behind the expeditions and the conquest of the West. Unlike the British settlements, where the colonists sought freedom of religion or escaped political persecution, the Spanish hidalgos had different social positions. They emerged from a feudal system where nobility was status and the natural right to own servants was granted with the title, yet they did not inherit wealth from their lineage.

The lack of access to resources was more of a stratification problem than a class struggle. New World adventure became a window of opportunity for hidalgos. Aspiring knights could accrue wealth if they were faithful to the Crown. Although traditional authority stemming from their "pedigree" did not guarantee economic prosperity, hidalgos, as I have explained, were "sons of somebody" Hijos de algo. They were loyal to the Crown; in exchange, the royal family sanctioned their position as critical officials who represented the Crown on the periphery. Acquiring nobility titles, whether by lineage or privilege, was an established practice in Medieval Spain. The New World would open a different chapter and change the tradition of granting nobility titles, wealth, and power. For example, in Spain, "La hidalguía, according to José Antonio Guillén Berrendero, was achieved by privilege *and merits, or by blood* (de sangre o de privilegio). To change the status from plebeian to hidalgo, one must provide militia services for the Crown. [67]

> *In the case of the kingdom of Castile and its jurisdiction rights, the change of status, from plebeian to noble, was operated mainly through the militia, where there was a need to promote repopulation in complex and border areas with the Moors, which required an army of solid cavalry, able to be quickly disposed of.*

Hidalguía in Spain had although another dimension. Hidalgos were *cristianos* and died as cristianos; when not fighting the infidel, they prayed for their salvation.[68] Hidalguía was built on three pillars that determined their place in the social order. First, belonging to the nobility had an economic benefit, the right to own land and servants. Secondly, the nobility status gave hidalgos legitimacy in their political and military position. The third pillar was morality and integrity. If it were not for the code of honor, hidalgos would not have been able to represent the Crown in two significant endeavors – *la Reconquista and la Conquista de las Americas.* Argimiro Ruano writes:

> *"The Spanish society of the sixteenth century with six hundred thousand nobles among eleven million inhabitants is governed by this nobility that -whether it lives a lie or the truth- is lived as a philosophy of life."*[69]

By the 1500s, the Spanish Crown had a clear vision of their country. They were aspiring to build a nation by cleansing the government of the infidels[70] and expanding in the Americas. It was perhaps an ambitious enterprise, yet the Catholic monarchs worried about governing the new territories. They were not as confident that the regions would be under the rule of the Crown. A system of checks and balances of power in the colonies was yet to be established. Overseas enterprises were far, and the honor code was not enough to govern. Fearing that distance and the unknown would weaken the Crown's control, the king and queen had to declare their absolutism as nonnegotiable and introduced a new system of incentives for hidalgos much more generous than prior practices during the Reconquista. Reinforcing old rank and nobility practices became a much more pragmatic solution. Those willing to travel far, conquer, and expand the empire were entitled to wealth, nobility titles, and a military and political career.

This enterprise adds another dimension to the role of hidalgos and completes the "triad" Hidalgo-Cristiano-Conquistador. Granting them an honorable status and the opportunity to acquire wealth turned the "Spanish Hidalgo" into a new ideology in the colonies. The valiant Hidalgo, born to conquer, belonged to the arms upon his birth. He became the dream of each aspiring squire to enter the nobility rank but foremost identified with Spain as the motherland (Madre España). These feelings sparked the first signs of national identity. The Hidalgo would become the future caste of peninsular at the top of the hierarchy in the colonies. [71] Moreover, there is a great debate between two distinct views on the colonization of the Americas and their legacy - North American colonialism and its counterpart – Spain, the undefeated empire for almost four centuries. The debate is a classic ideological trope; as defined above, it is a matter of perceptions and hegemony. The two interpretations about the Indies have become one of the reasons we see split loyalties in Puerto Rico's political dilemma since 1898. It is pretty apparent how these two interpretations play out in the identity debate. The nationalist proponents see themselves as aligned with the Hidalgo ideology. It is a question of the "superiority" of the imperial blood and self-realization of "who we are" as descendants of the Spaniard Hidalgo. The nostalgia of Madre España is not only about the "glorious past" but also about the peninsular blood in the Puerto Rican identity. "El hidalgo sabe perder," says Argimiro Ruano, meaning the Hidalgo loses with honor. But does he? [72] How and what did hidalgos lose, and did they ever accept the defeat of their Anglo-Saxon counterparts? The hegemonic and anti-colonialist rhetoric nowadays revolves around the presence of the Anglo-Saxons as the *other* in the Puerto Rican identity.

Juan Ponce de Leon, the founder of the Puerto Rican Settlement

Juan Ponce de Leon was part of Columbus' second expedition in the fall of 1493. "A poor squire yet loyal to the throne, Ponce de Leon had ambitions for power and glory as many of the hidalgos did once they embarked on the new journey. Juan Ponce de Leon, after quarrels with Columbus' son, sailed to Florida and founded the first continental settlement in Florida. His achievement has been overshadowed by competition and clashes, much like after death. Ponce de Leon has been portrayed as naïve, an adventurer, a curious traveler more than an honorable hidalgo. *The Puerto Rican Boletin de la Academia Puertorriqueña de la Historia* gives another account of Ponce de León. His role as one of the most influential figures in the early history of colonial Spain has been reduced to romanticized tales of wealth and gold, completely overlooking his political, gubernatorial, military, and administrative achievements.[73] Van Middledyk represents Ponce de Leon as a squire thirsty for gold and riches. He writes, *Ponce de Leon made known his desire to see the places where the chiefs obtained the yellow metal for the disks which, as a distinctive of their rank, they wore as medals around their neck.*[74]

Documents show that he was well-balanced and a man of honor. Hidalgo's duty in the New World was to serve the Crown and God and be compensated for work. Like many military men, they were aware of danger and death while they conquered every city and claimed in the name of God and the king. [75] Ponce de Leon was only nineteen when he crossed the ocean for the first time in 1493 during Columbus' second expedition. Born in 1474 in San Tervás de Campos, Diocesis de Leon, Provincia de Valladolid in Castilla, Ponce de Leon was a distinguished military man who fought in Granada at a very young age. In addition, Puerto Rican academics and historians argue that the figure of Ponce de Leon has been distorted and limited to his desire to get rich, overshadowing his leadership skills as a diplomat and governor.

> *Up until a few years ago, all the stories of America made it appear as described by the chronicler Gonzalo Fernández de Oviedo, "A poor squire when it happened, but in reality, he was already a veteran of the Moorish wars, having participated in the taking of Granada."*[76]

During his mission in the Hispaniola, Ponce de Leon distinguished himself during the rebellion of Taíno Indians in Salvaleon de Huguey. Nicolas de Ovando[77], the governor of the Hispaniola from 1501-1502, made him the lieutenant of Juan Esquivél.[78] After Esquivél engaged himself with the conquest of Jamaica and left Salvaleon de Huguey, Ponce de Leon was promoted to captain. While in Higuey province, Ponce de Leon learned from the Borinquen natives that there was gold in the rivers. In 1508, with Ovando's permission Ponce De Leon embarks on the journey toward the island of Borinquen with a caravel, a handful of men, and a few Taíno Indians as interpreters.[79] Ponce de Leon landed in Aguada.[80] The natives of Puerto Rico showed hospitality in expectation of a reciprocal attitude upon his arrival. Having learned about the atrocities the Spaniards had committed on the Island of Hispaniola, the mother of the local cacique had asked her son to avoid conflict and show kindness and hospitality.[81] Ponce de Leon established peace with the natives after years of disputes between the settlers and the indigenous population. He'd had a reputation for soothing the turbulent relationship of the Spaniards with the natives in the Hispaniola. Choosing a subtle strategy over violence resulted in reciprocal hospitality and reverence.

"It is deduced from these facts that Ponce de León possessed knowledge that today we call military engineering magnificent for its time. He was an unparalleled organizer, and thus we see how, in his first expedition to Puerto Rico, he drew villages, established governments, surveyed the new ports, built maps, and had knowledge of metallurgy, which allowed him to discover mines in the new lands."[82]

In Borinquen - just as he was promised, Ponce De Leon found a place rich in gold and changed its name from San Juan Bautista to Puerto Rico (Rich Port). As a reward for his calm temperance, while dealing with the indigenous population, Ponce de Leon received the sister of the Cacique Guyabana I in marriage. He kept a sincere relationship with the Spanish Crown. The calamities and the transgression were common in Spain's settlements. Settlers found guilty of mistreating the natives were often arrested and shipped to Spain, especially after the denouncements of the genocide by the Dominican Friars.

Ponce de Leon was known for his diplomatic skills, and that did not go unnoticed by its rivals. Many documents reveal the struggle and his relationship with Columbus' sons. Diego Columbus, around 1508 challenged the legitimacy of Ponce de Leon as Governor of Puerto Rico. Diego claimed that his father, Columbus, had claimed the island first. Thus, he was entitled to the gold and other resources as his son by an initial contract signed before the first expedition. The quarrel soon reached the Crown. The ongoing disputes over the island and the frequent correspondence with the Crown from both parties led to a final decision. Ponce de Leon was a dear and trustworthy person for the Crown. Yet the Columbus family was part of the deal he signed with the Catholic King and Queen.

Ferdinand, himself ended the dispute by ordering Ponce de Leon to leave the island, but he must remain untouched - in favor of his loyalty to the Crown. Thus in 1511, Ponce de Leon left the Island in the hands of Juan Ceron, Miguel Diaz, and Diego Morales (Diego Columbus' allies) and embarked on another journey. By King's decree, Juan Ponce de Leon was awarded the title of *Adelantado* of Bimini and Florida's expeditions. A few months later, Ponce de Leon headed north to Saint Augustine, Florida, and in 1513, founded Florida, the first colony in North America. He became the first Governor until he died in 1521. As one of the prominent figures in US history, Ponce de Leon has been overshadowed by the legend of Bimini and the Fountain of Youth, minimizing his role as the founder of two major settlements, Puerto Rico and Florida. Ponce de Leon is the classic hidalgo representation in the early Spanish settlements. Like Hernan Cortes and Francisco Pizarro, Ponce de Leon built his career as a military man, one who was born and raised to arms. Ponce's loyalty, much like Cortez and Pizarro, remained to the Crown Catholic faith and prospering in the name of Spain. In his figure, we see the first seeds of Spanish nationalism and identity transplanted in the New World, even though it was declared in the name of the Crown. Unlike the Columbus clan, who had no loyalty, identity, nobility titles, or affinity with Spain, hidalgos were mere nationalists, and later on, their successors would flock to the conservative Creole elites. Columbus' clan transgressed the boundaries of human behavior. They were there to exploit only, yet hidalgos carried out the task of building the Empire in the name of Spain, the Crown, and God.

Taínos: Beyond the Legend

Much of this chapter constructs a narrative depicting the encounter between Boricuas (Tainos of Puerto Rico) and the first Spanish settlers. Constructing a comprehensive narrative about the Taíno Indians is quite challenging. With the rise of the Neo Taíno movement in the last twenty years, the rhetoric has shifted from mestizaje or assimilation to Taino Nation and Revival. Taino activism claims indigeneity as an ethnic group and indigeneity within the group (mixed ethnicities or races). In agreement with the UN's definition of terms, Taino activism seeks to revive or give light to the indigenous element, and the loose UN definition fits their cause. Added in 1986, the UN definition of indigeneity includes: *"Any individual who identified himself or herself as indigenous and was accepted by the group or the community as one of its members was to be regarded as an indigenous person."*[83] This is very problematic for the Puerto Rican identity and undermines the triad or the mestizaje. The Taino Activists separate themselves from the Puerto Rican identity. They have emerged as an indigenous entity and fight for acceptance and adherence in a much larger community, the North American Native Community. [84] Hence, one would ask, who can claim indigeneity? The vagueness of the UN definition can create legal-political implications. Such ideologies can create *fictitious identities*, ethnic entrepreneurship or sub-groups, and territorial claims. Various sociologists and anthropologists have approached the problem on many levels. Among other approaches stand out, linguistic reconstruction of Arawak utterances, social constructivism of Taíno ethnicity, and establishing a network of Taínos with other Native American nations or tribes. Reconstructing linguistic utterances of the Arawak tongues is even more challenging. As a branch of many Arawakan languages, Taino disappeared in the 16th century. [85] The complexity of constructing the narrative by revitalizing Taino languages has major inferences. The language was not inherited or transferred. Taíno language ended with the population around the 1600's. The utterances were represented on symbols and lacked basic structures such as morphology, syntax, lexicology, and other linguistic components. The people who claimed to have escaped the Spanish genocide were not able to preserve the utterances (the spoken language) and pass them along. The second implication to claim indigeneity is that the population has assimilated, and those sustaining to have *sangre pura* Taina – unmixed- are merely claims or founded mostly on ideology and political agendas. Taino's presence as an ethnic or racial in Puerto Rican identity is often contested, and the controversy that surrounds their survival has become a political debate. The Puerto Rican identity, among many claims, shows incongruity and struggles to find common ground between studies on identity and ethnicity. Neo Taíno claims are fundamentally sociopolitical- about recognition of survival. In the Rise and the Decline of Taínos, Irving Rouse, the people who greeted Columbus defend the argument that Taínos have not disappeared. A few had escaped the genocide and fled to the hills or the tropical forest. Neo-Taino activists use this claim to further their agenda and claim autochthony or perhaps recognition as the other Native American tribes or nations. [86] Hence, it is not only a symbolic claim. Many researchers recognize that Taino's contribution to the Puerto Rican identity is crucial. Neo-Tainos maintain a sizable population of Tainos on the Islands of Puerto Rico, Cuba, and Hispaniola, who claim indigeneity based on reconstructed language utterances and other cultural and archeological sources. The groups claim that this identity is independent of the triad represented in mestizaje. To sum up the argument, the ambiguity around Tainos as people leaves the researcher with a few hypotheses. One is the assimilationist view that Tainos vanished or assimilated in the triad. Gabriel Haslip–Viera argues that Tainos have disappeared, and the remaining population assimilated in the first decades of the Spanish Conquest. The other interpretation is the *conceivable indigeneity* theory supported by the Neo-Taino activists and researchers such as Sherena Feliciano Santos, Maximilian Forte, Lynne Guitar, and Pedro Ferbel, who claim that Tainos still exist as an ethnic group. The blood quanta – David Cintron argues - should not be exclusive nor a membership requirement. Taino ethnicity is a mere cultural-social construct, and it is malleable, according to Cintron. [87] With the rise of the "Taino Revival," the debate has become political. Indigeneity is not the only claim beyond the Taino activist groups. Ethnicity comes in two forms. Ethnicity for profit and for meaning- Cintron quotes. [88] The claims of the activist groups are not only about survival but also legitimacy, self-definition, and self-determination. [89] Hence, the indigeneity claim has turned the identity debate into a masquerade. Sherena Feliciano Santos questions: Have Tainos assimilated into a new identity, or were they silenced by erasing away their existence? She approaches the indigeneity claims, backing up the Neo-Taino activism. Feliciano Santos argues that Taínos - the first inhabitants of Puerto Rico - never faded. More importantly, the "Taíno" element is, in fact, more present than it is thought. They have assimilated into the new identity and have become a part of the process of mestizaje. [90] She writes:

> *"In conventional histories of Puerto Rico, the designation of Taíno is often reserved for the aboriginal inhabitants of Puerto Rico before Spanish conquest and colonization. In these histories, Taíno political, social, and cultural organization was largely decimated in the early 16th century through warfare, disease,*

slavery, and assimilation of the colonizing process."

Then, she uses the dialectic approach to challenge the Afro-Antillean identity proponents. Her counterclaim depicts romanticizing the pre-Columbian period in the Antilles as a sophisticated effort to cultivate an identity that delineates the presence of indigenous factors within the margin of a group that no longer contributes to an identity. It is a political effort to create a perception that the indigenous presence is absent.[91] Henceforth, erasing the indigenous factor from the Puerto Rican identity is a biased interpretation and shifts the focus from determining individuality within a larger, collective identity framework without considering the hypothesis that Taíno individuality is present beyond the survived symbols.[92] Of course, Puerto Rico is a lab of conflicted identities, Argimiro Ruano argues. Other Taino Revival proponents argue that Taino ethnicity is a macro-social construct. By criticizing the assimilationist view, such arguments rely on the social-constructionism (constructivist) theory, which frames race and ethnicity as socially invented. The theory blows Taino primordialism and undermines the pre-Columbian civilizations as unmixed ethnicities. Such claims exclude race and ethnicity as kinship categories, and it presumes that groups can socially construct their ethnicity based on pre-set membership norms and values and how they define themselves as members of a particular group. [93]

Scholars such as Haslip-Viera argue that claims by Maximilian Forte, Lynn Guitar, and others erase or diminish the African contribution from the Afro-Antillean identity. Haslip-Viera argues that whitening Puerto Rican identity by boosting the indigenous factor (much lighter skin than the African factor) threatens the Puerto Rican identity as part of a much larger Afro-Antillean identity. Proponents of this theory –as we introduced in the introduction- are Jose Luis Gonzalez as well as Stuart Hall, who sustain that whitewashing the African factor is, in fact, a forged identity claim that aims to present the Antillean as lighter or European. The claims are also ideological and, as discussed later in the book, dwell on the classist division of the Antilles societies. [94] Gabriel Haslip-Viera mentions that based on historical evidence, "The pre-1492 indigenous population (unmixed with Spaniards, Africans, and others outside the Americas) became extinct in Puerto Rico, Cuba, and Hispaniola by the early decades of the 1600s."[95] The proponents of this theory –according to Haslip Viera- base their arguments on the misuse of evidence and claims that Tainos and their pedigree are still living on the islands of Puerto Rico, Cuba, and Hispaniola. [96] The argument is used to fuel circles of Neo-Taino groups who fulfill their political agenda by antagonizing the assimilationist view. In other words, here we have a few scenarios to worry about. Based on evidence and documents, I agree with Haslip-Viera's claim. The historical narrative of Tainos reveals that physically, as people, they became extinct in the early decades of the 1600s. Cited in Haslip Viera:

"As noted above, there are no actual Taínos in Puerto Rico, the Dominican Republic, and their Diasporas at present, nor at any time since the early 1600s, with an apparent very minor immigration that took place in the eighteenth century, and Forte provides no support or evidence for his assertion aside from his acceptance of the unsupported claims by the Neo-Taínos, Lynne Guitar, Pedro Ferbel, Tony Castana, and a few others. Forte's claim that Taínos are present in the modern world is also articulated in a simplistic and self-serving manner without analysis and based on his other simplistic view of the transition that takes place beginning in the period 1550-1600

when the decimated remnants of the pre-Columbian indigenous begin to merge with incoming Africans, Europeans, and others to form the ethnically mixed creole population that we see today."

Moreover, as Haslip-Viera continues, *"A relatively small subset of the pre-1492 indigenous population mixed with Spaniards, Africans, and others during the 16th and early 17th centuries. This population became the basis for the hybrid Creole population that is seen today."* [97]

Then, how do we construct narratives based on symbols, relics, and archeological sites? Puerto Rico's recent history testifies to something that cannot be seen but conceived. San Juan's aggrandized colonial fortresses are touchable and real. The narrow streets of San Juan, their names, the well-kept colonial buildings, the architecture, and so forth make up the pieces of the puzzle.

The very military character of Old San Juan gives evidence of a reality with a purposeful existence. However, there were Tainos and their dwellings before El Morro and San Cristobal. We can only imagine, nevertheless, they were there. Nowadays, Taino symbols have become part of Puerto Rican pop culture. *El sol, el caracol, el niño, and el coqui* are well-known, famous relics, visible and accessible all over the island in souvenir shops. It is a way to embrace a heritage and a sense of belonging. Taíno, according to Pedro Martir de Angleria and Diego Alvarez Chanca, means "Bueno" and "noble." It was first heard on the coastal side of what is now Santo Domingo, and it was - probably- part of the language spoken by "Indios" under the rule of the "cacique"- chieftain- of Guacanagarix Island, what is now the Dominican Republic. Taínos populated the Greater Antilles and were the ones to greet the explorers when they set foot in the Caribbean islands. What is left in the historical narrative is how we identify Tainos in Puerto Rican cultural nationalism today, and that has been the core of the debate between scholars and the Neo-Taíno movement.

The Pre-Columbian societies, especially those of the Antilles, continue to intrigue historians and archaeologists.[98] It is still an unexplored world. Due to the rapid decline, much of their narrative has yet to be constructed. The public perceives that Taínos seemed a mystical people whose mirage faded rapidly in the hills and the tropical rainforest after Spaniards colonized the island. Irving-Rouse has worked for many years to reconstruct the migration of people in the Antilles and has developed a few theories based on the evidence collected in the archaeological sites of three islands of the Greater Antilles: Cuba, Puerto Rico, and the Dominican Republic. *One of his claims sustains that the first migration came in what Rouse called the "lithic" age, which happened around 6,000 years ago based on the dates of the earliest sites on the islands. The second significant migration occurred during the Archaic Age, the third during the Ceramic Age, and the final during the Historic Age.* [99]Proving indigeneity remains a debatable topic nowadays, with the Taíno activist movements claiming that the thesis that the Taíno race has been extinct is a farce. [100] In one of the many Arawak languages, Boricua means "Brave Lords." They were also called Taíno Indians and, like many Arawak tribes, emerged in the Greater Antilles from the delta of the Orinoco River during the migration era around 5,000 B.C. The population process of the Antilles lasted thousands of years as the tribes moved up the archipelago until they inhabited most of the islands of the Caribbean, especially the Greater Antilles.

After the settlers took over the Greater Antilles, things changed drastically. In the tumultuous period that followed the discovery of the New World, little is known except for the "chronicles" the friars and historians gathered before the natives declined rapidly.[101] The first historian to have written the history of Puerto Rico was Fray Íñigo Abbad y Lasierra (1788). While he served in Puerto Rico, Fray Íñigo Abbad y Lasierra recorded the everyday life of Puerto Ricans, including costumes, climate, geography, flora, and fauna. It was considered the first work of the modern history of Puerto Rico. Hence, the debate nowadays over the Taíno people evolves around two claims; first, it recognizes the presence of Taínos in today's Puerto Rico culture and ethnogenesis. The second view is that Taínos disappeared entirely in the first years of colonization, around the first decades of the 1600s. Both views support the existence of Taínos as people and as a sub-culture inside a larger construct that of the pre-Columbian civilizations in the Antilles.

Historically, Columbus' first encounter was not as much about the natives as it was about the beauty of nature and the hidden treasures. [102]Upon Columbus' arrival in Puerto Rico, Taíno huts were empty. They had fled up in the hills. [103] Perhaps Taínos were not as gullible as the Spaniards thought but somewhat cautious and diplomatic. After all, "La Hispaniola" was hours away, and Columbus had left his crew behind a year before, in 1492. Taínos from Hispaniola and Puerto Rico visited each other daily.[104] After settlers imposed the encomienda system,[105] many Tainos escaped from Hispaniola to Puerto Rico because of the easy access and the proximity to the Island. Physically, Taínos were short people with straight black hair but well built. Taínos of Puerto Rico entered a category of natives called Classic Taínos living in the Hispaniola and Puerto Rico, as opposed to Sub-Taínos who dwelled in lesser-developed societies in the Antilles. *Taínos de Puerto Rico "tenian el pelo negro y lacio, eran bajos de estatura con cuerpos bien formados... andaban siempre desnudos,"* Rafael Gonzales Muñiz writes. [106]

The study and the reconstruction of the Greater Antilles' pre-Columbian population must rely on three primary sources of data collection, according to Karen Anderson Córdova: Ethno-historical, documentary, and archeological. For this study, I've relied on the work of Irving Rouse for the archeological sources and various researchers in the field of anthropology for the ethnogenesis and history parts. Geographically, the Caribbean islands are organized in three regions: The Greater Antilles (Cuba, Hispaniola, Puerto Rico, and Jamaica), the Lesser Antilles Virgin Islands, a chain of islands, and the Bahamian Archipelago. The large mountains and fertile soil make the Greater Antilles capable of supporting dense populations. Physically positioned in a favorable setting, Cuba in the West, Hispaniola in the Center, and Puerto Rico in the East enabled the natives to travel short distances in the chain islands of the archipelago. [107] When Columbus set foot in the Caribbean Islands, especially in the Hispaniola land of Classic Taínos, he encountered permanent villages, each governed by a chief (cacique). The villages had approximately two thousand people living in huts made of wood and thatch. They were loosely organized, and each had approximately fifty houses. [108] *El Cacique* had the more significant, better houses in the middle of the village. Demographically, the villages were organized into districts, each with its chieftain. Like many Pre-Colombian civilizations, the society had stratified into two main divisions, the ordinary people and the n:bility or the ruling class (*naborias and nitaínos*)· Ethno-genesis and group formation of Classical Taínos starts with the population of the Antilles.

The Contradicting Views

By the time Columbus set sail, the societies in the Antilles were well-established. [109] The Taíno existence – part of an unexplored culture due to the drastic historical mishaps – is left ambiguous, and most of this gap results from different interpretations. The discussion is entirely ethical and a matter of perceptions. The view about the West Indies' discovery is an important debate, unsolved. The other dimension of the discussion relies upon a political debate, a dichotomy professed as (*civilizacion y barbarie*). This argument is deemed a philosophical matter, which can well be, but it is also a not so silent war between two very distinct worlds, hispanofilía and "Anglo-Saxonía." Based on Domingo Faustino Sarmiento's work (Civilización y Barbarie: Vida de Juan Facundo Quiroga), *civilization* is associated with the Anglo-Saxon mentality, Northern Europe, their life, costumes and traditions, whereas as *barbarie*, Karen Ball,[110] identifies Latin America, and Spain. This taxonomy is, in fact, the center of the philosophical debate that has haunted the two imperialist powers in their quest for expansion. The conceptual understanding of the Colonial Spain stems in the medieval era, the chivalry, war virtues, honor, loyalty, idealistic interpretation of what the world is, whereas *el gentleman* is quite different, cold, collected, profit oriented and without ideals. [111]

Becoming an Imperialist Power with Private Enterprise

Castilian imperialism begins in 1492 with the fall of Granada and the end of the Reconquista. On January of 1492, Isabella and Ferdinand entered gloriously in the city of Granada, after seven centuries of Moorish rule. Now the Conquest of the Americas became a reality. The period marks an important era in Spain's history- the colonization of the New World in the name of the Crown and Christianity. This age also marks one of the most notorious yet transcendental undertakings in the modern history – the culmination of Castile expansionism, which had started long ago. [112] The actors involved in this juggernaut were operating in different realms of institutionalized imperialism where they each had a vested interest. The Crown, the clergy, the adventurers, the hidalgos, all intermingled in one of the most daring endeavors in human history. The crossing the ocean and taking land in the name of the Crown, from the people who had de facto judicial rights over their territory. Yet the Crown was not anew to this practice either. La Reconquista had served as a precedent where Ferdinand and Isabella had combined private enterprise and public (state institutions) in the conquest of the Moorish territories and the Canary Islands. The monarchs financed the *adelantados* [113] where they could, but largely, the conquest of the Americas was left in the hands of private enterprises. Elliott mentions that *"The leader of an expedition would also expect to enjoy the spoils of conquest, in the shape of movable property and captives, and to receive grants of land and a title of nobility, like his predecessors during the Reconquista."[114]* This practice, enabled military men to gain wealth, land, titles and power in the new acquired territories. They established their legal authority overseas, through capitulaciones even when the expedition was entirely financed by private enterprises. Such contracts guaranteed the power of the Spanish Crown and at the same time rewarded the settlers for their services. Unrestricted settlement had proven to be a disaster during the takeover of the Canary Islands thus Ferdinand and Isabella tried to reinforce the control while allowing the private enterprises to proliferate before other European settlers claim land in the name of other imperialist powers. [115]

"The problem of jurisdiction in America was both moral and material. The Spaniards could only survive in the New World by exploiting native labor, in the fields and the mines, but on what grounds could this exploitation be justified? This question raised the whole problem of the basis and extent of Spain's rights in the New World – itself an old problem posed in a new form."[116]

After cleansing Spain of the Jews, Moors and Gypsies the Crown confiscated what it could, established new economic policies among others financing Columbus' voyages. The ethnic and religious cleansing along with the new acquired territories marked the dawn of a new era, that of the Modern Age and more importantly, the establishment of a state through institutional coercion. Columbus' second expedition was a powerhouse. Along with conquerors, the vessels carried priests, medical doctors, historians, mapping experts. It was a very different expedition from the previous year (1492) when three small caravels carrying only one hundred twenty people accomplished the most transcendental event in the history of humanity.[117] The new expedition comprised three galleons and fourteen caravels of many sizes. The fleet was well equipped with all the requisites for the establishment of a permanent settlement in the lands that had been discovered the year before.[118]

The first encounter with the Boricua Taínos happened in the late fall of 1493. Columbus left Cádiz, Spain on September 24th. It was his second voyage to the West Indies. Enthusiastically, along with a crew of well-known names, the admiral was well prepared· [119] The expedition was founded with wealth confiscated from the Jews.[120] The immediate intentions, perhaps well-masked under auspicious

70

beginning, made up one of the major endeavors in the history of the discovery of the Western Hemisphere. November of 1493 found Columbus on his journey seeking to settle in the Hispaniola. After making brief stops in many islands of the Lesser Antilles, Columbus sighted the island of Puerto Rico. He stopped in the island briefly, and after christening it San Juan Bautista appointed Vicente Yañez Pinzón as Governor of the island. From the sources, it appeared to have been a quiet encounter.[121] Columbus then, headed west to the Hispaniola and according to documents, he'd forgot about the island of Borinquen.[122]

> *"On the thirty-third day after leaving Cadiz I came into the Indian Sea, where I discovered many islands inhabited by numerous people. I took possession of all of them for our most fortunate King by making public proclamation and unfurling his standard, no one making any resistance."* [123] *Adapted from Spanish.*

During the first years of his governorship in the newly founded settlements, Columbus dealt with insurgency amidst his men whom for the most part were unruly convicts, greedy scoundrels in search for what the Admiral had indirectly promised them; but instead, had found hunger, sickness and suffering. The bitterness of these men crossed the boundaries of transgression and crime in the years to come. [124]

> *The Admiral, who had indirectly promised them these things, to mitigate the universal and bitter disappointment, had recourse to the unwarrantable expedients of enslaving the natives, sending them to Spain to be sold, of levying tribute on those who remained, and, worst of all, dooming them to a sure and rapid extermination by forced labor.*[125]

The Columbus experience gave an overview of what the Europeans thought of the islands: A strategic position situated in the heart of the Caribbean, halfway from Florida and Colombia, a mountainous terrain with romantic views enchanting the heart of the traveler. After all, the island was called "La isla del encanto." The exploration, discovery and conquering era was nothing short of a period filled with uncertainty, adventure, greed and endless struggles. Parallel to the Spanish Crown's superiority and close to a perfect mercantile system of trading goods including slaves, the imperialist powers of modern Europe had more or less similar ambitions but a milder approach of conquering new territories and empires. Ferdinand of Aragon and Isabelle of Castile, in the late 1400's celebrated a feeling of victory and perhaps the birth of Spanish nationalism. The hidalgo euphoria was too large to be contained within Spain's territory. With the triumph of re-conquering Spain, the need of expanding became urgent.

The Genesis of Spanish Colonial Experience

Upon the arrival in the New World, Spaniards implemented all systems inherited from the Reconquista, the takeover of Granada once under the jurisdiction of the Moorish. However, the dominions of New World were not close to the metropolis, nor was it easy to establish a socio-political order and transfer state institutions. Once the Spaniards had arrived, they were aware that from a legal perspective the indigenous population was to be recognized as the sole legal proprietors of the land they owned and cultivated. The rest of the land immediately became state property. Based on Medieval practices and prior contracts, the Crown was obliged to reward the settlers and collect the profits. Thus, the need to structure the political and economic power called for the building of the administrative towns and cities as well as the urbanization of the communities following a Spanish model and architecture. This endeavor was fraught with legal, political and moral complexities. Physically, the towns followed the same model as the towns of Castile yet were more spacious. The moral question that the Crown faced was the case of the "pagan" population that came with the land. They were treated the same way as war booty. Nevertheless, the Crown struggled to maintain a balance between the Catholic moral values and settlers' greed for gold and glory.

The expansionist policies along with the establishment of a classist, and hierarchical order changed the communities and the dwellings of the indigenous population which imposed an urban plan much like Spain of the 1500's with the elite in the center and the lower class in the periphery. The transformation as a process was a simple model. The change agents, or the oppressors, forced upon human subjects their will until they had submitted to the new social order. This change happened on many levels until it culminated with the unrecognizable, and slaughtered indigenous communities. Once an idyllic and indolent lifestyle, it became a living nightmare. Settlers occupied the top of the hierarchy whereas the enslaved people of indigenous and Africans at the very bottom of the social caste. The newly created order was so aggressive that it transmuted in the first thirty years the indigenous population beyond recognition. The racial mix, known as mestizaje yielded new identities. What now sold as the unity of three cultures is an effort to diminish the devastating effects of colonization in the first thirty years in the Antilles. The history of Puerto Rico during the colonial period is a part of general transformations in the Greater Antilles colonized by Spain and under the model of the Reconquista.

Spain had no other option besides the private enterprises and contracted adelantados to advance as an imperial power. Thus, it was an agreement that suited both, the privateers and the Crown. By 1509, the indigenous population had completely lost their liberties. The turmoil and the struggle to govern the islands among the immediate family descendants of Columbus and other settlers proved to be an account of distrust and calamity. The Hispaniola and Puerto Rico were not only rich in gold, but also favorable in the cultivation of other profiting crops. The Spanish crown established absolute monopoly over its colonies and quite fretful demanded integrity and high fidelity in gold smelting and transportation. The conquerors depended heavily on the native's hard labor to survive. The "sistema de encomienda" was first introduced by Columbus in the Hispaniola and later implemented arbitrarily by Ponce de Leon in the Island of Borinquen. Under the encomienda, the natives were distributed among the Spanish settlers.

"These creatures were suddenly called upon to labor from morning to night, to dig and delve, and to stand up to their hips in water washing the river sands. They were forced to change their habits and their food, and from free and, in their own way, happy masters of the soil they became the slaves of a handful of ruthless men from beyond the sea. When Ponce's order to distribute them among his men confirmed the hopelessness of their slavery, they looked upon the small number of their destroyers and began to ask themselves if there were no means of getting rid of them."[126]

Distribution of Natives Among Spanish Settlers,

"100 to Vicente Yañez Pinzon, on condition that he should settle in the island , 100 to

Lope de Conchillos, King Ferdinand's Chief Secretary, as bad a character as Pasamonte, 100 to Pedro Moreno and Jerome of Brussels, the delegate and clerk of Conchillos in Boriquén, 100 each, (200), to the bachelor-at-law Villalobos 80, to Francisco Alvarado 8." [127]

Rivalry arose amongst the settlers especially in the first twenty years of the conquest. The struggle to gain gubernatorial control over the Island of Sanct Johan[128] lasted from 1493 to the 1520's. Juan Ponce de Leon and Cristobal de Sotomayor a young hidalgo - took upon themselves one of the most complex tasks facing the settlement in Sanct Johan - that of keeping the indigenous population under control, crushing potential rebellions. Under the system of "encomienda" and during a brief period the indigenous population honored their own nobility titles and developed hatred toward the Spaniards. The two entities co-existed momentarily in a non-parallel world. The lack of military power from the indigenous population weakened their position and legitimacy. [129] The new social structure was merely a rearrangement of the strata. These requirements included the creations of a new work force, and the development of a mining industry as the most beneficial of the economies. The settlers changed the natives' social status from free men and women to slaves under the system of "encomienda." The first of the economic policies the settlers implemented in the Española during 1490's was gold (smelting) and cotton crops. Hence, the natives of the Hispaniola refused to comply with Admiral's[130] demands. Many had fled to the woods and mountains to escape the submission to slavery.

The liberalization of measures and policies to increase the percentage of white population in the Indies were done diligently by the Crown. In a series of decrees, which justified the will to spread the Christian doctrine, the Crown allowed anyone without distinction to settle in the Indies. As long as they were introduced simply as Spaniards, no questions were asked, and no information was given or required. The interracial relationships became a widespread phenomenon. The people of color introduced with the slave trade started to engage in interracial marriages or relationships with natives. The introduction of African slaves into la Española was considered as a necessary mean to have continuity in the colony. With little regard for the disappearance of the natives, the settlers proceeded by introducing the African slave trade as a replacement for the fading indigenous people. The slave trade progressed pari passu with the gradual declining of the natives. Around 1502 Juan Sanchez entered five caravels of African slaves into the Island of Hispaniola, free of duty. The economic and migration policies encouraged the promotion of peninsulares (Iberians) whom through the political system would outnumber the people of color. This policy continued until the late 19th century. By the first half of the 19th century, the liberal laws of commerce, trading, taxing of property, goods, and services, import and exports enabled the settlers to accrue wealth and establish satisfactory social status. The colonists were encouraged by the Crown to remain on the island through the free land, slaves, and tax exemption. "The quantity of land allotted was in proportion to the number of slaves introduced by each new settler. The new colonists were not to be subject to taxes or export duty on their produce or import duties on their agricultural implements." Thus, the economic policies alleviated the condition for the stratification of the population into distinct groups of privileged Peninsulares, creoles, jibaros, and slaves. Many of peninsulares married wealthy Creole women and sought their fortune in the island. Under this stratum were merchants and shopkeepers, Catalans, Gallegos and Mallorquins who resided in the island temporarily and found wealth in

76

commercial affairs and business. This social group along with Garrison soldiers made-up the transitory population who'd returned to the peninsula as soon as their service time was over. Lastly, there was another stratum of white people which lawbreakers had sent to serve their time on the island. They wandered in indolence and mingled with the people of color. Regardless, historical sources sustain that it did not affect the social upbringing of people of color, nor it improved their social status. [131]

The population process of the Lesser and the Greater Antilles is consistent with many anthropological arguments from two perspectives: First, the perception that the island was a well-established society and at the same time part of a greater existence and an unexplored world, existential, in a continental setting. Secondly the argument relies on the philosophical debate between Western Civilization and the indigenous societies; a dichotomy of profuse yet bias opinions, refuted as the clash of two distinctive worlds. With many theories and debates on the Taino population as a contributor to the Puerto Rican identity, I argue that as a group, Tainos assimilated into the triad. They were a primordial group before the arrival of the Spaniards. Tainos were organized and had a society ranked by two distinct groups, nitainos and naborias. The social status was important. Tainos relied on trading and kept close relationships with Tainos of Hispaniola. In the first twenty years of the conquest, they were decimated as people and as a community. They forcefully submitted to a new social order, new diet, worked beyond their physical capacity, got hit with disease, which ultimately resulted in their decline. The evidence shows that Tainos physically ceased to exist in the late 16th century. Assimilation into the triad happened via the interracial relationships as *modus vivendi* with two other contributing races. Anthropologists sustain that today's Puerto Rican carries that genome. In approximately three dozen of testimonies that I have recorded from people of Puerto Rican ancestry, (both parents), it resulted that on average, Taino presence ranged from 8 to 13%, African presence (including many regions of Africa) accounted for 18-24%, and a range of 50-65% was of European ancestry mainly from the Iberian Peninsula and Italy. Hence, Taino does exist in the triad. In addition, by early 1700's as anthropologists[132] would argue, it was hard to find a person who was not of a mixed race. In other words, Tainos faded as an ethnic group, unmixed pre-Columbian people. However, I do not exclude the possibility that some fled up in the hills, tropical forest or even escaped to other areas as many indigenous populations did. This is a known fact, and supported by historical documents.[133] Geographically, Tainos – especially those in a small island such as Puerto Rico- had fewer opportunities to escape and reemerge as an ethnic group without interacting with the rest of the population for almost five hundred years. The language also disappeared with Tainos around the time that they'd ceased as an ethnic group. Evidence supports the interaction of indigenous population with Spaniards and African slaves.

The new architectural and social settings enabled Peninsulares to design communities that will fit their colonial status and needs. Like in many of the colonial towns, Peninsulares and Creoles settled in the center and indigenous moved to the periphery, where they had huddled up with African slaves to survive extinction. In addition, the hypothesized claims that Tainos abandoned their ethnicity for economic and political purposes is a long shot. If ethnicity is limited only to social constructivism then it can be claimed, abandoned and reclaimed, as people please, but this is merely an ethical question. The social order did not advance by whether men agreeing or not to cooperate to achieve a harmonious society, more so that to answer the question of why everyone is in conflict with everyone. Perhaps partially, yet systematically the new order was achieved through crushing rebellions until almost the drastic reduction of the Taínos and the introduction of two other dominant contributors: White and African. In this system, the enjoyment of their liberty no longer applied. The indigenous population in the colonies was forced to perform hard labor and excessive working hours, change their food, and their habits. Economic growth and division of labor during the colonial period is based on the relationship between the metropolis and the periphery. Once the Crown established absolute control over the settlements, it had also enabled the colonies to establish their own social order and select the economies that would most benefit the Empire. The vast multiplication of capital was attributed not only to the wealth distribution, but also to the division of labor and the slave distribution system. This form of social order enabled the settlers to accrue wealth very rapidly and it served as an incentive to increase the white migration - the peninsular population- in the Antilles. The division of labor was solely based on hard, unskilled labor in gold mining. Industries were flat and the continuity was only secured by replenishing the dying indigenous population with African slaves systematically.

The uneven, unequal distribution of goods and products yield the depletion of social class on which the settlers depended. The narrow vision of a future coupled with the greed to accumulate; the failure to establish a society with basic norms of human conducts expedited the decline of the Taíno Indians and their gradual replacement with the African slaves. The lack of skills and lack of specialized industries prevailed. Gold mining resources replenished in the first centenary of the Puerto Rican settlement.

A society strives on shared norms and values. Consensual behaviors indicate that the norms and values established are accepted foremost by its adhering members. The disjointed societies created in the Antilles early 1500's demonstrated a lack of cohesiveness regardless of the will to establish a society. It appeared that the rapid and unplanned arrangement of the society was based on a lack of norms and values. The second voyage comprised a well-thought plan of action which upon arrival especially in the Hispaniola did not translate into forming a society based on creating a set of standards. The supremacy of a class over the other warned a change in the social order and the transformation of identities. The conformity to the new social order did not occur consensually, rather through violence and rampage. The expediency was not unknown among the natives, yet it became a survival mechanism, such was the case of Ponce de Leon marriage earlier with the sister of the First Guayabana. The morality, a matter of perception became problematic much later when groups started to mingle because of the need to procreate and progenity (among races) became superior to the pre-set moral values. Promiscuity and unions among races on the lower social stratum drove the mixing of groups and the birth of a new genetic identity, which will be discussed in later chapters.

The Christian moral values in the first half of the 16th century became inclusive in the Greater Antilles. Through the doctrine of Christianity, the ordinances included worshiping as the promoter of continuity of the social order and order in the society. The moral commitment came as a top-down, hierarchical scheme, from the masters to the slaves, either native or African. Children upon birth were declared Christian per Crown ordinances. Thus, the strive to establish a state based on Christian doctrine following the model of the metropolis indicated a simulation of Spain's inside politics transferred into the new settlements.

THE IDENTITY CONSTRUCTION DURING 1508-1898

In this chapter I examine the identity forming under the Spanish colonial rule. I describe how the colonial system functioned in the periphery considering the laws, the systems, and the ordinances imposed by the Crown to create a society ruled directly from the metropolis. I examine the role of the clergy during the colonial rule and how it impacted the daily communal life in the early settlements. The most important part of this chapter is the analysis of the newly formed social caste and the stratification of the colonial societies. I analyze the ethnic and racial factors that contributed to the forming of the Puerto Rican people's identity and of other *pueblos* of the Antilles. Lastly, by taking a look at the socio-genetic components I will determine how society had shaped on the verge of the Spanish American War.

This chapter will help the reader create an imagery of the Antillean societies and evaluate in his own perspective one of the most transcendental periods in human history. Neither the age of the exploration, nor the voyages of Columbus, had given this era the attention and a particular place in the study of the social sciences. It was in fact, the birth of an entire "race" also known as "hispanoamericanismo" that Spain claimed to have engineered by colonizing the New World.

I take into account the historical narrative, the philosophical debate between the European stratified society opposed to (somewhat) egalitarian, Arcadian indigenous living. With the presumed "ending" of the process of mestizaje, the chapter will consider how the euro centrism mentality and the stratification of the society impacted the gradient process of mestizaje and its salient outcome toward the end of the 19th century. There are two concomitant concepts that this chapter will discuss; the homogenization of the sociobiological components, and the unification of their respective cultures.

Before analyzing the role that the Crown and the state had in the formation of the Puerto Rican identity during the colonial period, it is very imperative to establish a thesis that will explain how the transferring of power from the metropolis to the periphery occurred; understand how the structures that enabled and ran a day to day colonial system were framed. What was the nature of the institutions and their complexities; and finally, what constituted the rule of law. By explaining the structure of the colonial system, one might be able to understand how the identities were formed and how the colonial system impacted the new emerging *social caste* not only in the Caribbean Islands, but universally, in all the Spanish viceroyalties of Latin America.

The chapter is organized in various sections according to the theoretical framework and the continuum of the identity building narrative of the first chapter. I start with the colonial model where I give an overview of the Spanish mercantilism compared to other forms of colonialism especially that of the Great Britain. It is very important to explain how the early governing efforts by the clergy consisted in the establishment of societies with Christian values for the indigenous people, but also moral values and teaching of penitence to the settlers. As a result of the colonization, the urban centers were created, and the urbanization of the Indies is an extension of the first chapter where I have touched upon the building of new cities to fit the need of the settlers. I analyze class and racial modifications explaining the social fabric of the Antilles and the Americas after the colonial societies had settled. Finally, I give an account of the conflict between the Creoles and the

Peninsulares which marked the end of the "genetic" identity evolution in the Antilles pertaining to Spain's claim on the engineering of an imperial race.

The Colonial Model

The colonial "takeover" by Spain, Portugal, France, and Great Britain was a pervasive effort to dominate new lands, new markets, find cheap labor, exploit resources, and people in order to strengthen their imperial power and use the commercialism system as a way to control the world economy and order. The success of the model used by Spain and Portugal relied on an economic partnership between the adelantados[134] and the Crown. "The Columbian project was an economic partnership between the Crown and Columbus's private interests, self-consciously modeled on the Portuguese feitoria system." [135]

There were substantial differences between the British Colonial with the Spanish Colonial in regard to the economic model. In the colonial political and economic system, Spain was a stakeholder as opposed to the British Crown which was more like a shareholder. [136] Spain had absolute control over the colonies and in the 16th century had the most wealth and was the most powerful state in Europe. As a result, Spain was also the wealthiest colonial Empire. Theoretically, colonialism depends on dividends to proliferate and maximize profit. Economically, colonialism has two forms; mercantilism and liberalism: As a system, it is perhaps the most prevalent way for empires to expand their gains, and their territory exponentially. Production of goods and natural resources come as a result of the systems imposed and the role of the state (metropolis) over the conquered territories. Unlike Great Britain, Spain had a different approach, and we will see later how the absolute control of natural and financial resources turned out to be a beneficial system for the Crown, for the young "hidalgos" and the peninsulares in search for economic opportunities. This suggests that "colonialism impacts the institutions that regulate commerce and markets (e.g., the extent of free trade), political authority (e.g., the degree to which a rule of law is present), and race and ethnicity (e.g., the degree to which all groups have the same rights). [137] It is worth mentioning that race and ethnicity cannot be reduced only to the degree to which all groups have the same rights, but to the degree in which enabled the creation of social strata based on interactions and relations. Here the argument cannot be reduced to the distinctions between Peninsulares and Creoles. The hierarchical social order had come in shades[138] from top to bottom, lightest to darkest.

The impact that the metropolis had on the periphery, as far as creating the institutions and the entire bureaucratic cast system to exercise absolute control, proved to be beneficial for the Crown and enabled the viceroyalties to economically and administratively self-sustain their territory. Apart the cast of bureaucratic institutions, whether military or civil, Spain had created a high level of mercantile system that had an impact not only on the economy but also on the social development. In terms of social development, it had established labor institutions and sociocultural conventions to transform the indigenous population (or an imported worker population) into an exploited ethno-racial group that often lacked access to health care and education.[139] To be noted here is how social scientists present the idea of the process of mestizaje as an "ethno-racial" group formation. It sustains that this new population of mixed races was at the bottom of the social ladder and as a result of the systems created under a mercantilist model, the "exploiters" offered very little or nothing to the lower class regardless that the group represented a large percentage of the total population. The elite groups were usually unwilling—to provide competitive markets, education, a rule of law, health care, and other public goods to non-elite groups.[140]

Puerto Rico was one of the oldest colonies. Regardless of the size, it was considered of a high military importance and it was almost never defeated. With two castles, San Felipe de Morro and San Cristobal, Spaniards were able to block attacks from the Dutch, English, privateers and pirates.[141] Yet the island had no economy to self-sustain and more importantly, it was a beneficiary annex of the New Spain as opposed to the other strong holds such as Mexico, Guatemala and Peru which were at a high development level in the pre-Colombian era and remained at the high level of the mercantile system.[142] Antonio Pedreira, in his essay "Insularismo" recaps the history of Puerto Rico as documented for the first time by Friar Inigo Abbad. Cited in Antonio Pedreira:

> *"... in the fifth and last chapter of those devoted to studying the state of Puerto Rico at the end of the eighteenth century, it deals with public finances and affirms that the island is very burdensome to the Crown, that it does not cover its expenses and that the treasure, like everything else, is crying out for reform. It is known that since 1586 our treasure was nourished with the money sent annually by Mexico."[143]*

Historical sources reveal that the island was considered a dumping ground and a sentencing "facility" for convicts. The economies on the verge of the 20th century after Spain lost control, were the sugar cane and coffee. Once the gold mining industry was exhausted, it was never replenished by another profiting industry. Hurricanes and storms were a disruptor to the agricultural development whether crops were for consumption or for trading. [144] Early sources of literature, especially the work written on the verge of the Spanish American War sustain that the sociobiological transformation did not happen at the upper social strata such as the Peninsular Spaniards and their immediate descents (the Creoles), yet it happened at the lower strata; a class of native Indians, African slaves and white convicts from Spain serving time on the island. This thesis posits a few claims of group formation in Puerto Rico. First, it describes the role of institutions as a predominant factor in determining social interactions and preserving the classist society, while it searches for occurrences within the groups, meaning that; the concept of belonging to distinct identities and social clusters will promote the need to procreate within. A clear example from the upper strata preservation of class and rank society was the continuum of the white race enabled by the union between the Creole women and Spaniard Peninsulares while the lower strata of colored and indigenous population "huddled" together to survive extinction. The essential question remains whether the Puerto Rican identity was formed as part of the social order imposed by the first settlers, enabled the state policies established during the colonial period, or the identity was merely independent of the social order, the state institution and laws, meaning; it just happened! [145]

Early Governing Efforts

The lack of the state's presence during the first thirty years in the Antilles resulted in a period of benightedness and suffering for the natives, more so than the settlers whose fate was also determined by calamities, ill intentions and ambitions. More importantly, the lack of institutions, and the private governing of the Antilles by the Columbus clan, resulted in a lawless society that mirrored their intentions. Columbus' histrionic attitude in the letters of the king and queen no longer covered up the expunging of a race.

Understanding the Spanish colonial model holds perhaps the "key" to many questions about the historical transformations of the Americas. "Crown-licensed adelantados (expedition leaders) led self-supported expeditions of conquest during which successful conquistadors were rewarded with allocations of land and the servitude of the native people who occupied it." [146] *Among the most prevalent factors to have impacted the establishment of an entirely new social order, were the centralized government and the economy under the Spanish Monarchy, the impact of the Catholic clergy and religion as social regulators and catalysts, the structure and the model of the new city-provinces and dwellings, and lastly, the framework used to define class and race, also known as la casta social.*[147] The struggle to control the settlement reached the Crown and decisions were pragmatic at times favoring the settlers. One of the catalyst powers that impacted the social life and order in the Antilles was the Catholic Church. The role of the missionaries was multidimensional and guided the colonial life regardless of the turn that it took after the society changed beyond recognition.

The Catholic Church: Its role in establishing the colonies in the Americas

The role of the clergy was paramount in creating a social order that benefitted the Crown and also the settlers. However, the role of the Catholic Church must be considered and analyzed in a few dimensions. It is crucial to understand the relationship of the Church with the Crown throughout the entire colonial system as a benefitting relationship between two powerful entities: The clergy, and the secular institutions. In the beginning, the relationship between the church and the settlers was deemed by historians as one of the most unsettling relationships in the New World. More pressure the settlers put on the indigenous population, greater were the Clergy's efforts to end the system of encomienda. The clergy -outraged by the decline in number of the indigenous people- questioned the actions of the settlers, their loyalty to the Catholic faith, and their devotion in practicing Christianity during the troubling years (1492-1518). In addition, the Church used the doctrine to alleviate the irreversible pain and suffering caused to the indigenous, Africans and also mestizos and Ladinos. The role of the church in respect to its mission must be divided between two-time segments: 1) During the colonial period and, 2) at the beginning of the independence movements in Latin America. For the purpose of this study, I will focus solely on the first period. Using this framework, it will enable us to understand in depth the important role that the Clergy had in shaping an entire civilization.

Early missionaries played an essential role in slowing down the massacres and the slaughter of the native population. Such is the case of Friar Bartolome de las Casas, the Hieronymites Order, Antonio de Montesinos and others, whose assignment was to govern the settlements temporarily and stop the extinction of the indigenous people. [148] Confronted with atrocities and violence committed by the settlers, the Dominican Friars launched a series of actions where they had demanded the end the system of encomienda.[149] Hence their mission was not as easy, ending the encomienda threatened the economic incentives and violated the terms of the contracts signed with the royal crown. The settlers openly refused, and their resistance was firm. The Crown also had a reluctant attitude toward the problem in the beginning stages. Having an important role in the expansion of the empire and reassuring the flowing of the dividends for the Crown, the king and queen sided with the settlers and demanded the Friars not to interfere. Settlers felt endowed with the right to own slaves and exploit them. The Aristotelian doctrine of natural enslavement was an idea that played out in the entire Latin American continent throughout the colonizing period. Angry at the deplorable situation in the Hispaniola, on December 21, 1511 the Dominican Friar Antonio de Montesinos held a sermon for the Spanish settlers and delivered one of the most alarming accusation stating: (cited in Lauren Elaine MacDonald)

> *"This voice says that you are in mortal sin, that you live and die in it, for the cruelty and tyranny you use in dealing with these innocent people. Tell me; by what right or justice do you keep these Indians in such a cruel and horrible servitude?"*[150]

The following Sunday, Montesinos performed another sermon with an even harsher tone than the previous one. The settlers, offended, demanded an apology. Yet Pedro de Córdoba, the Head of the Dominican mission in the Hispaniola, and the first Spanish inquisitor in the New World responded that the Order would not issue any apology. Annoyed by the Dominican Friars, the settlers complained to the king and the Head of the Dominican Order in Spain which deemed Montesinos' and Cordoba's comments as harmful.[151]

In the following year, Cordoba sent Montesinos to Spain to lobby against the encominedas and advocate for the protections of the Natives. Pressured by the Dominican friars, King Ferdinand issued a set of laws known as "Laws of Burgos" to ease the pressure and improve the relationship between the settlers and the Natives. Nonetheless, the settlers were interested in sub-humanizing the natives in order to exploit and use their service for cheap labor. It is paramount to understand that religion in North America had a very different position and view from Hispanic America. North American colonies were refuge for religion freedom such was the case of Protestants and Catholics fleeing persecution. In Hispanic America, settlers sought fortune, and land, and not necessarily religious freedom. In contrast with North America, the Catholic clergy had a very dominant role in converting the native population into Catholics and also serving the early Creole societies.[152]

Friar Bartolome de las Casas and the Denouncement of the Genocide

The treatment of the Natives and the process of pacification in the first twenty years reached new levels of atrocities and greed. The pain and suffering inflicted among the Taínos resulted in the rapidly decreasing number of inhabitants and the debilitation of their physical and emotional health. Many had fled the island refusing to be submitted under the system of encomiendas, others died from the harsh working and living conditions, while others committed suicide (source). The deeds of the settlers soon reached Spain. The clergy concerned about the human factor and the disappearance of the Indians brought the case to the Crown testifying not only about the atrocities committed but concerned with the ceasing of their existence. Accusations were tense and the Crown confided in the clergy to govern the Island of the Hispaniola. The Jerome Friars (Hieronymites) governed la Hispaniola for a period of time and removed the natives from the Spaniard dwellings and placed them into villages.[153] To be noticed was the work of Bartolome de las Casas, the Dominican friar who had come to the court with the sole purpose of denouncing the system of "encomiendas" and the cruel treatment of the natives. [154] On July 12, 1512, Las Casas received perhaps the most important concession on behalf of the indigenous people which recognized that they are born free, the redistribution no longer needed to be applied, the Natives whom work in non-resident Spaniards are ipso-facto free to reside in their own villages under the authority of their respective caciques. Yet the concession faced opposition by the settlers sustaining that the right to own slaves is ingrained in the right to conquest.

> *"And thus, in spite of the philanthropic efforts of Las Casas, of the well-intentioned ordinances of the Catholic Kings, and of the more radical measures sanctioned by Charles V, the Indian's lot was not bettered till it was too late to save him from extinction."*[155]

With the Indians dying out, between 1530 to 1536 the Crown made a last effort to save those remaining. In 1538, the king decreed that all Indian slave owners should build stone or adobe houses for them, or they will lose them. In 1543 the Council declared all Indians still alive in Cuba, la Española, and Puerto Rico, are as free as the Spaniards. [156] Regardless of the royal and clergy recommendations to treat the natives well, pay them for their labor, or teach them the Christian doctrine, the masters continued to mistreat them. Thousands of natives were slaughtered for refusal to work or resisting to follow orders or organizing insurgencies.

The Hieronymites Order

The system of encomienda imposed the harshest conditions upon the natives that no human would be able to survive. The conduct of the settlers had been denounced earlier by the friars and the missionaries. The Cardinal of the Franciscan Order Francisco Jiménez de Cisneros after the great debate and dispute of the settlers and the Dominican Order about the treatment of the Natives needed a neutral set of actors to investigate the situation in the Hispaniola and implement social reforms. [157] Thus, the Hieronymites Order found in 1373 was not as influential as the Franciscan and the Dominicans yet had established a good relationship and connection with the secular powers.[158] In 1516, Francisco Jimenez de Cisneros asked the General of Hieronymites Order, Pedro de Mora to embark in one of the most difficult tasks; commit his order to Spain's colonies. [159] Pedro de Mora reluctantly accepted the invitation, after a few hesitations. The problems in the Antilles were many. While the Native population was rapidly declining, the King Ferdinand and the Crown had already been informed of the atrocities. However, caught in in the middle of a quagmire, and quarrels, between the church and the settlers, King Ferdinand allows Cisneros to alleviate some of the problems in the Antilles, by establishing a Hieronymites Order in the Hispaniola to offer relief to the native population. [160]

> *Mora at last selected three Hieronymites representatives–Luis de Figueroa, Alonso de Santo Domingo, and Bernardino de Manzanedo–and sent them to attend upon Cisneros and the impatiently waiting Las Casas. In Madrid, the Hieronymites received a detailed set of instructions from Cisneros, including the necessity of resettling Taino Indians into concentrated villages that would facilitate Spanish access to their labor. [161]*

The role of the Hieronymites in the Hispaniola did not consist as much in the governing the island. Friar Bartolome de las Casas had his reservations. He thought Hieronymites did not do enough to protect the indigenous population. In fact, they'd done as they were instructed. In the following years, the Hieronymite Order investigated through "El interrogatorio" close to fourteen encomenderos, among them two Dominican Friars who were opposed to the system of encomiendas.[162]

Urbanizing the Colonies: Class and Race: The New Social Caste

To be noted, sources sustain that the founding of the city's center impacted the social structure but also impacted the socio-genetic factors. As mentioned before, the huddling of natives and African slaves advanced the process of mestizaje. Yet, this was not the only factor that contributed in the creation of a new physical identity. The establishment of towns for both Spaniards and Indians were central to the Crown's imperial strategy for upholding social, political, and economic control in the Americas. Hence, towns were the idealized setting for "civilized" life. The newly established municipalities mirrored the adherence to general spatial patterns promulgated in the ordinances. [163] The rural areas and the frontier of the empire were vastly overlooked, thus establishing civilized Christian life was not as feasible. There was little social integration of colonized people in these areas into the empire beyond the symbolic acknowledgment of imperial and Catholic dominion.[164] Hence with the settlers, a good number of ecclesiastic servants and missionaries had found the parishes and convents. The relationship between race and class among the colonies was overwhelmingly supported by a certain type of arrangement that Ferdinand of Aragon and Isabelle of Castile disseminated in the first ordinances. More than a social adjustment effort, documents support that the Crown, as years went by, not only worried about the fate of the natives in all aspects, but they also worried about the reckless behavior of the settlers. After the denouncement of the genocide committed in the islands of Hispaniola Puerto Rico and Cuba, Fray

Bartolome de las Casas demanded that the Indians be treated with care since they were on the verge of extinction. Interracial relationships were unavoidable, especially at the bottom of the social ladder, hence the Crown and the clergy were more so concerned about the racial mixing which raised the concern that the unions must be between men and women of Catholic faith. Hence, converting became mandated in the first governing efforts promulgated in the Laws of Burgos in 1512 issued by Ferdinand of Aragon. Later, intermarriage and consensual relationships among Spaniards, indigenous, and African women created a new trend in transforming the social fabric of the Spanish-American colonies. [165]

The Trajectory of the Creole Pioneers: [166]

"El criollo dejó de querer a Europa y se identificó con la nueva tierra."[167]

"The creole stopped loving Europe and identified with the new land."

It is worth mentioning that while describing how the identity of the Creoles emerged, this chapter will have two major interpretations. First, it is the Anglo-Saxon view which mirrors the American Revolution and the rebellion of the colonists against the British. The other interpretation is based on the Hispanic perception of the emergence of the Creoles as a class with questioned identity and not enough stamina to build a strong case of nationalism but remains in the framework of the state building based on republicanism. Let's begin the argument with Benedict Anderson and his Creole Pioneers. Introduced in "Imagined Communities," Creoles, by the 19th century have realized that their social status was much more than being descents of the Spaniard "Peninsulares." Creoles saw themselves solidified economically as landowners, but politically weak. As it was the case of Bolivar in Venezuela. They lacked legitimacy as a political class. Kathleen Deagan sustains that it was a gradual self-realization that they'd no longer identified with Spain but felt entitled by birth to a whole new identity associated with land and wealth. [168] This awakening came because of the discontent from limited access in the political and gubernatorial positions strictly reserved for the Peninsulares. Thus, the discontentment produced a sort of cultural self-affirmation.

Creoles of the Americas were sons and daughters of the Europeans, (Iberian Peninsula) born in the colonies, but could not prove that they were of Spaniard blood. In Europe, creoles were disregarded as provincial and considered unfit to govern. Here is the key that later separated the Creoles from the Peninsulares. By the 1800's, over the longue durée Creoles no longer sought themselves as European descents. They were presumably a class of influential wealthy landowners– economically, who believed they had held all the rights over the land and territory of the Americas. [169] We see the same argument in the universalism of Bolivar. This vicissitude came as a result of the promulgation of the universal human rights, and illuminist ideas of John Locke, Jean Jacque Rousseau, Adam Smith and of course the Revolution in North America. [170] Primarily, the movement for human rights and liberty were a catalyst for the independence movements in the Americas, but the political structure of the colonies was considered unfavorable for the Creoles. Hence, it gave birth to this new American identity that had no longer associated with Spain.

Creoles were, without a question, a wealthy class of landowners and merchants without political power, and the changes they sought applied only to that class, which meant: The independence was not a social movement to change the entire system. Creoles hoped only for the replacement of the Peninsulares and the seizing of power. They sought to end the ranking order established by the Crown, yet to keep a classist society.

> *"The Creole Aristocracy identified with the free commerce, self-determination, a government for the governed, the concept of free market economy, etc. However, these aspirations were limited within the Creole (social group). Thus, Creoles did not aspire for a radical change of the system, but the replacement of the Peninsulares in charge of the positions."*[171]

For the first time, Creoles saw themselves as a solidified identity, that of the Americans with natural rights over the territory. From this moment, the Creoles considered the peninsulares as "extranjeros" (foreign). This change in ideology marked a pivotal moment in the identity revolution of the American Creoles.

The Long Overdue Conflict

The Crown created a system where Creoles were subject of a ranking-social caste. Creoles were mainly in the upper scale. They had accumulated wealth, land, slaves and servants. What Creoles did not have was political power. For instance, Simon Bolivar, a wealthy Creole, one of the Caracas most prominent Creole families, was a military officer before he'd led the independence war in Nueva Granada.[172] Various points of view portrayed the conflict between Creoles and Peninsulares rather a struggle for power where the battle was forged and aggrandized by the insurgent press. The existential conflict between the Spaniards and the Creoles was a matter of gaining legal and political control over the continental territories in the Americas. Defining nationalities was farfetched. Peninsulares and many conservative Creoles identified with Spain. The essential question about Creole uprising is as existential as their emergence as a dominant class on the verge of losing privileges to the angry Spaniards. Yet at what point did the Creoles identify the Americas as their mother land. When and how did the Creoles break the barriers and end their loyalty to Spain? [173]

Anderson mentions that the Spaniard "pure blood" could no longer be proven and that made Creoles apocryphal for the Metropolis. Creoles could not hold positions exclusively for Spaniards hence, this was not paramount for the uprising. The gubernatorial exclusion was one fraction of the problem the Creoles faced. The hegemony of Peninsulares over the Creoles along with the invention of separated memories [174] became the breaking point of the side switching from *amigo to enemigo*. Tomas Perez Vejo in *Criollos contra peninsulares: la bella leyenda* [175] gets ahead of Anderson's "Imagined Communities" concept. While Anderson deemed the communities as imagined, but relied on common memories, Vejo suggests that Creole memories were invented separate from the Peninsulares to make a case of a distinct identity, that of the authentic American. Here we have an irreversible dichotomy, Creoles felt authentic to the Americas, yet were considered second class citizens in Spain. This was a perception and reason strong enough to extract the Creole – soul- from the Spaniard. Controversially, Vejo debunks the Creole myth of identity by writing:

"Above all, the result of the invention of separate memories inside a group that if it was characterized by something, it was because of its racial and cultural homogeneity. In a pre-national world, characterized by heterogeneity, the elites of the Catholic Monarchy were strangely homogeneous; they shared language, religion, memories of origin, etc."[176]

With this affirmation, the Creole identity was bound by the territorial implications and the birthplace but left out the common culture, ethnicity, (race), language, religion and the previous association with Spanish nationality. Did the Creoles evolve together as a group inside of a supra-national identity? Will the binary nature of this supra-national identity allow this primordial sub-group to expand into a nationalistic entity? It is argued, and not without a reason that Criollismo was conceived out of the necessity to legitimize the political power more so than a pre-national movement. After all, Creoles born in the four virreinatos of the Spanish Crown did not have a specific nationality that pertained to the virreinato they had belonged to, until (perhaps) after the independence. Apart of the hidalguia [177] status, Creole class identification was separate from the lower class of indigenous population, mestizos, and all combined. They were a subgroup that emerged from one homogenous group and sought differences beyond national ideology. In fact, Creoles were born in the Americas and their status was nothing short of wealthy landowners, local bourgeoisie, merchants, and intellectuals. However, the question of nationality vexes the researchers to define Creoles as group and the salient factors that determined their new loyalties.

The Historical Occurrence: The Mestizo and the Mestizaje

In this book I will use the terms interchangeably. El mestizaje, beyond the biological fusion of more than two races (bloods) is an ideology which will serve later on as a unifier against not only Spaniard Peninsulares but it will also serve as an auxiliary by the political elites to arouse the population and create that uniqueness in front of the North American hegemony. Hence, before there were mestizos, there were social groups and races, very distinct from one another. Many studies simplify el mestizaje as a mere product of the unification between two people from different races, mainly Spaniard men and indigenous or African women, but later on the term expanded to cultural products and perspectives. With that said, Peter Wade categorizes the process of mestizaje as nationalist ideological movement. But before I jump to the ideology, let's break down the concept and explain the ontology. This perhaps will show the attitude that distinguished the mestizos as a social group and later rank, from the rest of the colonial society especially in the Antilles. The disdain for mestizos was not a sheer classist attitude; it was in fact the birth of an entire race that neither Spaniards, nor natives, or Africans knew how to deal with at the time and at the moment of the racial blending. Ronald Soto Quirós and David Díaz Aria in *Mestizaje, indígenas e identidad nacional en Centroamérica: De la Colonia a las Repúblicas Liberales* had offered an etymological approach. The first definition of mestizaje, according to Ronald Soto Quirós and David Díaz Aria has appeared in the dictionary of Julio Casares[178] in 1959 and it describes the word as:

"Mestizo, za. Adj. Aplícase a la persona nacida de padre y madre de raza diferente. Corromper las castas por el ayuntamiento de individuos que no pertenecen a una misma."[179]

Adaptation:

Mestizo

1. It applies to a person born from parents (mother and father) of a different race.

2. Mestizar: v. to corrupt the casts by adding individuals that do not pertain of the same.

Whereas other definitions describe the term as:

"mestizaje.1 Mezcla de razas diferentes (...) 2. Mezcla de culturas distintas (...) mestizo, za .1. Que resulta del cruce de dos razas o de dos tipos diferentes (...) 2. Referido a una persona, que ha nacido de padres de grupos étnicos diferentes, esp. si uno es blan-

co y otro es indio (...) 3. Referido a la cultura, que es resultado de la mezcla de varias culturas diferentes (...) Etim. Del latín misticius (mezclado, mixto)." [180]
Mestizaje:

1. *Mixture of different races. 2. Mixture of different cultures, 1. That results from the crossing of two races, or different types. 2. Refers to a person, that is born from parents of different ethnicities, (if one is white, the other is indigenous). 3. Refers to the culture that is the result of the mixture of various cultures. (Etymology: Latin misticius)*

In Portuguese, mestiço refers to the mixture of bloods (sangre mesclada).

Nowadays a random search will generate various results such as:

Mestizo: Del latín tardío mixticius (mixto, mezclado), mestizo es quien nace de padre y madre de distinta raza. El término suele utilizarse para nombrar al individuo nacido de un hombre blanco y una mujer indígena, o de un hombre indígena y una mujer blanca. [181]

Mestizo: Cruce de razas diferentes.
Conjunto de individuos que resultan de un mestizaje.
Mezcla de culturas distintas, que da origen a una nueva. [182]

Adaptation:

Mestizo: From the late Latin, mixticius (mixed), mestizo is the one born of father and mother of a different race. The term is often used to name the individual born to a white man and an indigenous woman, or an indigenous man and a white woman.

Mestizo: Crossing different races.
Set of individuals that result from a miscegenation.
Mix of different cultures, which give rise to a new one.

The definition of mestizo and mestizaje had derogatory notes and it was in congruence with the social position of the mestizos. Many social science researchers use the term Latinization in lieu of mestizaje. The term was adopted from the North American researchers in the 1930's [183] who used it to refer to mestizos, mulattos, zambos (African and Amerindian ancestry), but also the blacks or "Europeanized" Indians and poor Spaniards. [184]

Mestizaje came about as various combinations of racial or interethnic mixes. There are merely seventeen combinations according to Carlos Alberto Echanove Trujillo. But their distribution varied from one place to the other.[185] In reality, regardless of the laws and ordinances issued by the Crown to segregate the Spaniards for the indigenous population, it would have been impossible to prohibit the sexual interactions between them. The lack of Spanish women forced the Spanish men to engage in conjugal relationships (or even relationship) with indigenous and African women. Later, the Crown sanctioned the union of Spaniard men and indigenous women, yet the legitimization of mulattos, or mestizos in a caste society became very problematic. Pelaez Martinez writes:

> *"Así, las leyes definían y restringían las posibilidades económicas, políticas, educativas y sociales de las castas con una clara meta de exclusión. La preocupación principal era mantener marginados a los ladinos."[186]*

Translation:

Thus, laws defined and restricted economic possibilities, policies, educational and social of the castes with a clear goal of exclusion. The main concern was to keep out the ladino outcasts.

Yet more problematic became the proliferation of the mestizo variations in Centro America. Hence, the mestizo not having a fixed place in the social hierarchy became subject of marginalization. In fact, (he) did not have a legal status, or an ethnic characterization. More importantly the mestizo was not considered pure blood, thus it lacked social and political power. Mestizos were stripped of any

102

human accounts except for their existence. Merging in the social strata (casta social) as undefined race, mestizos were seen as negative elements in the society and subject to derogatory definitions cited above. Stigma came with discrimination, and maltreatment."[187]

Nonetheless, Ladinos, mestizos – also in alignment with the North American interpretations - enjoyed a certain degree of freedom as outcasts. This marginalized stratum of people of various combinations lived in the trenches, yet was pursuing freedom continuously, and that freedom came with the price of stigmatization of living in vice, and libertinage. In addition, mestizos, were not part of the institutionalized religion and feared no king (assuming the law), or God. Cortez and Larraz wrote:[188]

"It is thought to live in blacks, mulatos, and Latinos a perverted and abandoned life, without any fear of the King or God."

During (1500-1700), the interaction between Ladinos and the indigenous population, became very problematic according to Cortez and Larraz. Ladinos and mestizos had taken advantage of the indigenous people who have settled mostly in el campo (hills). The disputes over the land became tense as mestizos grabbed land from the indigenous people, or settled in their territory causing clashes and destabilizing entire indigenous communities (especially in Centro America).[189] By the 1700's the Crown implemented a series of reforms called (Reformas Borbonicas) which meant to strengthen Spain as a power. The reforms affected a great deal of Spain's possession overseas. Among others, there were changes to the military, the establishment of viceroyalty of Rio de la Plata, and Nueva Granada. The reforms meant to establish an efficient administration but most of all encourage the production and commerce in the colonies which until that point were only resources to fund Spain's military operations. [190] The need to build roads, the infrastructure, increase production especially in the agriculture sector changed the social order and gave mestizos, black, and ladinos an opportunity to integrate in the society. By 1750, after centuries of marginalization and living in destitute, mestizos sought multiple opportunities for integration.

> *"En definitiva, observamos que desde 1750, tras siglos de marginación, los mestizos, mulatos, ladinos o castas ven abrirse una mayor posibilidad de participación social, económica y política."[191]*

> *In short, we observe that since 1750, after centuries of marginalization, the mestizos, mulattos, ladinos or castes see a greater opportunity for social, economic and political participation.*

Thus far we have treated the mestizo as it is defined in the social science and we have seen the term in congruency with the historical narrative. Mestizos or Ladinos were a hybrid identity, a homogenous race created by the mix of more than two races. Socially, mestizos and ladinos were seen as products of immorality, humanly unacceptable for the whites (Spaniards) but also the indigenous. The intimate relationships between the groups, apart the stigmatization, were a disloyalty to the pertaining group. For example, indigenous women who slept with Spaniards were considered traitors. On the other hand, Spaniards whether, married or not, were practicing Christians and indigenous people were seen as heathens to the Crown and the Catholic clergy. However, the hybridization of the heterogeneous groups will become a class which will take a political position later on especially in Centro America, where mostly mestizaje occurred. Peter Wade sustains that el mestizaje has been seen as the base for the construction of national identities in many Latin American nations. In that sense, Wade continues, the nation fundamentals in a post-colonial Latin America was none other than the mestizaje, the product of three races, Spaniards, African and indigenous.

Many interpretations of mestizo contribution to nation building in the viceroyalties pertain to different points of views. For example, mestizaje in Brazil and Mexico had given a positive view of the society. In Brazil, the post-colonial nation was considered a cohesive union between the three races. In other countries such as Argentina, the Afro element was problematic. For the nationalist elites in Argentina it was very important that the Afro element was invisible in the perception of the nation. As mentioned before, even el mestizaje had shades. Thus, el blanqueamiento [192] or race improvement became paramount for the creole elites. The white population was still very significant.[193] Stutzman (cited in Peter Wade) sustains that el mestizaje in itself is a racist ideology where the nationalist elites (inevitably) seek to whitewash the population elimination of the other two races. In 1981, Strutzman defined as "the all-inclusive ideology of exclusion."[194] Peter Wade reinforces the idea of exclusiveness of the Afro and indigenous factor from the nation building's rhetoric. Among others, Wade refers to mestizaje as a hidden nationalist ideology of race whitening both in physical and cultural terms. The politics of inclusion in Nueva Granada, and later Columbia - considered liberal- Pedro Fermin de Vargas proposed an assimilationist theory into creating a Columbian nation, but not a nation of mestizos. This strategy yielded a pacifist yet nationalistic, racist approach in itself. Anderson [195]quotes Fermin de Vargas.

"To expand our agriculture, it would be necessary to Hispanicize our Indians. Their idleness, stupidity, and indifference toward

the normal endeavors, causes one to think that they come from a degenerate race which deteriorates in proportion to the distance of its origin... it would be very desirable that the Indians be extinguished, by miscegenation with the whites, declaring them free of tribute and other changes and giving them property in land."[196]

Later on, we will see that even in Puerto Rico, where the indigenous population vanished rapidly, the Puerto Rican jibaro, is portrayed more as white than Afro. Or for example "La Borinquena," the Puerto Rican anthem, completely excludes the African factor, from its identity. There are no attributes in the lyrics that pertain to the African heritage. The attempt to exclude the Afro element from the mestizaje is rooted in the old social cast model where the African slaves were at the very bottom of the social ladder, and the whitening of the population became necessary to give the new Creole nations a character other than the mestizo factor.

Identity Evolution in Puerto Rico

In continuum, I will sum up the trajectory of the Puerto Rican identity by explaining how the ethno genesis occurred and by revealing some of the particularities of the island. From 1887 Census, done by the Spanish government, Puerto Rico had the following statistical indexes: Blancos (472,230 hembras y varones)[197] Pardos (mixed race) (244,996 hembras y varones) and Morenos (colored of African descent) (76,404 hembras y varones). The population accounted for approximately 793,632. Out of this number around 321,400 were colored and mestizos thus 40%.[198] In 1899 after the Spanish American War, or more precisely, when United States took political and legal control of the territory of Puerto Rico, the island had a population of 953,243 with the most populous cities of Aguadilla and Ponce. According to the US Census,

7,690 of the population were born in Spain, 14,000 were foreign born and approximately 1,000 were US citizens, 470 African and 68 Chinese. 600,000 were whites, and 350,000 were colored (with 304,000 mixed blood).

Thus, 61% of the population was white and 38% colored. Only 21 percent of the population (203,792) lived in urban areas, including Ponce, Mayaguez, Aguadilla, and Arecibo, Humacao, Bayamon and others. The median age in 1899 in Puerto Rico was eighteen. [199]

Summarizing the data: The island's population had grown by leaps and bounds over the course of the century to 953,243 in 1899. It was a young population: 31 percent was under ten years old, as compared to 24 percent in the United States. Only 11 percent was over forty-five years old; the comparable figure for the United States was 17.2 percent. Only 2.8 percent of Puerto Rico's residents were Spanish born. Blacks and mulattos represented 38.2 percent of the population, somewhat higher than the 36.2 percent which inhabited the American Atlantic southern states.[200] Observing the patterns of other settlements, identity and the ethno-racial makeup of the societies, the accuracy of the census leaves room for different interpretation. Many sources sustain that the mestizo population in the Antilles and Centro-America proliferated with a greater percentage than the white population. But when taking into account that the mestizos who lived in the fields and hills (jibaros) could have well been registered as whites, and then it can be inferred that, the claim of Stutsman about the mestizaje as a whitening ideology of the Antilles had solid foundations. In the next chapter we will see the argument defended by two prominent figures in the study of the identity in Antilles, Stuart Hall and Jose Luis González which both claim that "el mestizaje" is a concept used by Creoles to omit the

African and indigenous factor from the identities emerging from the colonial rule in the Antilles. The discrepancy between the social casts and what the census reported, yields a "whitewashing" phenomenon occurring in the Antilles; a phenomenon previously treated as an ethno-nationalist ideology.

In the *longue duree*, the Indio transformed genetically and culturally. The key to the debate nowadays is the presence of the Native factor in the Puerto Rican genetic identity; apart the great debate of the Afro-Caribbean factor. Sherena Feliciano Santos argues that the extinction is a myth that excludes the Taíno presence from Puerto Rican identity, but in reality, Indios never disappeared. Instead they assimilated and became part of the Puerto Rico's three blood identity. Proving this fact would not exclude complexities. However, beyond the fact that Taino language as part of the many Arawak languages or dialects was based on symbols, not much was left to discuss based on the language. The argument had gained popularity and has become one of the major defining point and the institutionalized deconstruction of the Puerto Rican identity.

In "Languages of Pre-historical Antilles" Cranberry and Vescelieus argue, "Nothing has survived of the lengthy utterances of Taíno Language." Thus, in many of the islands of the Caribbean after the conquest of the Spaniards, languages were wiped out along with the population, and it is therefore very difficult for researchers to study these dead languages. Little is known how developed the languages of great Antilles were when the explorers first arrived in the islands of the Caribbean.

Genetic Transferences

The understanding of the Puerto Rican identity is part of an entire philosophy based on historical occurrences whether they were spontaneous or premeditated.[201] Nevertheless these occurrences caused the transformation of the societies in the Antilles. The historical narrative of el mestizaje bases the assumptions on the genetic transformations during the first fifty years of the Spanish settlement. Inherently, three contributing races formed the first interracial products which later expanded in variations (*see Ruano's and Feliciano social cast*). When the Europeans set foot in Borinquen (Puerto Rico) and the rest of Latin America, their attitude toward the Indios was not necessarily racist. [202] The European mentality was classist. The society was divided in classes, low and high social stratum. Those at the bottom were at the service of those on the top. Thus, on December 20, 1503 Isabelle of Castile decrees obligatory work for Indios at the service of the Christians.[203]

Ethno-genesis of a Puerto Rican stems in an ideological purpose that Spain implemented in the Antilles, and then got out of hand with the process of mestizaje. Europeans were convinced that they were the predominant blood, yet by the 1800's the Crown allowed the interracial relationships with the African population, and then the proof of blood was derogated to hold political office. [204] In Ruano's "La identidad de los puertorriqueños" Díaz Soler, a Puerto Rico historian writes:[205]

> *"Racially and culturally, the small Antillean land is a hybrid with deep Indo-African roots that Spain undertook to agglutinate by imposing on its overseas domains the Greco-Roman culture along with the experience of long centuries of coexistence with other peoples with which they mixed. That attitude transplanted to its overseas colonies gave rise to mestization, which in the case of Puerto Rico*

has been rather a long and uninterrupted process of mulatization."

The moment when one race met the other, resulted one of the most important moments in the history of Puerto Rico. In 1493 Columbus and the settlers came to the Antilles with dreams for titles and glory. Peninsulares willing to risk their lives and cross the Atlantic asked the queen that she grants nobility titles as an incentive. Etymologically Hidalgos (hijos de algo) means sons of someone/somebody. Historically hidalgos were royal blood, but without any rights to inheritance or title.

Coll y Toste writes: [206]

"Mestizaje began in the same year that colonization, in 1509. According to the laws of anthropology, a new generation comprises thirty years that is considered as the average duration of each generation of the human race. A century comprises, on average, three generations. So, in 1539 there were already 50% mestizos in the country with white blood and 50% indigenous."

When understanding the Puerto Rican identity one must have a clear picture of what Argimiro Ruano calls sangre ideologica en Puerto Rico (ideological blood in Puerto Rico), in other words the stratification of the society following the Spanish conquest of the island after 1493 according to the European mindset: "inequality vs. equality" by blood.

The justification of homo homini lupus, the Aristotelian postulation that slavery is just part of the human nature, changed the social strata and the social order drastically within the Spanish colonies. Thus, with the stratification of the society hierarchically, the peninsulares remained at the top of the pyramid. Creoles came under the Peninsulares and the rest were the caste system. This social order continued until the wars for independence.

Is there an ethnic Puerto Rican, and if so, is there an ethnic homogeneity, or a culturally unified heterogeneity? The understanding of the "puertorriqueñdad," implies a new construct, that of cultural uniqueness instead of the homogeneity of the race. Such concepts no longer apply to the case of neither "isleños" nor the -separately considered - contributory bloods from Europe and Africa. Armiro Ruano argues that the process of mestizaje takes roots in the colonization period in a certain way that by approximately forty years after the Spanish conquest of the island, the mestizos had half indigenous blood and half white (Spaniard blood).

The commercial sexual interaction between Spanish men and indigenous women became routine and by 1567, the indigenous element was reduced to twenty-five percent. In the 1800's the process of mestizaje had entered a new phase that of the racial balance and homogeneity. Andre Pierre Ledru, a French scientist who had visited the island in 1797 noticed that the population was so mixed that is was hard to find a white person with Spaniard blood without being mixed with a different race. Hence, the true ethnicity of the Puerto Rican is caught between genetic and anthropological definitions. Criollos v. Gíbaros has been in the center of the argument of the Puerto Rican ancestry. Perhaps the argument is more cultural than genetic. But the question remains how an islander perceives his or her identity in the midst of the racial combinations and genetic trasvasadades (transferences) in the blood spectrum.

Regardless of many interpretations, the cultural argument has settled the complex perceptions. Puerto Rican identity is not a disputed construct. The people identify with a unified genetic mixture of three bloods which has created the homogeneity of racial heterogeneity. The conscience collective [207] in Puerto Rico became evident throughout the nineteenth century with the efforts of the political elites to gain autonomy from Spain. Following the ongoing quest for political autonomy self-identity struggles were concentrated on an individual level more so than a collective identity. Creoles landowners, merchants and businesspersons who were not part of the political discourse started to awaken and see Puerto Rico as a distinct community of people bound by the same culture and background rather than a stratified society with wealthy Peninsulares at the top, and so forth. Creoles had strong economic interests with Spain.

The last half of the nineteenth century marked an ongoing battle to grant Spanish citizenship to the islanders. [208] However, the liberal Creole elites wanted to form a collective, common identity and status distinct from Spain. For the Creoles, both liberal and conservative political identity was a mere split of loyalties. It determined who identified with Spain, and on the other hand who saw themselves as belonging to the Island and therefore to the Americas. Lastly, the societies of Latin America were imagined communities waiting to construct their own identity, their own collective conscience. Unlike Puerto Rico, the continental Latin America and the former virreinatos had to successfully transition from imagined communities into nations.

Meanwhile, the social and political changes not only in Spain, but in the periphery dictated the success or the failure of the newly formed independent states. The settlements – after getting rid of Spain - broke into countries, and countries later into nation-states. However, they were fragile and very weak political units often devastated by violence and lack of leadership. In the early 1900's, the newly formed left ideological groups engaged into deadly clashes with the conservative elites competing for land and power. The war for land converted into deadly conflicts, and violence became the culture in countries such as Colombia and Venezuela with large mestizo, and campesino population.[209] The elites, land grabbers and bandits struggled for power in various Latin American countries. The lack of political culture and governance made the new republics very weak and unstable. Whereas Puerto Rico became a territory of the US. After the passing of Foraker Act in 1900 and Jones Act in 1917 which regulated, corporate owned land, and sanctioned the economy. Rule of law had become prevalent and the violence between landowners and villagers was inexistent. The mestizo once a cultural and socio-genetic construct built in the second half of the 19th century, became the exploited agrarian class of the 20th century.

The construction of the collective identity in the newly formed states –under the new political leadership of the Creoles became a multifarious process. The process of identity formation expedited in the second half of the 19th century with a drastic change in international relations and world politics. In other words, after 1898, pro-independence elite sought to form an identity opposite of the North American identity. The promoted identity mirrored social, genetic and cultural incongruities between the island and the US. The cultural corollaries that emerged in Latin America and Puerto Rico, as a result of colonialism shaped the mentality, the ideology of what makes the Hispano-American different from the North American other, *el estadounidense*.

Inexperienced in domestic and international politics, fraught with inside problems, Creoles succumbed to calumnies, insurgencies, and conflict amidst the efforts to grab the power. The old and new global actors doubted the rise of the new republics in the southern continent. Creoles had no other options but to invent national identities using the emotional attachment of their communities, to the historical land, to the prevailing culture, myths, and symbols. The United States remained an existential threat to the newly created Latin American states. Thus, the double task consisted of creating an overarching Latin American identity and the sub-cultural identities in each of the newly created states. The social fabric component of the Latin American communities served as a unifying factor, but also a shield to protect the countries from annexation by the United States. The overarching identities that emerged from colonialism in the western hemisphere opposed one another. Ibero America and North America were distinctly large and different. The vernacular and shared history drew the border between two large imagined communities. In other words, throughout the 19th century, Latin American countries started to construct their own myths and national symbols. Such is the case of the first indigenous Mexican President Benito Juarez now "preeminent symbol of Mexican nationalism and resistance to foreign intervention." On the verge of the 20th century many of these imagined communities had already formed a cultural identity and were building their national identities.

THE ROOTS OF CULTURAL NATIONALISM

How does cultural identity become the foundation for national identity? In this chapter, I will examine the process of the construction of the Puerto Rican cultural identity under the Spanish rule, and its subsequent transformation to a national identity after 1898. There is a strong thread of continuity between the colonial and post-colonial periods wherein the process of the identity formation, the presence of "other" becomes central. Similarly, I explain that the new collective identity after 1898 is fundamentally different from the prevailing identities of the past. In this specific political circumstance, Puerto Rican people transform the cultural identity into a new form of nationalism.

The Puerto Rican people exhibit one of the most striking dichotomies of national identity. They have developed a strong national, cultural identity yet national identity does not seek an independent state. Theories of nationalism tells us that nations should seek a state. Puerto Rican people, as Guzman Font shows, have been able to maintain the schism between the strong cultural nationalism and US citizenship. Her approach is legalistic. However, there is another side to the problem. The economic reforms and incentives that Puerto Rico received as concessions from the US Government during the significant economic reforms led by Luis Muñoz Marin downplayed the nationalist movement of the 1950's and the self-determination efforts. Other scholars like Juan Manuel Carrion and Arlene Davila argue that this choice was forced upon the Puerto Rican people and they have not been able to express their own true identity under

the commonwealth status. There is no question
that all of their work is an excellent contribution to
understanding the national identity in Puerto Rico.
The general assumption is that if nationalism was
to unfold without any inhibitions, it should have led
to independence. The evolution of the identity
under the political and economic circumstances
has been one of the factors that Puerto Rican
national identity has remained in the framework of
cultural identity and cultural nationalism. I argue
that Puerto Ricans have a powerful national
identity, yet their choice not to support political
nationalism is due to the logical decisions of elites
using the cultural identity to unite people around a
political objective. Scholars of Puerto Rico's
nationalism see the case through the lens of an
anti-imperialist interpretation downplaying the role
and the pragmatism of the elites.[210]

In other words, I look at the evolution of identity
and show how Puerto Rican people chose to
preserve and cultivate a strong cultural nationalism
all the while, drifting from the independence
rhetoric and building on the commonwealth status
instead of a nation state.

Construction of Cultural Identity under the Spanish Empire

People of Puerto Rico always had a cultural
identity which became politicized and laid the
foundations for national identity when the US took
over the island in 1898. When one takes a look at
the identity formation during the longue durée,
something is striking about Puerto Rico. Puerto
Ricans had a cultural identity and national identity
before the US takeover. However, while the cultural
identity seemed to evolve within the same pattern,
the national identity became much more
problematized and contested under the
commonwealth status. What did it mean to be a

116

Puerto Rican under the Spanish rule and later on, under the commonwealth status? In this chapter, I observe the pattern of identity changes during the two periods: The identity construction during the Spanish colonial and the identity-shaping after the inclusion as an unincorporated territory of the US. Until the mid-19th century, people in Puerto Rico related their identities to their social status and class. However, during the second half of the 19th century, as mentioned earlier, we start to see the distinct and inclusive "puertorriqueñidad" take shape with el Grito de Lares and Manuel Alonso's "El Puertorriqueño." During the 20th century, this identity became the foundation for the national identity. This evolution of identity has theoretical implications in our understanding of Puerto Rican identity. I argue that the critical factor that influenced the cultural identity shaping in Puerto Rico was the role of the Creole elites, not just the bourgeoisie. Prominent Creole intellectuals educated in Europe, writers, doctors enlightened by French Illuminists and the independence movement in Latin America sought an identity inherent to the island. The rising of the Creoles in other viceroyalties had influenced the Puerto Rican elites, and at the same time, it had fueled a war of loyalties as we will see on the verge of the Spanish American War.

The chapter is organized in subsections that emphasize the role of culture, traditions, formal and non-formal institutions in shaping the identity of Puerto Rican people from the early settlements until the 1950's. In the first section, I bring a panoramic view of the state and clergy sponsored institutions built during the first thirty years of colonization when the indigenous population was still existent as a community or as an ethnic group. I describe the beginning of an institutionalized society striving to obey the rules and ordinances transferred by the Metropolis and designed for the "conquest" settlements. Furthermore, I discuss the standardization of the cultures. The dialectic approach of standardization is based on a reluctance to homogenize the high culture and the schism that existed between the high elitist culture and the peasant -jibaro culture that later became a symbol of the pop culture. It is essential to mention in the chapter the establishment of the first cultural institutions founded by Puerto Rican intellectuals that will later serve as a source of pride and cultural identity. Lastly, I touch upon the shifting of authentic culture to a government-sponsored culture that gave Puerto Rico a new perception of what the identity should be under the commonwealth status.

Cultural nationalism and collective identity are interrelated. They are products conceived under political and social changes. In other words, society shapes cultural nationalism. Arlene Davila argues that policies also shape cultural nationalism such as the case of Puerto Rico after 1950's when the pro-commonwealth political party after the ratification of the Constitution (1952) promoted the nation as a cultural nation. [211] This way, the commonwealth proponents preserved what they believed to be the national identity under The United States. Smith has argued that the cultural nation must become the political nation characterized by a political culture. With political culture Smith understands policies, institutions, national symbols, flags, anthems, ceremonies, festivals etc. [212] Davila notes, national identity in the case of Puerto Rico, in the absence of a nation-state, is defined in terms of identification with a culturally distinct community. *The conception of national identity drawing in on the identification with a culturally distinct unit rather than a nation-state is particularly relevant for the case of Puerto Rico.* [213] In the light of her argument, the chapter offers a distinctive view on how the policies shaped cultural nationalism and at the same time cultural nation failed to become the political nation.

Institutions and Culture during Colonial Puerto Rico

The building of heritage in Puerto Rico, as in many Latin American settlements started with the building of the religious institutions to establish moral norms, values and cult practices. It is perhaps the richest heritage from the old Spanish days. After the founding of ICP[214] one of the tasks was the renovation of the churches and the cult objects as one of the island valuable patrimonies. However, the building of tradition in the island of Puerto Rico was quite inherent to the religious tradition in the upper stratum.[215] In the lower stratum the tradition was more versatile. Due to the ever-changing character of the lower stratum made of Indios, African slaves and white's evolving nature was not a linear process, nor was it consistent. Francisco Serrano argues that the flux of immigrants, were not only made of Africans, but also European. The new order, and *la casta social*, changed drastically the social fabric of the Antilles. Religion became the driving force and the institutionalized doctrine. With the founding of the settlements, and as Laws of Burgos specified, settlers were encouraged to provide spiritual guidance to the enslaved Indios and Africans. Instead, they failed entirely to protect the indigenous population, whereas African slaves were instrumental to their survival and enrichment in the New World. Antonio S. Pedreira in "El Insularismo" explains,

> *"La raza blanca era legislativa, la negra ejecutiva; una imponía el proyecto y ordenaba; la otra ofrecía el brazo y obedecía; mientras la europea era dueña de vidas y haciendas, la*

africana no podía disponer ni siquiera de sus sentires."[216]

With the emergence of mestizos, whose social status was much more complex, because they were at the frontier of the two races,[217] we have a new social class that was utterly living in the trenches of the society. Mestizos were seen as a hybrid race and deemed unacceptable for the early societies of colonial Spain. As a result, mestizos formed a social stratum at the lowest level of the social hierarchy, prone to libertinage and poverty. It is not until the Constitution of Cadiz (1812) and the liberal policies that mestizos began to integrate and obtain the right to a more dignified social status; meaning that they were able to own land, or even have some sort of administrative employee status. Also, according to Francisco Scarano, the social fabrics and demographics of Puerto Rico wavered frequently with the arrival of African slaves as well as European profiteers - mainly whites- who settled on the island. [218] The establishment of religious institutions was necessary for the Spanish solders and officials, as well as for the indigenous population and the African slaves to maintain spiritual practices after conversion to Christianity. Clergy's role became paramount in applying rigorous ordinances to establish a Christian doctrine. Teachings of obedience, admission of guilt, penitence, and remorse were used to configure social behavior which also helped to keep the population under control to avoid pacification. Many ordinances such as the "Laws of Burgos" 1512-1513 (in the Hispaniola and the Island of San Juan)[219] established for first time behavior practices based on Christianity. The laws were merely a regulator to institute a daily routine and a spiritual life for the indigenous people. Spaniards thought they lacked morals and considered them heathens.

"Whereas, it has become evident through long experience that nothing has sufficed to bring the said chiefs and Indians to a knowledge of our Faith (necessary for their salvation), since by nature they are inclined to idleness and vice, and have no manner of virtue or doctrine (by which Our Lord is disserved), and that the principal obstacle in the way of correcting their vices and having them profit by and impressing them with a doctrine is that their dwellings are remote from the settlements of the Spaniards who go hence to reside in the said Island, because, although at the time the Indians go to serve them they are indoctrinated in and taught the things of our Faith, after serving they return to their dwellings where, because of the distance and their own evil inclinations, they immediately forget what they have been taught and go back to their customary idleness and vice, and when they come to serve again they are as new in the doctrine as they were at the beginning..." [220]

The Laws of Burgos became a landmark in the recognition and the beginning of human rights. [221] However, life in the colonies, regardless of the Catholic King ordinances of 1512 continued to be harsh as the encomenderos[222] did not comply with the laws. The ephemeral impact of the ordinances in the early society came as a result of the indigenous population's rapid decline. The settlers continued to mistreat and deprive them of their daily rituals and practices including spirituality and tradition. As it is noted in the ordinances, the Crown issued statements that the native people must preserve their culture and must be allowed to perform their dances (ayretos).

"...we order and command that they shall not be prevented from performing their dances on Sundays and feast days and also on

Later on, after the conversion to Christianity, Indios –in most of the settlements of the New Spain - started to integrate into the newly designed social system, including those who settled in the hills (*en el campo*). The earliest ethno-cultural native relics included embroidery and needle work decorations for the newly built Catholic churches in the Island of Puerto Rico. The natives used the artisan work as their contribution to the cultural blending that later on would include the African factor as well. Christianity and clergy in general in the early stages, reduced the opportunities for the participant groups to construct their own identity. [223] The institutional culture - promulgated by clergy and the military - shaped the public culture not only from a functional point of view but it also stratified the population.

Architectural features of Puerto Rico reveal a military style that Spaniards inherited from la "Reconquista" and used it in the New World to protect the settlements from the attacks. Hence Puerto Rico was a small island and had two of the greatest castles: El Morro and San Cristobal, located in Old San Juan. The city walls between El Morro and San Cristobal were built as a defense from the attacks frequently by the Dutch and the British. In 1630, the Gubernator Enrique Sotomayor began building the walls that would encircle the city but left the slave dwellings outside the walls. The castles were completed in 1635 under Captain General Iñigo de la Mota Saramiento.[224] Now they are one of the most important landmarks in Puerto Rican culture and heritage. Puerto Rico, just as the rest of the Caribbean was considered a strategic point by the Spaniards maintaining the island safe from frequent attacks was a priority. [225] The island was considered more as a fortress more so than a profiting colony. Puerto Rico was a benefitting settlement. Meaning, the economic impact it had on the revenues and the dividends for the Crown was minimal. The identity was associated with Spain and the metropolis up to the second half of the 19th century.

Standardizing the Culture: The Common Grounds of High Culture and Low Culture

Historically, in Puerto Rico, the construction and the rise of cultural nationalism was a product of the elites in search for identity. The Creole movement throughout Latin America was characterized by the feeling of belonging to an entire continent – territorial meaning -and not necessarily to a nation. National identity needed to be invented. Hence, what Creole elites were not able to accomplish was the closing of the gap between the masses and the elites around a national project. Creoles did not perhaps realize the importance of inclusion of all components of the social caste around the national project. Due to a deriding attitude toward the jibaros and mestizos– as Scarano notes, the Creoles saw in jibaros an uncultured *"personaje"* worth scoffing for what el jibaro was in reality, the face of the masses, mainly the rural population.[226] By 1898, Puerto Rico's society was classist and the gap between the masses and the elites was not only economic. The illiteracy level was at a staggering 82%. The discrepancies between the intellectual elites and the jibaros and farmers were significant. [227] The Creole cultural elites in the mid 19th century emerged as the representatives of the island's elitist culture, yet it was far from the culture of the masses. [228] The elites admired a European bourgeoisie mentality, and a European culture. Many of the Creoles aspired of transferring the European elitist and intellectual culture to the island. Thus, the intellectual elite in 1876 founded el "Ateneo Puertorriqueño. By the early 1900's el Ateneo became the cradle of culture and politics of Puerto Rico. [229] It was modeled after "El Ateneo de Mardrid." The importance of el Ateneo remains in the efforts to institutionalize the nation's cultural identity. It was in fact the most important cultural institution until the founding of the ICP in 1956. In contrast with the ICP el Ateneo was highly elitist whereas ICP created a new cultural identity which included the masses and put the cultural triad at the forefront of the Puerto Rican identity. El Ateneo remains an elitist institution and was farfetched and not accessible for the common people.

Substantial efforts to build a national heritage was dated in the second half of the 19th century. The intellectual circles understood that the importance of a national identity relies on a shared common past. The efforts to build a national identity started with the founding of the Society for the Gathering of Historical Documents of the Island of San Juan Bautista of Puerto Rico. However, just as "Grito de Lares," the ambiguity of the past of the island overshadowed their efforts to establish a solid national identity. This uncertainty was also mirrored in the Betances' view of the Puerto Rican identity as part of a Greater Antillean identity. In the excerpt below[230] the ambiguity of *raices de nuestro pueblo* leaves room for many interpretations about the Puerto Rican identity and loyalties. It has yet to clarify whether the elites identified with Spain, the island or had embraced the concept of "el americanismo" like the Creoles of other virreinatos.[231]

Disagreements arose among the elitist circles on the search for a cultural identity. On the verge of the Spanish American War, conservative elites advocated for a strong relationship with Spain, and liberals for an autonomous Puerto Rico.[232] Cultural nationalism by definition is ambiguous, and once it is politicized it will split loyalties due to the divisive nature of the elites. [233] Politics became a divisive factor in splitting up the elites among autonomistas, anexionistas and independentistas. [234] When politics influence cultural nationalism, then the loyalties become complex under the same identity; Carrion argues that symbols can be ambiguous, nonetheless they hold power. The power struggle intensifies when political entities interfere in order to impose their hegemony to the point that it can turn the war of symbols in "banal nationalism." [235] At the end of the 19th century the division did not only exist among the elitist circles, but they also existed among strata or classes, such was the case of Creoles vs. Mestizos and so forth. Their cultures were united by the same vernacular, yet distinct by the social schism. The dilemma defined the island of standardized culture. Will it be the Spanish (peninslular), or a nativist creole or mestizo culture? By this I infer that the popular culture became the culture emerged from el mestizaje and not the high elitist Creole culture. Cultural nationalism developed in many layers and strata. While the lower stratum moved toward a cultural identity unique to the island based on celebrations, tradition, and music indigenous to Puerto Rico such as Bomba, and Aguinaldo, the upper yet very small strata of peninsulares still identified with Spain's high culture and therefore Spain was a source of pride and nationalism. The local nationalism -in the periphery - was somewhat passionate about the island, whereas' the national identity was nothing less than a sense of pride for the Spanish nation and for Spain the metropolis. [236] The distinction among the two layers relied on self-perception and the social status each had. Up to the mid -1920's there was no national project and the dilemma was how and when the elite and non-elite groups –which in reality made-up the social strata- would come together, with the same interest and agreement on national symbols, public rituals, codes, language dialect unique to the island.[237]

The lower stratum of mestizos, jibaros, and farmers were quite overlooked during forming of their identity. It was not until Manuel Alonso's poetry book "el Jibaro" that the Puerto Rican farmer had entered the scene as a major player, but of a lower social status. The dichotomy Creole and mestizo was problematic. Francisco Scarano in *The Jíbaro Masquerade and the Subaltern Politics of Creole Identity Formation in Puerto Rico*, 1745-182, notes that the printed press in the 1810's revealed a scorning attitude of the Creole class toward the jibaro. The jibaro was portrayed as uncultured, lacking depth and sophistication. In contrast with the folk culture, the jibaro was portrayed as poor, witty and clever.

In the late 1800's mestizos in Latin America had slowly began to integrate as a vital part of island's society. Many owned land living in the hills (campo). The mestizo became conventional and widely accepted. However, the mestizo did not only come with the typical islander look, as described in Manuel Alonso's book. Instead it came with the mentality, culture, habits inherited from the Spaniard blood, the African blood and the remainder of the indigenous blood. The mestizos lived completely segregated, but they had become a prominent cultural construct that could no longer be denied or erased from the identity debate.

As mestizos were rising from the trenches, Creoles found themselves in an awkward position regarding their relationship with Spain. Metropolis saw in Creoles a tarnished identity. Their peninsular blood could not be "proven,"[238] and that had become a problem for the wealthy creoles in Latin America. More importantly, pro-independence and nationalist voices were racially mixed. Starting with Ramon Emeterio Betances and later on with Pedro Albizu Campos, the nationalist movement were led by people of a mixed race, with a dominant Afro factor. Thus, a disconnect existed in the way the identity was interpreted. Who were the true Puerto Ricans, Creoles, or mestizos, and what did they have in common?

Was the true Puerto Rican identity only the stratum impacted by the mestizaje? In the lower stratum the mestizo was born to various combinations.[239] The question of how and when "el mestizo" became the new identity is tightly related to the philosophy proponed by the Puerto Rican political elites and intellectuals in the mid-20th century. For most of the 19th century, the upper strata of Creoles and Peninsulares did not have a sense of solidarity. Loyalties started to split. Spain – the mother land- was now losing the colonies in the New World. The "spiritual" transition from motherland Spain to Puerto Rico, is found in the 1940's in the political discourse of the nationalist leader Pedro Albizu Campos.

During the Spanish colonial era, symbols and flags were associated mostly with the crown and the deep colonial system. Scholars offer few models to frame the role of cultural nationalism and the construction of national identity: [240]Anthony D. Smith uses Armstrong's binary concept of cultural nationalism. First, individual symbols, myths, memories and values of which they were composed; the mythomoteurs that underpinned their polities, and secondly, the different kind of ethnies that formed the bases for subsequent nation formation.[241] This framework can be appropriate for the case of Puerto Rico, but also, it has many implications due to the very complex nature of ethnie formation under the Spanish colonial rule. The construction of symbols, myths and memories was a prolonged process and controlled by two compelling structures: The Catholic Church as the social catalyst, and the Crown with imposed colonial set of structures and systems. Their impact on society and institutions determined how cultural nationalism prevailed from the early settlements until the first half of the 19th century.

After the Treaty of Paris (1898) when Spain lost the last dominions to the US, the national identity became more complex. The future of the island's identity, nationality and citizenship became more multifarious than before and even uncertain. Thus, for the elites, the invention of the national identity became a necessity. More importantly, for the nationalists, the Puerto Rican identity to oppose assimilation into North American culture needed to put an emphasis on the schism that spiritually and culturally separated the North American (mainly Anglo-Saxon) identity, and that of the hispanophilia. As Francisco Scarano explains: *"I suggest, therefore, that from its inception the identity trope was plastic and dynamic. The drastic political changes that followed the U.S. invasion and takeover of Puerto Rico in 1898 placed these attributes in bold relief."*[242] Thus the identity trope became an effort to refute the assimilation into the North American culture, idolize Hispanic roots, and maintain the Spanish language as the vernacular. [243] After the US takeover, a new culture was introduced to the island: The North American pop culture, none other than Anglo-Saxon customs, traditions, and consumerism.[244] This was a substantial threat to the hispanophilia in general and Puerto Rico's identity. The opposition of the North American culture was open and bold. It was manifested in the cultural and the linguistic resistance.[245] The relationship between the two cultures will remain problematic for most of the 20th century. North American and Hispanic people and cultures are inherently different. The hegemony was never a matter of the strongest power defeating the weakest. It was entirely a metaphysical matter that required much more depth in understanding why North American cultural hegemony failed the first years of the US takeover.

Ethnie and Race as Cultural Constructs

As I explained above, the struggle to construct a national identity had many underlying factors. The cultural nationalism in Puerto Rico for most of the 20th century has traveled parallel with the search for national identity and political nationalism. Another underlying factor in determining identity was the complex nature of Puerto Rican ethnicity. Symbolic elements of ethnicity, unique for the groups or ethnies, and what separated them from other groups, relied on the growing need to understand the inner world of each other. Anthony Smith explains that,

> *"...it was necessary to account for the durability of ethnic groups in terms of symbolic boundary mechanisms such as words, signs, languages, dress and architecture, the manner in which elites communicated symbols and the successive mythic structures in which such symbols were embedded. Myth, symbol and communication – the 'myth–symbol complex' – provided the essential conceptual tools for the analysis of ethnic groups and nations over the longue durée, as well as for grasping the central function of mythomoteurs – sets of myths constitutive of an ethnic polity."*[246]

In the case of Puerto Rico, ethnie and race are more or less ambiguous. In this book, I use the terms interchangeably since they convey not only a socio-biological meaning but also a constructed cultural significance. Ethnie intercepts often with "race," yet they are not the same. La raza has a powerful meaning in Latin American culture, and Puerto Rican people have embraced this term. La raza is a much larger and inclusive concept used as a unifier of Latin American countries who emerged out of Colonial Spain as products of mestizaje. Ethnie applies only to the island and carries that particular uniqueness that is determinant in the nationalist rhetoric. Both terms can lean toward a cultural definition more so than a socio-biological fusion. Looking closer at how the race and ethnie differ in this case, we must argue that the European settlers did not have ethnic individualities. In the late 1400's or early 1500's, Spain was just emerging as a nation, but not based on ethnicity, but religion. Spaniards, after seven hundred years of Moorish rule, and a substantial Jewish population, had very little to claim in solid ethnic roots. The same assumption can be made of African slaves who were traded in different ports and came from different part of the African continent. Race, as we will later see, was considered a cultural appropriate term to unite three groups into one called "la raza." Yet, ethnie becomes relevant later on when the Puerto Rican identity is confronted with the North American *other.* La raza in this denomination does not only refer to the interracial population but to the culture emerging from these interactions. It was the social outcome, the product of four hundred years of colonialism. Spain took pride in creating "la raza imperial" and this argument became their rationale during the U.S interference in Cuba before the Spanish American War. Lastly, the Taino Indians under the inclusive Arawak (a multi-tribal) denomination, among others, Ciboneys, Tainos, Caribs, were mere tribal societies, geographically isolated and hostile at times. [247] Thus, these distinct groups created the base of the mestizo identity, and the base of the folk culture known as "el mestizaje."

From Early Myths and Legends to the Puerto Rican Jíbaro

Early myths and legends include folk stories and tales such as of Guanina and Sotomayor,

Salomé and Aruaca (the story of the daughter of a Creole landowner who falls in love with the last of the Indian warriors), La Leyenda de Coqui – the singing frog. Also, the myth and legends from the past included religious and spiritual tales such as La Rogativa, La Capilla del Cristo etc. Another *personaje* that is very authentic to the island is Juan Bobo[248]. Juan Bobo, *el jibarito puertorriqueño*, is one of the most identifying folk figures. He is a boy around 9-10 years of age which represents a wise, witty and naïve character in one. Juan Bobo has become a cultural construct studied in US and Puerto Rican children literature. The adventures of Juan Bobo mirror the country life in Puerto Rico. His character draws his roots in the Spanish picaresque novels of 1550's and particularly Lazarillo de Tormes.[249] This also can be interpreted as an effort to whiten the jibaro and exclude the Afro-Caribbean ancestry.

Cited in Sarai Lastra:

> *"Behind the facade of this 'jharo manso' lurks the mind of a Puerto Rican superhero whose wit, brilliance, thespian proclivities, and bravery in the face of danger make him the ideal seeker and defender of justice for those who experience little of it in their real lives."* [250]

Thus, the myth, symbolism and tradition were invented through folk tales in the lower stratum. These myths and legends were unique for the island. On the other hand, the invention of the mythomoteurs was a challenge for the elites. The mythomoteurs were folk tales circulating in the lower stratum. Their communal nature excluded the elite. [251]The intellectual elite, and their high culture was not unified with the folklore; it was in fact exclusive and a classist ideological division.

Since el Gibaro was first introduced by Manuel Alonso in 1849 it had then remained a dynamic yet problematic figure as the standard of cultural identity of the Puerto Rican people. Scholars of

Puerto Rican background seemed to have different perspectives on the figure of jibaro. El jibaro has been the center of many theoretical arguments and interpreted from many points of view. *La casta social* implies that el jibaro is a mestizo of many combinations (hijo de un chino y mulata). Arlene Davila uses the term interchangeably for Creole (culture), she argues that el jibaro has been portrayed as campesino,[252] however, of white Spaniard look. Sherena Feliciano Santos argues that el jibaro is portrayed more as a Taíno than any other contributing races. Yet underlines that considering el jibaro the Puerto Rican identity, it is an effort to frame the people as savages, uneducated and uncultured. On the other hand, Jose Luis Gonzalez deems el jibaro as forged identity and an attempt of the Creole elite to whiten the Puerto Rican identity by eliminating the Afro-Caribbean factor. Francisco Scarano treats the argument using Gramsci's view on subaltern politics. Scarano argues that el jibaro is a subaltern identity casted by the dominant (class) on the oppressed. [253] Scarano notes that –as many studies from the SSG[254] sustain- the dominant often casts these identities to ridicule the lower class of slaves and peasants. His take on the jibaro questions the entire authenticity of the jibaro as the Puerto Rican identity.   This argument brings us to the root of the problem, when and how el jibaro became an "image" of cultural identity. The Creole Manuel Alonso, while in Barcelona Spain, publishes a transcendental work titled "El Gibaro:" a collection of verses depicting the poor Puerto Rican country man. Puerto Rico.

El Puertorriqueño

Color moreno, frente despejada,
mirar lánguido, altivo y penetrante,
la barba negra, pálido el semblante,

rostro enjuto, nariz proporcionada.
Mediana talla, marcha compasada;
el alma de ilusiones anhelante,
agudo ingenio, libre y arrogante,
piensa inquieto, mente acalorada.
Humano, afable, justo, dadivoso,
en empresa de amor siempre variable,
tras la gloria y place siempre afanoso.
Y en amor a su patria insuperable
Este es, a no dudarlo, fiel diseño
para copia un buen puertorriqueño[255]

Written in 1849, el Gibaro marks one of the first documents that reveals a Puerto Rican constructed identity and it was a mere description of el mestizo. Not only el Puertorriqueño was of a brown color and of a mixed race, but he was the representation of a lower social stratum. Defining the Puerto Rican cultural identity is quite a multifaceted task and socially must include the transferences from the considered subcultures, folk cultures, the pre-Colombian cultures, and the Spanish colonial culture. The cultural homogeneity yields a unity of the three dominant groups. This cultural archetype allows the Puerto Rican - as product of history - to introduce the three worlds with little regard to the *sangre pura* once the dominant trait of pre-Columbian inhabitants of the Greater Antilles. Such cultural modifications are expressed in many writings and essays in the early 1900's. The sailor Victor *Rojas in Coll y Toste (Boletin historico de Puerto Rico 7, 169) is described:*

> *"Victor Rojas was a sailor from Arecibo (arecibeño) who had the perfect conjunction of the three races that populated the island; he had the agility and the sharpness of the Indio, the strength and the humbleness of the black (African), and the intelligence and cleverness of the white (European). He was an ethnic mixture of the White, Indian and Black."*

The identity - according to Coll and Toste- is a balance of the three races genetically represented in the (jibaro) the countryman of a lower social status (el Puertorriqueño)[256]. El jibaro represents the new Puerto Rican socio - cultural identity. Belonging to a lower social stratum, el jibaro is very unlikely to climb up the social ladder. As we will see in the later chapters the jibaro shifts from the cultural identity to a class identity – with the emergence of populist politics in mid 1900s. Hence by the beginning of the 20th century approximately 75% of the population lived in the countryside and made up not only the largest social group, but also the agrarian class. Thus, cultural traces of this social stratum can be found in the music and other traditions.

In fact, as the title of this book suggests, identity in Puerto Rico is one of the most disputed constructs that creates schism among groups whether cultural or social or genetic. El Jibaro also has become part of the identity debate. The typical Puerto Rican, in the variations of the social caste - reveals more or less the same patterns and racial combinations. I conclude that due to the heterogeneity in the Puerto Rican ethnogenesis, it is very ambiguous to trace, but also impossible to deny the presence of the Taino race. [257] El Jibaro – theoretically -is a mix between a Lobo (Chinese man and a mulatta woman) and a mulatta woman is the mix of a Spaniard with a Black woman.[258] El Jibaro is of brown skin. The controversy according to this scheme stems from the lack of Taino presence and is argued from a few sources which I have explained in the previous chapters and has to do with the mestizaje as a process of race improvement or el *blanqueamento de la poblacion mestiza*. [259] Later, we will see that apart from the blanqueamento efforts by conservative Creoles, the mestizo is at the center of the mulatization debate. More importantly, nationalist elites in the 1940's

134

emphasized the presence of the three bloods in the Puerto Rican mestizo to promulgate an identity inherently, genetically and culturally different from the Anglo-Saxon identity of North America. The etymology of the word jibaro according to Feliciano Santos comes from jiba- presumably hill in Spanish, and the suffix "ero." In reality it translates to hillbilly – Feliciano mentions, and it is considered as a derogatory effort to portray Puerto Ricans as savages.[260] The debate about el jibaro is political and of many perceptions. It has been associated with the Puerto Rican identity, yet it has also been fraught with difficulties. El jibaro is perceived as unsophisticated, uneducated and uncivilized, along with a hot temperament of a *pendecinciero* [261] character.

The liberal elites with the help and convenience of the printed press were established in Puerto Rico in 1806. They'd made an attempt to build a cultural identity, other than the one associated with Spain. Diverting from the metropolis had given the Creole elites the sense of political power but also an identity inherent to Americas, known as *el americanismo.*[262] This identity needed to be an expressive form of a nativist perspective. Furthermore, the elitist circles used the printed press to diffuse their political views. On that note, elite divergences were not unknown in Puerto Rico at the end of the 19th century. The elites were profoundly divided, and their split loyalties mirrored their political beliefs and pragmatic attitudes toward Spain but also the United States as an emerging power. [263] Secondly, although the identity building was a mere historical process, it was authentic to the island due to the inherent set of social conditions. The elites needed to forge an identity to separate them from Spain and they invented the jibaro identity (the Puerto Rican peasant farmer). As we will see later on, the jibaro figure remains a very conflicted identity, yet my argument is that, regardless of the elites' pragmatism, el jibaro endured as a cultural construct, native to the island, and in spite of the efforts to "whiten" the jibaro, he remains a widely accepted identity. El jibaro turned out to be a populist ideology by the commonwealth proponents in the 1950's and continued to be a popular figure among the folk music genre.

La cultura jibara gained popularity and became not only a nativist perception but brought a spiritual connection among people and the urgency to identify as part of that culture. As a culture, it was as authentic as it can be. Even the urban culture of the earlier 20th century was not as authentic as la cultura jibara. For example, el Aguinaldo, (Christmas Carol) performed by "el jibaro" remains a cultural construct; a cultural name for the Puerto Rican mestizo even though it has a geographic etymology. Jibaro was a true representation of the authentic Aguinaldo puertorriqueño. The urban Aguinaldo was tamed by the Northern American influence.[264] Let's discuss Raphy Leavitt's song "Jibaro Soy."[265] Raphy Leavitt (1948-2015) is of Jewish and Catholic ancestry from San Juan, Puerto Rico, far from being a Jibaro. The lyrics of the song reveal a strong connection and identification with the Jibaro puertorriqueño. The lyrics divulge the frivolous spirit of the typical jibaro and reinforce its personality traits and the desire to be known and accepted as a humble man, *bien orgulloso*. Leavitt brings forward the social contrast and distanced the Jibaro from "el señor," since el jibaro is a widely accepted folk *personaje* more so than a man pertaining to a lower social stratum. In fact, the two texts (el Puertorriqueño and El jibaro soy) emphasize "love" as a concept, but in Manuel Alonso's the love is toward la Patria - the country, whereas in Leavitt the love is toward el Borincano- the Puerto Rican.

Building cultural nationalism in Puerto Rico after the US takeover was a consistent battle between the island's will to remain a Spanish speaking community and the overflow of the North American media and technology. David Gleason writes:

> *"During this era, Malavet Vega asserts that the Christmas music of Puerto Rico also came under the cultural influence of the United States. As the economy of Puerto Rico modernized, the island experienced the growth of mass media in the form of phonographs and radio. The control of this mass media, however, was in the hands of U.S. companies."*[266]

In congruence with the claim that Davila makes in *Sponsored Identities* of the need to build a cultural identity in Puerto Rico, it drifted the folk culture to consumerism. Cultural nationalism in Puerto Rico, as I've mentioned before, had many influences from the overarching Latin American community. In the last one hundred years, the presence of the North American pop culture is evident. Yet, Puerto Rico remains a Latin American community of people sharing a common past with many countries of the Caribbean, Central and South America. With the flooding of these influential sources, the question of cultural nationalism in Puerto Rico is a matter of defining the part of the culture identified with the Latin American community, and what the intercultural factors were? The countries that declared independence from Spain in the 19th century from had in common apart from cultural components, the sociobiological component through el mestizaje, even though el mestizo was versatile. Thus "la hermanidad", more than a sociobiological unifier, was also a cultural unifier.

The Puerto Rican pop culture began establishing itself in the second half of the 19th century. One of the most recognized songs is the Aguinaldo Jibaro, "Si me dan pasteles." The song dates back to the

19th century and has no composer. It is played during the Christmas season. The song has been recomposed and used by many artists. In 1970 Willie Colon a New Rican (New York born Puerto Rican) in collaboration with Hector Lavoe Puerto Rican from Ponce released "La Panameña." La Panameña is a tribute to the Latin American brotherhood and culture and culminates with the introduction of Borinqueña. But, la Borinqueña is also the name of the national anthem of Puerto Rico. The authors remastered the music of "S*i me dan pastles*" to give it a new note and a nationalist meaning.

Unifying Nation's Culture: The ICP Experience

Culture, as a term, is ambiguous and it can be exclusive and inclusive at the same time. A modernist view emphasizes the importance of institutionalized culture. Davila notes that in Puerto Rico, institutionalizing cultural nationalism did not start until the PPD overwhelmingly won the election in 1952 and shifted the rhetoric from building a nation-state (political nation) to cultural nation.[267]

Thus, under the auspices of Luis Muñoz Marin, El Instituto de la Cultura Puertorriqueña ICP (founded in 1955) oversaw the so-called Operation Serenity, a policy of promoting cultural institutions to reinvigorate the national culture. Even though, the (Creole) elitist culture had decreased after the US presence, it kept its pro-Spain character. After the US takeover, we see a trend among the intellectual elites' pro Spanish heritage to counterbalance those in favor of annexation. The Nationalist Party used   the same approach to promote cultural nationalism. Gellner has emphasized the importance of the standardized culture as one of the building blocks of the modern nation. In the case of Puerto Rico, Gellner's concept of *high culture* and *low culture* takes a peculiar twist. Institutionalizing the national culture completely shifted from the modernist paradigm where the high culture of the elites dominates the low culture of the masses. Thus, the jibaro character became the standard Puerto Rican. El jibaro represented the masses in the Puerto Rican pop culture especially in the visual arts. This rhetoric proliferated and continued to expand until the economic reform in the fifties.

Yet when the industrialization of the island became a priority for the insular government and also the corporates, then a more inclusive character became necessary to represent the new Puerto Rican. This character was distinctive, authentic, and discernable in and outside of the island. To realize such a cultural project, it was essential to call upon the past of Puerto Rico's ethno-genesis. While shifting the rhetoric from the agrarian past and el jibarismo, to the concept of el mestizaje, Luis Muñoz Marin through had created a more inclusive image of Puerto Ricans through cultural reform. The three-race mestizo no longer was the jibaro, or the suffering farmer. Instead, the three-race mestizo was the painter, factory worker, artist, teacher, lawyer, student, doctor etc. And as the binder of the identity, Luis Muñoz Marin promoted the coexistence of the three cultures and three races in one which was highly visual and colorful.

Standardizing the "high culture" is a process that Gellner deems essential to create a set of institutions that will reflect nation's shared vision. Part of these institutions are public education, standardized language and all means of communication. As part of the agreement between the US and the Insular Government, after the ratification of the Constitution of 1952, the island kept Spanish as its official language and as vehicular language they had used it to promote the commonwealth status. Davila mentions that DIVEDCO (Division of Community Education), was another institution created to promulgate simultaneously the commonwealth status and at the same time assist the people with a basic education about the North American "modern life," consumerism, practices of market economy, industrial development etc. [268] This type of cultivation came as a result of PPD's leadership and United States Government to facilitate among others. The conversion of the island from an agrarian economy to an industrialized economy; a corporate haven after Operation Bootstrap was implemented as economic policy. [269] Thus, the national culture after 1950's headed toward a hybrid form of culture; a mélange between the image invented by the ICP with consumerism and exhibitionist practices such as festivals, shows, parades etc. The role of culture and its part in developing a national identity is related to the relationship of both; the low culture of the masses and the high culture of the elites or aristocracy. In the case of nations that are struggling for independence, it is rather significant to find a binding factor or a common denominator to unite the elites and the people around a collective identity and a unifying culture.

Preserving Cultural Nationalism

Preserving cultural nationalism in Puerto Rico started with the building of traditions. In the early colonial period, the Catholic clergy had sent missionaries whom served as a catalyst of establishing societal norms, maintaining a functioning colony based on Christian doctrine. After the Christian based society took shape, then a set of institutions emerged to reinforce these newly established norms. The first formal institutions promulgated and enforced the cult and the spirituality with obstinacy. In the 1800's the printed press was introduced to the island allowing the elites to promote various political views. As we

140

see the enabled political entities promote their agenda especially the Creoles.

> *"The introduction of the printing press to Puerto Rico in 1806 permitted the publication of a wealth of historical and political material throughout the 1800's. The result was the development of a national political discourse and the definition of a Puerto Rican cultural identity. Publications from the nineteenth century and the first decades of the twentieth century, including chronicles, historical essays, political debates, memoirs, government records, and newspaper articles, document the socio-political dynamics on the island during the last century of Spanish rule and the early period of colonial government under the United States."[270]*

The presence of the United States after 1898 questioned the future of Puerto Rico's cultural nationalism. According to Nelson Denis, American consumerism and pop culture in the early twentieth century became an imminent threat to the Hispanic heritage. The Spanish language, as the vernacular for almost four centuries, was immediately replaced by English, yet English had died a few years later. By 1898 the island's population lived mainly on the farms and owned modest land. After the corporate takeover, jibaros lost their land to expropriation. Once the jibaros lost their means of production, they became dependent on working for major sugar companies. The corporate and banking industry devalued their assets. It impoverished the jibaros turning them into a new proletarian class that later on would be the center of the Socialist Party rhetoric led by Luis Muñoz Marin. Education also became an assimilationist experiment. American teachers flooded the schools in Puerto Rico to teach English and shift almost 300 years of established Spanish colonial culture to a new, Anglo-Saxon culture and mentality. [271] The Puerto Rican elite still had close spiritual and cultural ties to Spain.

Regardless of the Northern American intervention and the great hope for democracy, the people were not quite ready to shift their culture and traditions.[272] In the early years of occupation, the acculturation of masses had proved fruitless. People were not ready to abruptly drop their culture and mentality to embrace a new one. The United States to the islanders' represented military might, democratic values, yet they've found it quite impossible to embrace Americanism. The English dominance over the Spanish language was farfetched. Nelson Denis argues that the people found the English language to be abhorring and refused to speak it. The liberal elites viewed the United States as the symbol of democracy, unlike the backward Spanish monarchy nevertheless, culture-shifting was far from reality. Michael Staudenmaier emphasizes that the early independence efforts and resistance to hegemony were among the enlightened and educated population as opposed to the rest of the community. Hegemony were among the population who was enlightened and educated as opposed to the rest of the population.

> *"The US quickly outlawed Spanish for use in official business and imposed English as the language of instruction in schools. In a society where literacy rates hovered below 10 percent, the small literary community produced most of the early pro-independence sentiment, often dramatizing its position with vivid depictions of oppression and the assault on Puerto Rican cultural identity."[273]*

From a cultural perspective, the political developments in Puerto Rico after the US takeover had a weak impact on the culture and the sense of identity. It created a rhetoric where Puerto Ricans would reject anything that was not part of their culture, tradition, and especially language.[274] English could not just replace Spanish as the vernacular and printed language since the 1800's.

142

On the other hand, the political landscape was an unsettling battle between groups competing for power. The relationship between people of Puerto Rico and the appointed "administrators" grew bitter, especially when the nationalist activism of the 1930's took the shape of a political movement. The nationalists had formed their chapters and structures.[275] The nationalists refused to give in to a neocolonial system. The American corporatist system was only acceptable if Puerto Ricans bought into the commercialized, and consumerist culture. It was not only a matter of replacing Spain's dry mercantile colonialism with more versatile consumerism. The culture resistance to the North American informal and formal institutions was significant. The nationalist elites and the people rejected everything "Yankee." In the second half of the twentieth century, the struggle for power became evident. [276]

The second period, and perhaps what we know now as the new Puerto Rican identity, or diaspora identity, came after commonwealth's political status was established judicially and politically. Once Puerto Ricans were granted US citizenship and elements of the civic (institutionalized) nationalism were extended to the island, it enabled waves of Puerto Ricans migrants to move up to mainland US, and seek better opportunities for most of the 20th century.[277] Puerto Ricans brought the local cultures and what they could; the myths, the symbols, the values, in a sense, completely detached from the island's nationalist rhetoric of the 1930's until the 1950's. The traveling of identity was purely cultural, enclosed in clusters and segregated communities mainly North East of the United States.[278] The rural population (campesinos) showed little or no interest in the political debate fueled by the political elites. The economic opportunities in United States were bountiful and regardless of the secondhand citizen treatment, racial or ethnic stereotype, Puerto

Ricans seemed to integrate in United States' low economic and working-class stratum. During the 1930's, the upward social movement north of the US, brought in seasonal and migrant workers looking to cash in capital and send it back to the island. Puerto Rican migrants were only driven by economic motives rather than using "American Exceptionalism" as a model to build a nation back in Puerto Rico.[279]

In this chapter, I have discussed a few concepts about the construction of identity in Puerto Rico. Stuart Hall and Jose Luis Gonzalez argue that Puerto Ricans were Antilleans, and that identity is represented in the "ethnic-racial" make of the Antillean Mestizo. I described how the ethno-racial identity has shaped the cultural constructs, and in particular, the Puerto Rican jibaro. When the island became a commonwealth, the rhetoric changed, and the paradigm shifted into a nationalist political agenda. In island politics, we were no longer looking at cultural nationalism. With the birth of the Nationalist Party, we see a clear political nationalist agenda and self-determination efforts. Thus, the perception of collective identity expanded and transformed into national identity. Pedro Albizu Campos, the promoter of the nationalist agenda, became the Insular Government's opponent and later on turned into a foe of the United States. The nationalist elites sought to remove the political tutelage the US had imposed on the island after the Spanish American War.

Cultural nationalism transformed quite drastically from the old Spanish traditions rooted in Catholicism, colonial architecture, rituals and fortresses to a more modern, inclusive political nationalism along the 20th century. [280] Arlene Davila explains that cultural nationalism is an ongoing and recurring process that can emerge and heighten at different historical states. [281] Political nationalism in the 1930's, emerging from cultural nationalism, was work of the political elites, mainly nationalist and independentistas [282] and it served as a solid base for the nationalist rhetoric. By the mid-20th century, political nationalism had become a problem for the Insular Government and also for the Government of the United States. [283] With the founding of liberal institutions Puerto Rican nationalists sought an opportunity to denounce the commonwealth status as a new form of colonialism and intensify the efforts of self-determination by proving that Puerto Rico and United States are irreversibly different cultures being unique from one another. At the core of their argument, nationalists used cultural nationalism, language, collective identity, historical past and territory. The rhetoric was quite heated. The nationalists introduced a completely new type of nationalism, it was inherent to the island and stemmed from the recognition of Puerto Rico as la patria (fatherland).[284] For many historical reasons, Puerto Rican nationalism flourished as a revolt against assimilation into a new culture; an argument made not only by Pedro Albizu Campos, but also, scholars of Puerto Rican background. Argimiro Ruano argues that the two (North American and Puerto Rican) cultures are irreconcilably different. As Arlene Davila noted, in 1950 after the commonwealth status was ratified, the nationalists were considered separatist, were shunned by the Insular Government and the political opponents *"Separatist nationalism was contained by repression and co-optation and different element of Puerto Rican culture were unequally incorporated into a culturalism definition of the nation embodied in folklorized images of a utopian agrarian past."*[285] The PPD (el Partido Popular Democratico) in the 1950's used the image of jibaro as a cultural construct to unify the people around the new rhetoric and had succeeded.

I also explained that the role of the institutions became paramount in promoting political nationalism. In states that emerged from the colonial rule, nationalism was weak for the reason that virreinatos were more or less imagined communities rather than political units, but the prevailing culture was strong and shared throughout Latin America. The elites in the second half of the 19th century had created a unified, cohesive culture which used as its base the mestizo culture even though the creoles were direct descendants of the peninsulares and were considered part of the white population. "The Antilleans" in the midst of the 19th century, were a product of many races, for reasons that I have discussed in the identity-forming chapter. The dilemma of this historical period was whether or not the elites chose the mestizo culture as the most identifiable trait of the Puerto Rican heritage to purposely contravene the white, Anglo-Saxon hegemony. [286] It was clear that the nationalist discourse of Pedro Albizu Campos based on "hermanidad e igualidad" belief, unified the people in one race, (la raza), that of "la puertorriqueñidad" – *"if you see one, you can tell by the eyes and the skin."* [287] Albizu Campos thought the Puerto Rican was the typical mestizo (which he was as well), the product of the three races, and that identity was not the Creole nor the white Spaniard, but the Puerto Rican mestizo. [288]

The construction of cultural nationalism did not occur in a vacuum, regardless of the geographical position and the defined territory very particular for Puerto Rico. Nevertheless, the island was an open system with a sizable cultural input from Spain, and a cultural impact from the African slave trade. After all, it produced an output of three cultures including the Taínos heritage in the form of the distinct identity known as puertorriqueñidad.[289] The role of the other neighboring settlements in the viceroyalty of the Nueva España cannot be denied. The construction of a cultural identity happened, independently, but as a result of the colonial system and its mere products. The mercantile system imposed by the Crown did not play a major role in institutionalizing the culture, it is just enabled social interaction among the ethno-racial groups. Creoles educated in Europe later on sought to westernize their cultural identity.   Anthony D. Smith argues that it is the task of an ethno-symbolic analysis to provide a cultural history of the nation. Furthermore, Smith states: *"By this, I mean an inquiry into the successive social and cultural self-images and sense of identity, the ideological conflicts and the social changes of a culturally defined population in a given area and/or polity."* [290] The dilemma of the Puerto Rican case is when did cultural history convert to cultural nationalism? Alonso Manuel's "El Jibaro" is the voice of the cultural elite educated abroad, but the face of the plebian; the Puerto Rican farmer. The self-perception of Creoles and the mythomoteurs forged (invented) by the need of authenticity and legitimacy which contributed to the building of the cultural nationalism throughout 19th century. To put Smith's argument into a historical context, the 1800's were characterized not only by the separatist Creole politics in the New World, but also the integration of the mestizos in the Creole society. The debate was more political than national. Creoles had felt closer to the people they resented; the indigenous and la casta social because they were looking for broad support to cast Spain out. Peninsulares treated the Creoles with disdain because of their birthplace yet considered them Europeans. [291] Smith writes: *"These self-images, identities, conflicts and changes stem from the interplay of competing cultural and political projects of the different classes, religious confessions and ethnic groups within a given area and population* and/or polity, as well as the political impact of external collectivities and events, especially, but by no means exclusively, in the modern era of nationalism."[292] The assumption that nationalities were forged or invented through the 19th century during the Creole movements of independence from Spain is in congruence with the argument that Anthony D. Smith presents in relation to defining a nation from the ethno-symbolic perspective. Thus, Creoles had to better invent a shared memory along with a supranational construct in order to separate themselves from the peninsulares. Evidencing Smith's argument, I would argue that Criollismo was never an ethnic movement, by all means, el americanismo was a forged supranational identity that related to the territorial claims and political control.

PUERTO RICO 1898 THE SHIFT OF THE POLITICAL ACTORS

In this chapter I will cover the Spanish-American War and the final political legal effort for Puerto Rico to become an independent nation. The argument develops around the attitudes of the political elites at the brink of the Spanish-American War and how well they've understood the importance of identity preservation in a different legal status. I will explain the international relations between Spain – as an imperial power in decline – and the United States. This chapter reclaims the idea of comparative domestic politics inside Puerto Rico; how this colony manifested its will to self-determination against Spain and how they had approached the independence cause after the Spanish-American War. More importantly, I explain that due to the new world order in the 1900's, the Western Hemisphere was in a vulnerable position. The new states and nations had domestic issues that weakened them in the international arena and made them vulnerable. After the Spanish American War, the United States used Puerto Rico as one of its strategic interests to secure control over the Western Hemisphere by prohibiting other world powers in their search for new markets.

The commonwealth status is as complex as it sounds, and the public are often confused about the relationship between Puerto Rico and United States. Puerto Ricans as US citizens are often caught in the politics of representation. Here in the States, many Puerto Rican parents have asked me to include Puerto Rico's history as a part of the curriculum. In fact, the historical narrative of

Puerto Rico - one hundred years after the War of 1898 - is absent from textbooks in the United States. The public's knowledge of Puerto Rico is limited to the political and economic ties to the United States. Many biases and prejudices portray the relationship as a one-way street, benefiting only Puerto Rico, and this has created a sort of animosity in the American public. And this perspicacity has been going on for decades. While explaining that the status of commonwealth excludes Puerto Rico of some economic burdens, yet it strips the island of economic sovereignty while it is still hard to explain the most asked question referencing this: "Why don't they ask for independence?"

The nationalist rhetoric and the quest for independence in the 1950's hardly made it to the American public, and many believed that nationalists were part of a terrorist organization trying to overthrow the insular government. Also, the Puerto Rican nationalists were educated in the United States institutions whom had understood the commonwealth status will yield problems in the future of both the island and the United States. But in order to understand what really transpired between Puerto Rico and United States in the 1950's and how that shaped Puerto Rico's nationalism, we must go back to the beginning of the relationship between the US and Puerto Rico. The rapport is part of the international relation theories and precisely, the Just *War* doctrine in the Spanish-American War. The war ended with the defeat of Spain and the loss of its last territories – Cuba, Puerto Rico, Philippines, and Guam. Cuba and Philippines – after all - obtained their independence through negotiations, whereas Puerto Rico's sovereignty was transferred from Spain to the US. Puerto Rico has since remained an unincorporated territory of the US.

One of the driving forces inside of the world politics and intentional relations is war and conflict itself. A realist view of war is the paradigm that given the anarchist nature of the international community and the lack of a higher authority to regulate the same state of nature in which the world functions, from time to time, the use of war as a means to protect their interest is necessary. When it comes to war, scholars believe that Americans tend to be natural-born realists. [293] Briefly, given the history, the United States has fought in dozens of major wars, and countless small-scale military interventions.

To what extent was the Spanish-American War necessary, and what justified a belligerent act, is very important to understand the implications of world order on the verge of the 20th century.

In the late 1890's, Spain had weakened as a hegemon in the Caribbean and the Philippines. The economic ties with the colonies had debilitated. Once a high-level mercantile system with rigorous rules and policies came about, their economic strength through trading was slowly dying as the US was emerging as a new economic and military power in the region. Inside the social life of the colonies, the contrast between the *Peninsulares* and the *Creoles* had deepened and became poignant. The peninsulares occupied the most important positions in the colonial system and that upset the Creoles. The elites contemplated the American democracy from a distance and lamented about the lack of the political power and decision-making. Educated Creoles blamed the conservative monarchial rule for its backwardness, the lack of democratic values and the violation of human rights. Inside of the colonies, testimonies of gross human rights violations had reached the international community.

The Spanish-American War had different dynamics depending on the region and the various types of uprisings. It was a multidimensional war and the interests were not the same in the three last colonies: Cuba, Philippines and Puerto Rico. Essentially, the main interests were far from being economic. US Military and strategic interests were at stake. The Spanish-American War was not all about acquiring territories, but the reassurance that the US emerged in the international politics as a world power. As such, it had all the capacity to not only acquire new territories, but to establish a new world order and a new balance of power with its European counterparts as well as the newly emerging Latin American nations. Thus, it was paramount that strategic holds in the Pacific Islands, South Asia and the Caribbean remained under the strategic and military control of the United States.

Puerto Rico has since remained one of the United States' strategic interests in North America. On the verge of the Spanish-American War, the politics inside Puerto Rico were as problematic as the vulnerable position of if left without the protectorate of a world power such as Spain at the time. The idea of becoming a sovereign state in the western hemisphere was farfetched. Puerto Rico did not have a strong inside insurgency, nor did it have unified elites. The elites in Puerto Rico were highly divided. While political insurgencies emerged in Cuba and the Philippines, Puerto Rico's parties held different positions within the new reality. El Partido Republicano - led by Jose Celso Barbosa - sought annexation within the US. El Partido Unionista, founded in 1904 by Luis Muñoz Rivera, sought full independence and sovereignty of the island. The conservatives sought a political status, allowing Puerto Rico to remain a province of Spain with fully autonomous legal, political, and economic rights as the other autonomous provinces. Such status suggested that the status-quo be preserved. That meant the autonomy granted by Spain in 1897 remained intact. Spain granted autonomy to Puerto Rico with the right to self-govern shortly before the US declared war. It was not a coincidence. An autonomous status allowed Spain sovereignty over Puerto Rico yet gave the Puerto Rican political elites the right to govern their island. Self-governing and autonomy were two different forms of dependency on the Crown, and none meant sovereignty. Secondly, "La Carta Autonomica" converted Puerto Rico into a province of Spain with equal rights as the other provinces. Puerto Rico was no longer an inferior colony.[294]

Article1 of Autonomy Cards mentions: [295]

The Government of the Island will be composed of an Insular Parliament, divided into two Chambers, and a Governor General, a representative of the Metropolis, who will exercise the Supreme Authority (adapted from Spanish) on its behalf. Thus, as in the old colonial tradition, the Governor would still be a high official from the metropolis, in other words, a peninsular. While the elites in Puerto Rico achieved autonomy, Cuba was in political and military turmoil. Rebels, with the help of the political activists in New York, among others José Marti, sought to oust the Spaniards from Cuba. Meanwhile, in 1895, the building of the battleship Maine was completed. It was the first US Navy ship named after a state. It meant to establish a balance of power between the United States and Latin American countries - newly emerging in the political scene. Maine was a response to "Rachuelo" a Brazilian battleship and the rising of Latin American naval forces. Despite a few disadvantages in technology, Maine was a high-quality American-designed warship. However, unexpectedly, on the night of February 15, 1898, Maine exploded and sank quickly, killing approximately 300 men on board. Maine was anchored near Havana harbor to protect American interests amid the Cuban uprising against Spain.

The American public, blown by the provocative Yellow Press, blamed the Spaniards for the sinking of Maine and demanded action against Spain. Throughout the 19th century, the United States had strengthened their position in the Western Hemisphere due to two strong ideologies - the Monroe Doctrine, and the Manifest Destiny. The expansion philosophy promulgated in the second half of the 19th century has already yielded results. Through a chain of territory acquisitions, treaties and vast land purchases, the United States has expanded its territory in the North American continent. Among others, the US purchased Florida from Spain in 1832; paid 15 million dollars in war loss compensation to Mexico; got almost half of its territory in the Treaty of Guadalupe Hidalgo and acquired almost thirty thousand square miles in the Gadsden Purchase. Nevertheless, what really mattered to the U.S was the prestige of being a military power, and the assertion of being the victorious party in every treaty and pact. *On December 2, 1823, President James Monroe used his annual message to Congress as an opportunity for a bold assertion: 'The American continents ... are henceforth not to be considered as subjects for future colonization by any European powers."*[296]

By the late 19th century, Spain has weakened its position in Central and Southern America due to the revolutionary wars in Latin America. However, there had always been a risk that Spain might seek to reassert the colonial rule in these regions. Spain's colonial rule and high-level mercantilism in Latin America worried the United Kingdom as well, but the United States had a different approach. At this point, the United States had no interest in engaging in a direct war with any of the European powers, yet it sought to establish boundaries and protect its interests. For example, before the Spanish-American War, American interests in Cuba had thrived as some of the main producers and distributors of sugar. US business interests indicated that, while Spain still held political authority over Cuba, economic authority was slowly shifting to the US. [297]

The United States' foreign policy, regardless of occasional military interventions in Latin America, was not geared toward European powers yet. The Monroe Doctrine's main concern was to reassert the role of the US in the Americas, the Caribbean and to make sure that European mercantilism could not be re-imposed in the regions where had established its economic and ideological interests.

In 1901, Roosevelt became President of the US and extended the Monroe Doctrine with his corollary. Roosevelt asserted that, hereafter "European nations would not be allowed to use force to collect debts owed to them by Latin American countries." Roosevelt's foreign policy, however, was focused on establishing governments in Latin America that would maintain 'order and fulfill their obligations toward outsiders more so than the European interests. Balance of power – theoretically - assumes that a certain equilibrium among the great powers promotes stability, since no state can pledge war and be assured of victory. From a historical perspective in late 1890's, the relationship between Spain and the United States had worsened, yet the United States had little interest in combatting Spain. The war in Mexico, the annexation of Texas, the Gadsden Purchase and many treaties signed to expand the US territories had given the country great confidence. However, the United States kept a close eye on Cuba, Puerto Rico and lastly the Philippines, where insurgency leader Emilio Aguinaldo led the rebels in two frontal wars: In independence from Spain and later against the United States' presence.

In this chapter I will cover the Spanish American War and the final political legal effort for Puerto Rico to become an independent nation. The argument develops around the attitudes of the political elites on the verge of the Spanish American War and how well they'd understood the importance of identity preservation in a different legal status. I will explain the international relations between Spain –as an imperial power in decline – and the United States. This chapter retakes the idea of comparative domestic politics inside Puerto Rico and how this colony manifested its will to self-determination against Spain and how they had approached the independence cause after the Spanish American War. More importantly, I explain that due to the new world order in the 1900's, the Western Hemisphere was in a vulnerable position. The new states and nation had domestic problems that weakened them in the international arena making them vulnerable. After the Spanish American War, the United States used Puerto Rico as one of the strategic interests to secure control over the Western Hemisphere and prohibit other world powers in search for new markets.

One of the driving forces inside of the world politics and intentional relations is war and conflict itself. A realist view of the war is the paradigm that given the anarchist nature of the international community and the lack of a higher authority to regulate the same state of nature in which the world functions, from time to time, use of war as means to protect their interest is necessary.

Spaniards called the Spanish American War "the unjust war." *Especially Puerto Rico, which ended with the transferring of the sovereignty from Spain to the United States.*"[298] However, before I start explaining how and why Puerto Rico ceded to the United States, it is paramount to analyze some of the causes of the Spanish-American War and some of the implications for the people of Cuba, Philippines, Guam and mainly Puerto Rico. There are a few points of view when it comes to the

Spanish American War and every one of them has a rationale that has to be considered in order to understand well what transpired. Spain's interpretation of the war was merely a belief that the long colonial rule was the genesis of a spiritual relationship that Madre Patria (motherland) had with all the colonies and dominions in Latin America and Asia. Spain supposed that the conflict with the United States was nothing short of "an unfair war." Nevertheless, the conflict was much more complex than independence uprisings. Soon the insurgents in Cuba and Philippines understood that the war had entered another dimension. Puerto Rico was in a very delicate position. After four hundred years of colonial rule, the pro-annexation elites revered American democracy and were not seeking independence.

The Pact of Zanjón ended the armed struggle of Cubans for independence from Spain that lasted from 1868 to 1878, known as the Ten Year War. On February 10, 1878, a group of negotiators representing the rebels gathered in Zanjón, a village in Camagüey Province, signed the treaty with Spain. General Arsenio Martinez Campos served as auxiliary to the treaty. Spain promised quite a lot, among others, abolition of slavery, but the situation became worse and Spain did not keep their promises. On the other hand, the North American investments had multiplied and by 1894. The American capital was in danger. With roughly fifty million dollars invested in the sugar industry, a potential conflict could jeopardize the production of sugar and rum. [299] A part of the economic interest, the United States worried about the dismal of the political situation, the atrocities that Spaniards committed toward the Cuban civilians.

W. Randolph Hearst of the Hearst Corporation used the Yellow Press to arouse the population into accepting the war as the only option to rid Cuba of Spain and eventually protect the American interests in the region. By the late 19th century, war had become one of the most important elements in world politics. The year 1898, marked the lowest point of the diplomatic relations between United States and Spain. The United States, a rising power, and Spain a "falling" empire, were disputing over the last of Spain's colonies: Cuba, Puerto Rico and the Philippines. [300]   In 1895, Spain appoints General Valeriano Weyler to control the insurgency in Cuba. Weyler also known as "The Butcher" earned himself a notorious reputation for the atrocities toward the Cuban civilians in concentration camps in order to separate it from the rebels. Many people died in the camps due to diseases and poor living conditions. [301] Spaniards defended the thesis that other nations have acted in such a way that it was –for the time– morally justifiable to control the rebels. Salvador Casellas sustains that Great Britain has acted in the same way with North American indigenous people and the population in South Africa the United States in the Philippines.[302] Spain wanted to protect the absolute hegemony over Cuba and was willing to use any means, whether by military pacification and perhaps negotiations, yet the President Cánovas Del Castillo reassured that Spain would not make a deal with the enemies and elements of the "black race."[303]

Spaniards had a completely different perspective about the causes of the war. It was a moral and metaphysical question based on the imperial "law" of what they called Spanish heritage and that Spain has "created a new race of people [304] after Columbus' discovery of the New World. [305] From the beginning, Spain claimed that the United States was "playing dirty." With the stationing of Maine near Habana's harbor, the Spanish claimed that it was a pretense; a premeditated plan to cause a mutiny or an aggression that would justify the war, and the sensational Yellow Press did nothing but to support that thesis. [306] Spain portrayed the United States as the real enemy and deemed Congress Resolution as the sentence of the sugar cane producers, the filibusters, and the market in which they buy and sell their conscience. [307] Spain used all the means to avoid the war and so did President McKinley, but he saw it coming. The public was prepared to go to war and Congress – mentions Salvador Casellas- controlled by jingoists granted the funds to cover the war costs to calm the public down whom were outraged by the explosion and the sinking of Maine. [308]

From the War to the Tutelary System: The Case of Puerto Rican Elites

There are different views about the Puerto Rican elites and their relationship with the United States on the verge of the war. It would be quite a challenge to draw a parallelism between the Cuban and Philippines' sternness to obtain sovereignty at any cost, with Puerto Rican elite's pragmatism. Julian Go has been very critical about the elites' attitudes and loyalties before and after the war. However, Julian Go does not take into consideration many geographical, political, logistic and cultural factors that account for elites' attitudes. Also, the takeover of Puerto Rico without resistance from the Spaniards justifies Spain's non-desire to pursue a war that did not want to fight in the first place. As for the islanders, it was farfetched to take arms and engage in any belligerent act against the United States. With seventy-five percent of a population of unarmed farmers, few latifondistas and a divided political elite,[309] any resistance would produce more destruction than results. [310] The faction between these two groups became a power struggle. While peninsulares occupied the main governmental jobs and had control over the island's finances, the insulares – (landowners, latifondistas) depended on

Spain's economic ties for trading goods and products. Keeping the flow of the capital preoccupied the economic elite greatly. When Spaniards left the island - to escape the financial devastation of the war- they'd taken their capital to Spain leaving the landowners and traders broke.

Nevertheless, since the elites had no political power, they'd completely overlooked the political question of the U.S take over. To understand the role and the behavior of the Puerto Rican elites, one must recognize that landowners belonged to a wealthy group of people, but their preconceived cultural constructs and perspectives had a deep root in a paternal form of governing, much more different than the North American democracy. This translated later on in their inability to implement democratic values in their first efforts to self-govern.[311]

Moreover, the last decades before the war 1870's-1890's the elites – used more sophistication than means of pressure to demand autonomy and constitutional integration as part of Spain.

Julian Go points out the elite's cultural upbringing and the lack of democratic culture during the colonial rule as the factors for the failure of the first self-governing efforts. The Puerto Rican elites revered the American democracy, and this did not go unnoticed by the Americans. Such is the case of *José Celso Barbosa*, a doctor and politician, born in Bayamón, Puerto Rico but educated in the United States with a medical degree. A member of the Autonomous Party once led by Baldorioty de Castro, in 1899 Celso Barbosa founded the Republican Party of Puerto Rico that advocated statehood for the island. Barbosa was openly pro American intervention on the island. In June of 1898, General Nelson Miles bombed San Juan for three days; yet, no resistance from the islanders was reported. Those who were pro US intervention rose to the occasion and as General Guy, Henry wrote to President Mc Kinley "Puerto Ricans called themselves Puerto Rican-Americans."[312]

Puerto Rican liberal elites warmly welcomed the American troops headed by General Nelson Miles. The local elites gave a warm reception to the American troops and offered their services by submitting themselves to their authority. [313] In fact, many were happy to see the Spanish rule end, and declared liberty and progress for the country upon the arrival of the American troops. The elites accepted the idea of tutelary rule and sought to design the concept of tutelage for the island and its population.[314] The complex case of Puerto Rican elites and their need to accept a higher legal – rational authority made it much easier for the transferring of sovereignty from Spain to the United States. A crucial role in the implementation of tutelage as another form of colonialism was not the fact that elites bought into that idea. The Americans had known exactly what the Puerto Rican elites wanted. The reasons were much more pragmatic and tightly connected to the interest of the elites as the ruling economic class. By the second half of the 19th century, the elites strengthened their economic position more so than their political position that was exclusive to the peninsulares. The landowners sought to find more trading opportunities with Spain rather than engage politically in the colonial system. On the verge of the Spanish American War, the Spanish bankers transferred their capital to Spain leaving the elites out to dry with no income. Along with economic vulnerability, the elites dreamed of a democratic system of governing, and General Miles in his speech gave the Puerto Rican elite exactly what they wanted to hear "the right to self-administer." But this right did not come the right way.

In 1897, Spain had already granted autonomy to Puerto Rico, however, the Americans after emerging as the winning party in Paris in 1898, did not recognize it nor did they recognize the Spanish citizenship for the islanders. Puerto Ricans had so many problems with their citizenship which was not recognized. In 1917 President Woodrow Wilson granted the islanders US citizenship – no exception. Julian Go harshly criticized the elite's soteriological attitudes toward the United States yet does not take into account the rising nationalist movement or the political resistance to the neo-colonial system implemented after the Foraker Act. In 1904, Luis Muñoz Rivera responds to the Foraker Act with the founding of the Unionist Party – a direct opposition of the US rule within the island. Also, in 1922, a branch of the Unionist Party, known as conservatives – a group of highly educated elitist men, founded the Nationalist Party. Dissatisfied with the granting of US citizenship to Puerto Rican people, the Nationalist Party openly opposed the US presence in the island. The questions remained why the Puerto Rican elites embraced the idea of the tutelage. There was of course a logical explanation. The wealthy landowners and the elites considered the arrival of Americans as a pathway to democracy and self-government. Others pushed for integration in the Union. [315]

The Spanish American War marked a very important period not only in the history of the United States, but also that of Spain, Cuba, Puerto Rico, Philippines, and all the territories granted to the US after the treaty of Paris. In fact, it was a multidimensional war, short in nature, yet paramount in exhibiting the might, the strength and the growing power of the United States. There are many elements that should be considered in the foreign policy and domestic policy of the United States while analyzing the real nature of the war and frame it according to the international relations theories. One particular factor that guided US expansion was the rising of the country as a nation and binding the population to the idea of civic nationalism, as opposed to jingoism and chauvinism. The building of the American Empire was nothing short of an ideology based on a peculiar combination of Christianity and Darwinism.[316]

On the other hand, the loss of the war marked a very important phase in the decline of the Spanish Empire. On an international level, Spain exhibited accuracy and great diplomacy to avoid the war at all costs and did so for many reasons. Spain had no interest in engaging in a war with the United States. The economic ties in Cuba, Puerto Rico and Philippines had weakened drastically. Militarily, Spain struggled in the Ten-Year War with the rebels in Cuba. In 1897, the Spanish Government granted autonomy to Puerto Rico and promised to do the same in Cuba. For most of the 19th century, Spain fought in the colonies to pacify the rebels and maintain the position of power and hegemon. The creole uprisings throughout the 19th century turned into bloody revolutions and wars of independence throughout Latin America. The domestic policies remained static, without much social or economic change. Spain could not contemplate the idea that colonial policies put in place with the early settling no longer suited the need of the population and their desire to self-govern. Four hundred years of colonial rule have not only changed the New World, but it had created many versions of the Latin American race through the process of mestizaje, in which the hierarchical nature of the social pyramid framed the strata according to the race, birth and status. Spain created an irreparable schism between the peripheral elites and the peninsulares reinforcing the social structure imposed by the metropolis, until the nationalist elites in the 1930's– especially in Puerto Rico - identified themselves as successors of the Spanish "Hidalgos" and rejected the North American "Gentleman" mentality. Spain's rationale about creating an entire race from Iberian roots became an ideology during the first half of the 20th century and continues nowadays in Cuba and Puerto Rico as another schism between Latin American (brotherhood) hermanidad, and North American hegemony.

During the colonial period, ordinances and constitutional power came directly from Spain and it did not allow room for the Creole population to participate in the political life yet enabled them to accrue wealth and economic strength. However, the elites depended on the Crown's economic tutelary and once the American interests and corporates expanded, elites saw an opportunity, completely overlooking sovereignty problem – especially in Puerto Rico.

NATIONAL IDENTITY

In this chapter, I present an overview of national identity in Puerto Rico. In agreement with the core argument of the book on contested identities, I explain how Puerto Rican people perceive themselves on the island and the United States, as individuals, and as an ethnic group. I argue that there are a few conflicting dualities in explaining the case of Puerto Rican national identity. Primarily, understanding the duality oneself and the other lays the foundation of national identity even in political circumstances where the hegemony of the other is perceived as an existential threat. Secondly, I contextualize the concept of national identity in the dichotomy: The Puerto Rican identity vs. the state promoted cultural identity. Thirdly and more importantly, I explain another duality that is related with the legal-political status of Puerto Ricans as US citizens. Thus, I show that the Puerto Rican identity as self and US citizenship as the other are concepts that must be separated and analyzed seorsum. Why is identity paramount to understand the construction of nationality, and how do people in Puerto Rico experience their national identity? To answer these questions, I describe how people of Puerto Rico apply the concept of self-identity and collective identity in their political setting, meaning - how they experience Puerto Rican nationalism under the commonwealth status. Lastly, I contrast the US citizenship to the Puerto Rican citizenship in the case of Juan Mari Bras and Alberto Lozada Colon to show that loyalties to the Puerto Rican identity have displayed a sense of dissatisfaction with the legal-political system of Puerto Rico.

National identity in Puerto Rico is one of the most complex issues in its contemporary politics and it is tightly related to Puerto Rico's legal-political status.

Puerto Rican scholars such as Juan Manuel Carrion and Jacqueline Font-Guzman have approached the problem from the dichotomy of self and the other, where self is the Puerto Rican identity, and the other is the US citizenship. I purposely use citizenship, instead of US as a sovereign over Puerto Rico. The US citizenship to Puerto Rico has long been a catalyst of economic prosperity for the waves of migrant workers. Thus, Puerto Rico's national identity is portrayed as the self, and the institutional North American nationalism, as the other.

The paradigms postulate that once people enjoy and experience their cultural identity, and the sense of belonging to a distinct nation, they share political aspirations and seek an independent state.[317] National identity uses formal and informal institutions to bind people who share the same political aspirations. Hence, for Puerto Rico national identity has always been problematic. An essential element that is often confused with national identity is the concept of citizenship, which is merely the relationship between an individual and the state. Based on the political status of Puerto Rico as an unincorporated territory, two issues overshadow Puerto Rico's national identity. First, it is the political status of Puerto Rico. In other words, Puerto Ricans are US citizens. Secondly, is the idea that Puerto Rico is a cultural nation without a nation-state. The second choice has been disseminated by the Puerto Rican diaspora to keep close ties with Puerto Rico as their cultural cradle while enjoying the benefits of US citizenship. The project led by PPD has converted Puerto Rico into a cultural nation rather than a nation state.[318] In nation-states made of homogenous groups, or one ethnicity, the individual can fully experience their national identity. While in Puerto Rico, national identity is unsettled. Guzman-Font explains that Puerto Rican people experience cultural nationalism as part of their cultural identity and use the US citizenship as a legal, political identity. The diaspora identifies as Spanish speaking Americans. This particular approach to Puerto Rican national identity fits perfectly in Anderson's framework of imagined communities, a cultural nation without settled boundaries and political aspirations. Whereas the nationalists and pro-independent activism in the island have openly rejected Anderson's approach seeking a well-defined national identity and a Puerto Rican citizenship.

Smith's Framework of National Identity

Without the slightest doubt, Puerto Rico is a cultural nation, and the puzzle we sought to solve in the introduction was the motive as to why this cultural nation is not seeking a state. Puerto Rico is also a homogenized nation that socio-genetically dwells on the mix of three primary cultures and ethnies over the longue durée.[319] Paradigms tell us that Puerto Ricans should be seeking their state. After 1989, many people who migrated to the mainland US chose an economical solution over a political one. Thus, loyalties split even deeper. In the mid-1900's, the political parties were not the only ones divided on the issue of the US. People who had already moved into the US have been economically established, and they were in favor of the political and economic relationship and their dependence on the American institutionalism. Diaspora in the US had taken a different approach than the nationalists on the island. While nationalists on the island sought a national identity, diaspora sought a Puerto Rican cultural identity and a US citizenship. This relationship was unacceptable for the nationalists and pro-independence parties

A national identity is a form of collective identity, and perhaps with the rise of criticism toward the terminology, it is more acceptable to use national identity instead.[320] Smith emphasizes that national identity is a sense of belonging to a nation. It is the group's desire to have an independent state and believe in its political aspirations. What we have seen so far in the Puerto Rican case, is a well-defined -distinguishable- cultural nationalism that people can identify with as an ethnic group. Furthermore, this set ethnic identity that I use interchangeably with the concept of puertorriqueñidad is a cultural nation and not a political-legal unit. Anthony Smith states that: "It was Friedrich Meinecke who in 1908 distinguished the Kulturnation, the largely passive cultural community, from the Staatsnation, the active, self-determining political nation." As Smith explains, even though Meinecke might dissent from the use of terms, the distinction is a valid one. To describe the national identity, Smith uses the allegory of Oedipus the King. "There was no nation in Ancient Greece, only a few city-states jealous of one another; however, there was a common culture and a Greek ethnic community, but not a nation." The question to ask is whether or not we can have a cultural nation without having a state-nation (nation-state). Secondly, are we able to apply Smith's framework in the case of Puerto Rico to define national identity? Thus far, we have seen that Puerto Rico is a cultural nation and is able to express cultural nationalism openly without inhibitions. We must not confuse cultural nationalism and national identity. Being that Puerto Rico is a commonwealth of the United States it makes the Puerto Rican national identity unclear.

Elements of National Identity

Anthony D. Smith mentions that the key to ethnic survival is cultural and demographic continuity. [321] Granted, the cultural continuity, and tradition, is what keeps an ethnie bonded together. But when it comes to national identity, Smith argues that it includes some sense of political community. Smith's theory and work comprise a cultural aspect as the driving force of nationalism.[322] Smiths' theory postulates that culture is paramount to ethnie and vice versa and goes to say that to have a national identity there must be a political community, a project that will bond the ethnie together in a national project. Both ethnie and cultural nationalism are precedents of the nation-state. However, the political community can be an elusive concept and for that matter fragile. Smith argues that nationality is the product of strong cultural identity with a political purpose and a political community. The political community entails traditional institutions, laws, and expectations for all the members. Most importantly, Smith underlines that the political community must live in a well-defined territory the members can identify with, and to which they feel they belong. [323] In other words, Smith deems the nation *as a community of people obeying the same laws and institutions within a given territory.*[324] According to Smith - the above definition is a Western perception of nationalism, which implies that the territorial nation – and the rational state are tightly related to one another. In Smith's perception, national identity requires a politically organized community with a set of codes, laws and a defined territory that gives the nation a sense of belonging. More importantly, national identity implies that the state as a legal- political entity ensures continuity and a sense of security for the nation. More importantly, Smith argues that national identity endows people in their homeland where they share common myths and historical memories. In other words, the political-legal community endows civil liberties and guarantees equal treatment under the law for all of its members. Lastly, people must have a shared economy free to move within their defined territory. [325]

Here the case of Puerto Rico becomes problematic for nationalists and pro-independence activists who seek a Puerto Rican national identity. Juan Manuel Carrion, in his work El Imaginario Nacional Norteamericano y el Nationalismo Puertorriqueño argues that the national identity in Puerto Rico cannot be interpreted without considering the presence of the imaginary North American nationalism. Carrion explains that these conflicting identities stem from the competition between the Puerto Rican nationalism and the imaginary North American institutionalized nationalism (referring to the statehood movement).[326]

Limited by the political and legal status of the island - the national identity of the Puerto Rican people will remain a contested subject. Meaning, the essential components of national identity do not all apply in Puerto Rico under the commonwealth status. Thus, Kulturenacion and Staatnacion have no converging points. In this case, Staatnacion in Puerto Rico is an elusive concept. The imagined political community is not Puerto Rico as the homeland or the historical territory, but the overarching set of institutions under the present political status.

The second element of national identity according to Smith is the idea of a Patria, a community of laws and institutions with a single political will. This assumption entails at least some conventional regulating institutions that will give voice to common political sentiments and purposes. [327] Due to the etymology of the word Patria, (Latin: fatherland), in Puerto Rico is a little ambiguous because it dates back to the colonial times where Patria, or Madre Tierra (motherland) implied Spain. The nationalists interchangeably used the terms referring to Spain as Madre Tierra and Puerto Rico as Patria. In Smith's argument, la Patria endows security and perpetual stability; a sense of national identity to the members. Can the US ever be la Patria for people of Puerto Rico? For Puerto Ricans in diaspora and the island, la Patria carries an emotional attachment, more so than political-legal connotation and it is always associated with Puerto Rico.

The third element of national identity – Smith argues - is a common culture and a civic ideology; a set of common understandings and aspirations, sentiments and ideas that bind the population together in their homeland. For many scholars and what is most considered as a perplexed idea is the separation of a nation from a state in cases where nations exist, but they do not have their state. The state, in Puerto Rico's case, is seen as the set of institutions, laws, and government under the commonwealth status and Patria (fatherland) is merely an element of cultural nationalism. The identity in Puerto Rico exists, but it is completely separated from the idea of the state as group membership. In this case, the self-governing powers granted in the Constitution of 1952, were not considered as an expression to common – nationalist – sentiments and political aspirations, rather a way to self-administer the territory. Moreover, the nationalist discourse of the 1950's brought forward self-determination with the aim to unite people and create a Puerto Rican independent, sovereign state. [328]

The national identity relies on a few assumptions that according to Smith are fundamental features, which define a community by the common historical territory, myth and memories, common mass culture, legal rights, and a common economy with territorial mobility for its members. Using Smiths' argument, we see that the national identity in Puerto Rico is fraught with complexities. Because the island limited political powers and the legal status, there is a significant discrepancy between national identity and citizenship. The disconnect theoretically – does not allow Puerto Ricans to fully develop a national sentiment and the sense of belonging to the United States as a nation because of the emotional ties to their historical territory. As Carrion argues, the North American nationalism is imaginary to the People of Puerto Rico. This relationship between people of Puerto Rico and American patriotism is merely a historical question and a matter of Puerto Rican ancestry, language, culture, and tradition and ethnogenesis. The fundamentals of national identity are primarily a manifestation and a transformation of cultural nationalism with a political purpose. Political nationalism can also fuel cultural nationalism with ideas and practices that relate to the revival of collective identity, public culture, and the refinement of the nation from a moral standpoint. The nation, in this case, is not seen as a political organization, but rather a cultural community striving to develop norms, ideals, rekindle the common past, and eventually lead to a national project. While nationalism bases its existence on shared memories and a sense of solidarity, it has enabled political agendas to use it as a unifying factor of people with a common political purpose.

The Historical Background of Puerto Rican National Identity

Ramon Emeterio Betances is known as the father of Puerto Rican nationalism. A doctor by trade, he was born in Cabo Rojo. His father was from Hispaniola, his mother was of Puerto Rican and French ancestry. Ramon Emeterio Betances' cry of independence was the first national project in Puerto Rico, and ironically, it was crushed in a matter of days by the Spanish army. Betances' national project was limited in scope and lacked a unifying ideology, precisely the nationalist ideology. The scrimmage to break up with Spain and declare independence stemmed from the limited understanding of Puerto Rican identity, and therefore it failed as a project. Without a national identity that would bond the people to the territory, a common historical past, language, tradition, and a clear political purpose, there cannot be a unified ideology or a successful independence movement.

Nevertheless, the movement sparked elements of national identity and is of great historical importance. As I have discussed before, Betances' convictions represented the typical Creole ideology where he'd seen the Puerto Rican as Antillean.[329] In his famous quote, Las Antillas para Los Antillanos, Betances joins the other Creole uprisings of Latin America to rid Puerto Rico of Spain, yet the Puerto Rican identity - separated - as national identity was farfetched. During the 17th and 18th century, the Creole and Peninsular elites stratified the society into a hierarchical the caste system. The ranking marginalized the mestizo, the indigenous and the African population. In the previous chapter, we have discussed that mestizos were ostracized for almost two centuries and deemed as godless people living in sin and immorality. Albeit, the elites ranked the population according to their socio-biological characteristics; in other words, practiced racial classifications and divisions. As we have seen in the process of mestizaje, the combinations of racial mixing were many. The darker the skin, the lower the social status, the lesser the economic opportunities. [330]

On the verge of the dissolution of the Spanish Monarchy in the colonies overseas, there were many social issues. But the issues that Latin American Creoles faced after they'd declared independence from Spain were two: determining nationalities and unifying their people –without racial and class distinction -around a national project. As we have mentioned in chapter two, the mestizaje was an obstacle in identity construction. The African factor in defining the socio-identity was problematic in countries with a more extensive European background such as Argentina. In the Caribbean Islands, the problem of defining identity was less problematic. The Afro-Antillean was not a divisive factor, as it was in Argentina, but it remained a debated identity.[331]

Nevertheless, the contributing groups were no longer ethnicities, and they were homogenized. Such is the argument of Stuart Hall and Jose Luis Gonzalez who deem the Afro-Antillean identity as the standard identity for the Antilles without considering the collective historical past, and culture thus group's similarities as opposed to others. The Marxist interpretations of Hall and Gonzalez are international ideologies founded on class struggle and anti-colonialist rhetoric. The argument is merely a deconstruction of identity; adrift from the uniqueness of puertorriqueñidad to an overarching, identity which is true, but inclusive and on a larger identity scale. What Hall and Luis Gonzalez argue is, in fact, a Pan-American identity which undermines the "self" of each culture or nation. Such interpretation tends to disregard the importance of historical territory, the political aspirations of people along with the mythomoteurs and their particular culture. Religion, language, class struggle and the colonial past – can create a supranational identity yet are not conducive to national identity therefore making it a weak argument.

The case of nation building in Latin American countries after their dissolution from the Spanish monarchy is quite different from the rise of nationalism in modern Europe. We hardly see national building from Gellner, Anthony D. Smith or even John Hutchinsont. More importantly, the political situation in Latin America was not compatible with Europe in many levels as prerequisite condition for modern nationalism. The industrialized societies and the urbanization to meet the need of the capitalist, the high standardized culture was quite absent. The Spanish colonial system was hardly a capitalist system. In fact, *colonos* were vassals of the Crown. The building of national identities in Latin American countries followed a different path. It was after virrenatos turned into states what gave birth to the national identity and not the opposite. With that said, when Spain lost the colonies, the colonies dissolved and created the states. Of course, Creole pioneers were at the forefront of the societies and the newly created political-legal units, but they were not nationalists. In fact, there were no nations in the virrenatos, but societies with a ranking caste system. Colonialism did not spark nationalist feelings among Creoles, and many of them identified with Spain as a nation yet did not share Spain's political aspirations. Granted, Creoles' economic interest became the pivotal cause of the wars for independence. National identity was a new concept. El americanismo as the ruling ideology of the Creole movement was far from being a national ideology it was more of a cry for freedom from economic constraints dictated by Spain and their mercantile system. The former colonies had many issues that they needed to solve before they became nation-states. First, many of these new countries struggled with power issues and inside politics. The political culture was entirely lacking, and so was the self-governing abilities. Western democracy, human rights, market economy were challenges ahead and they still remain. However, the biggest challenge was getting rid of the caste system and building a collective identity.

How the United States Became the Other for the Puerto Rican Nationalists

In 1900, when Congress passed the Foraker Act, the intentions of the United States about Puerto Rico were uncertain. The island had been a Spanish colony for five centuries with practically no experience in self-governing. On the other hand, Puerto Rico was very vulnerable to potential belligerent European powers and threats if granted independence immediately after the Spanish American War. A possible invasion of Puerto Rico by Spain or other rising forces would have changed the balance of power and the new world order. However, after Congress passed the Jones Act in 1917, the future of Puerto Rico became more or less clear. Puerto Rican men registered in the US armed forces to fight in WWI. Jones Act angered the nationalists which at the time were elitist men highly educated with conservative views. However, the political situation in Puerto Rico became heated and local elites advocated for three different political statuses at the same time, autonomy, annexation, and full independence. Michael Staudenmaier argues that the United States had no plan to grant Puerto Rico independence any time soon, and this fueled the nationalist elites prompting them to establish the Nationalist Party in San Juan in 1922. Staudenmaier writes: "In a society where literacy rates hovered below 10 percent, the small literary community produced most of the early pro-independence sentiment, often dramatizing its position with vivid depictions of oppression and the assault on Puerto Rican cultural identity."[332] Thus to retake one of the ideas that I've presented in the hypotheses, it is essential to mention that inherently, the resistance to the American rule stemmed in protecting the cultural identity at any cost and paving the way to independence to materialize it. Luis Gonzalez' argument that the fourth floor (Puerto Rico's Commonwealth era) is the new identity implication is undisputable. The Puerto Rican identity under the commonwealth status has entered a new era. The consequences are many, and the rhetoric is not the same in the US diaspora as it is on the island. While diaspora has grown roots and can experience citizenship with full voting rights in the mainland US - it will hang on to cultural nationalism on the island. Whether out of pragmatism or convenience, the middle class or even the Puerto Rican working class enjoys the political and economic benefits that US citizenship offers. In this case, Puerto Rican nationality becomes secondary. The island is the cultural home, but not the political homeland. Many proponents of independence agree with this argument. Just as my theory suggests- identities in Puerto Rico are ever changing, politicized, and balkanized. The lack of the unification ideology has proven to be the cause of the failing national identity efforts whether in referendums or through other democratic means. It's shocking that political structures promoting national identity, sovereignty and independence have the lowest turnout of the elections. This accounts for a disconnect between the masses and the nationalist elites. However, constructing nationality is much more complicated than unifying people around a cause.

The argument here is; can the shared culture, myths, and symbols unify the people of Puerto Rico in the quest for independence? This rhetoric is fraught with complexities, on the island and in the mainland US. Many discourses of the mid-20th century - especially those promulgated by the independentistas and the nationalists such as Pedro Albizu Campos- brought up independence rhetoric based on historical traditions, languages that separated the two different worlds. The dilemma lies in the split between nationality and citizenship.

The Symbolism of Juan Mari Bras and Alberto Lozada Colon

In the 1990's the US citizenship again became the center of the debate and a legal hurdle between the United States and proponents of the Puerto Rican independence. The insurgencies, rebellion, and anti-imperialist rhetoric no longer suited the political situation between the US and Puerto Rico. Thus, the independence activists relied on the national identity to extract the Puerto Rican factor from the US citizenship. The symbolic acts of citizenship relinquishment challenged constitutional courts in the US, the insular government and the government of the United States as well. More importantly, the act commanded statutory solutions, far from semantics and symbolism. In late 1990's, two prominent Puerto Rican lawyers, Juan Mari Bras and Alberto Lozada Colon, both proponents of the independence movement, renounced their US citizenship in the countries of the Dominican Republic and Venezuela - stating that the US citizenship does not represent them as Puerto Rican nationals. There were no precedents on either case, thus the cases demanded a solution that would legally recognize elements of national identity, a historical territory, a defined culture, language and some sort of political objective and unity. [333]

There is no evidence that the two cases were synced or linked to one another, yet they served as precedents for many claims of Puerto Rican citizenship after. On September 23, 1996, Alberto Lozada Colon appeared at a United States Consulate in the Dominican Republic and stated that he desired to renounce his United States nationality.[334] After legal hurdles and litigations, the US State Department did not recognize the renouncement of the US citizenship on the ground that the petitioner has not presented preponderant evidence to relinquish his citizenship. Alberto Lozada Colon decided to appeal the case at the Court of Appeals in the District of Columbia. Lozada-Colon requested a writ of mandamus to direct the US State Department to recognize his renouncement of citizenship. His request was denied, and the case went to the Supreme Court of the United States. After the writ of certiorari was granted, the Supreme Court dismissed his claim stating that the Court of Appeals cannot grant a writ of mandamus to force the State Department to issue a certificate of loss of nationality (CLN). The Supreme Court as well as the Court of Appeals for the District of Columbia maintained that the petitioner is welcomed to voice his strong political convictions about the independence of Puerto Rico in other forums. The case served as a precedent for Mari Bras' denial of the relinquishment of his US citizenship. [335]

On July 11, 1994, Juan Mari Brás had renounced his US citizenship at the American Embassy in Caracas, Venezuela. Bras assumed that by abandoning his US citizenship, he would have to be deported to his birthplace, Puerto Rico. As he declared "If I renounce my US citizenship, they will send me to the country of birth, and that is Mayaguez Puerto Rico." On November 22, 1995, the State Department approved Mari Brás' renunciation of his American citizenship. However, in 1996, Miriam J. Ramirez de Ferrer, a Puerto Rican politician took the case to the Supreme Court of Puerto Rico stating that Juan Mari Bras was no longer eligible to vote in Puerto Rico ever since he has renounced his US citizenship – a prerequisite to voting in Puerto Rico's elections. Puerto Rico's Supreme Court sided with Mari Bras stating that, as a citizen of Puerto Rico, Mari Brás was eligible to vote in local polls. With the ruling on Lozada Colon vs. the Department of State and Court of Appeals for the District of Columbia, the US Department of State rescinded Mari Bras' renouncement of citizenship stating that to renounce US citizenship one must live in a foreign country. Since Puerto Rico is a territory of US, such clause should not apply. Thus, the decision on Lozada Colon by the Court of Appeal and Department of State was upheld. Lozada colon served as a precedent in Mari Bras' court ruling. [336] The cases were symbolical, but gained attention and in 2007, for the first time Juan Mari Bras received his certificate of Puerto Rican citizenship. Since then, many Puerto Ricans have received their citizenship certificates while some have renounced their US citizenship in solidarity with the independence cause.

Citizenship as another form of identity is purely political, it is not always established by birth, but rather by states, and as such, individuals can either reject it or accept it. By definition, citizenship can be deemed as an individual or group relation to the state.[337] Thus, the relation to the state and citizenship is crucial in determining nationality. But when the individual considers the state as the *other,* then it becomes a political and legal problem. Theoretically, a democratic state protects the inalienable rights of their citizens and the citizen must fulfill the duties such as serve in armed forces, pay taxes etc. What perplexed the two Puerto Rican lawyers to renounce their US citizenship was the dichotomy of citizenship and nationality. Puerto Ricans are citizens of the United States, yet -many- do not identify with the American nation. Moreover, the rhetoric used by both lawyers is merely anticolonial and considers the United States as *the other.* The United States' civic and modern nationalism is not one of *the preferred group* [338] choices, and in this case the preferred group is the Puerto Ricans mainly on the island. Such ideology was propelled by the nationalists. Despite the efforts to label the rhetoric as separatists, in its core had more to do with a feeling of identity than separatists. It was a mere effort to show that the two nations are very distinct, and different. The pro-independence activists had a very modern - non-violent- approach to the independence cause, but the ideology and the rhetoric is exactly the same. Considering the United States as an existential threat to their identity, the nationalists and the *independentistas* emphasized that the Puerto Rican identity is inherently different from the Anglo-Saxon identity of North America. Thus, the Puerto Rican identity is "everything" but North American, or otherwise Anglo-Saxon, and that did not imply the socio-biological or ethno-genesis, but it implied a different ideology. [339] For example, the anti-colonialist proponents identified with Latin American Spanish speaking nations that were once under the Spanish Crown and now see the United States as a potential threat to their identity.

Another identity that was tangible, and inclusive to most of Latin American countries is "la raza". La raza implied all people in Latin America whom emerged from the process of mestizaje. This identity included all of those who once were part of the caste system – in the lower ranks. The Afro-Antillean was another identity layer that unified mostly people of the Greater Antilles predominantly with African roots. The Puerto Rican identifies – more or less- with all of the above yet does not identify with the North American identity even one hundred years after the inclusion. The split nature of Puerto Rican political spectrum has ranged from conservatives – those who hoped to keep the ties with Spain, to the annexationist - those who wanted to break-up with Spain and become a state or a commonwealth of the United States. Nationalists and independentistas were adamant and against a North American presence in Puerto Rico. At the same time, many identified as Ibero-Americans- meaning that they share the Hispanic heritage, the same language, the same historical territory and have the same political aspirations for self-determination.

To sum up the argument, in this chapter, I have covered a few key concepts and events to help better understand the national identity in Puerto Rico, and how that applies to its special political status. I also have contrasted the national identity and citizenship in Puerto Rico using the cases of Juan Mari Bras and Alberto Lozada Colon to show that in cases where the pre-requisites for national identity and citizenship are not congruent, then people will abandon the citizenship because it does not give them a sense of belonging. The case of Mari Bras and Lozada Colon have paved the way for scholars to contextualize citizenship inside of a modern state with multi-ethnicities. Mari Bras implied that holding on to citizenship that is not congruent with his national identity does not make any sense. He had explained his position to the public on nationality, independence, and sovereignty. The national identity - in a disputed society with split loyalties such as Puerto Rico is hard to fathom.

On the other hand, it is not hard to realize that social structures, political entities, and change agents are those who - whether give rise to the idea of Puerto Rican national identity or trade it for a lesser political version, - a cultural identity. Burke and Stets argue that social structures are significantly impacted by the actions and beliefs of its members and these are the actors or the agents.[340] For a national identity to flourish, we must have all the elements that Anthony Smith suggests, yet in everyday politics, things can take a twisted turn that will change the fate of the nation for centuries to come. In a modern world where nations seek their states in conventional ways such as self-determination movements, or non-conventional ways such as the case of Israel, the fight or struggle revolves around a sense of loss. This sense of loss questions the existentialism of tradition, culture, historical territory, shared past, language, and religion. In other words, everything that makes ethnicity one of the most powerful social groups, and collective identities conducive to national identity. In the case of Puerto Rico, many underlying assumptions will affect national identity building. The split loyalties, the "many" Puerto Rican identities, the lack of clear national project, the role of the elites, but most of all, the constitution of Puerto Rico are the factors that have impacted the slow process of national identity building.   Puerto Rican people have a strong identity, and a clear view of what the implications are for the island – given the three choices, independence, commonwealth, and statehood. Out of these three choices, the first one will promote national identity. Commonwealth and statehood can promote cultural nationalism and a cultural identity much like of what we see during the Puerto Rican cultural celebration of la puertorriqueñidad. Thus, la puertorriqueñidad, is only a cultural representation of the people of Puerto Rico. In this case, the historical territory, the language, the religion, the common past are only elements that will create a strong sense of identity but will not be conducive to national identity.

CLASH OF IDENITITIES: WHEN ETHNIES DO NOT SEEK THEIR STATE

In this chapter, I examine the rise and the fall of political nationalism led by the leader of the Puerto Rican Nationalist Party, Pedro Albizu Campos. I juxtapose the key question of this chapter remains: Why did political nationalism fail? To explain the collapse of the self-determination efforts, we must examine the inside politics in Puerto Rico and the role that the United States played in the future of the island. We have to consider many variables, such as the elites, loyalties, national identity, and the stakeholders vested in this endeavor. How the legal and political powers controlled these variables? More importantly, we have to look at the role that identity played in the failure of political nationalism. By retaking the identity path, I explain how contested identities have determined the political trajectory of Puerto Rico in the 1950's. I argue that when political nationalism fails, it is likely that the movement will shift in another direction or change its original path. In the case of Puerto Rico, political nationalism turned to a radical movement that brought the Nationalist Party to its political dismay. Examining the role of the populist elites, I show how the rhetoric from political nationalism in the 1940's and 50's, shifted to cultural nationalism to unite the people around a national project that would exclude Puerto Rico's sovereignty. This new form of sponsored identity also excluded the need for a nation-state, in exchange for economic incentives.[341] The populist ideology promulgated by Luis Muñoz became the moving force behind the cultural nationalism that we see today in many Puerto Rican parades across

184

the US. Luis Munoz engineered a form of cultural nationalism that did not require its own nation-state. He used a symbol and a fundamental identity construct, the Puerto Rican mestizo, called Jibaro. The jibaro is quite visible with many displays of graphite and artwork in Metropolitan areas of the island and also in the United States.

Nationalism is a feeling. It is often associated with displays of flags, intense rhetoric and does not go away as long as people feel strongly about their nation. People or ethnic groups become more problematic when a nationalist movement is silenced or crushed. The more the movement is silenced, the more intense the feeling grows. In 2015, Nelson Denis a former New York Assemblyman released a book called *War against all Puerto Ricans; Revolution and Terror in America's Colony*.[342] The book is an overview of the nationalist uprising of the 1950's on the island. The claims and the allegations in his book are severe and reveal factual information released by the FBI in 2004. The narrative of the book depicts an ongoing struggle of political rivalries between Pedro Albizu Campos and Luis Muñoz Marin, Puerto Rico's first elected Governor and the founder of modern Puerto Rico. These two political foes who were initially pro-independence grew apart. Their differences became opposing views on the future of the island. Eventually, the battle ended up with the crushing of the nationalist activism and the overwhelming victory of Luis Muñoz Marin as the Governor of the island.[343] Luis Muñoz Marin's pragmatism has often been criticized by scholars, political opponents, nationalists, and independentists. The well-thought commonwealth solution was embraced by the people of Puerto Rico and by the diaspora whom never wanted to break ties with the United States. In the 1930's Luis Muñoz Marin became one of the key players in Puerto Rico's politics. Once, pro-independence activist with a liberal Creole background, Luis Muñoz Marin, became one of the promoters of the Gag Law which prohibited any display of national symbols on the island in 1948. As the President of the Senate, Muñoz Marin shuttered and outlawed the pro-independence parties in search of a political solution that eventually changed the identity path of Puerto Rico again.[344] Knowing well that the political persecution in Puerto Rico was unconstitutional,[345] even under the overarching US Constitution, Muñoz Marin used the ambiguous situation to secure a victory in the 1952's elections.

During the 1920's and 1930's, the island's economy was in disarray. Many of its sectors changed drastically to meet the needs of the corporate and satisfy consumer demands in the mainland US, especially the need for sugar. Without a formal national economy, the raw materials and the resources were controlled by a handful of US and European corporates. The five major corporates that dominated the production of sugar paid the workers close to nothing. The poverty-stricken jibaros had no means to make ends meet, and soon, images from their harsh living conditions flooded the media and the popular culture. The political situation, on the other hand, mirrored the economic distress. The island struggled to find common ground between the new form of shared power between the US and the insular government. The Senate at the time mirrored dysfunctional and divided politics. By 1917, Congress conferred US citizenship to the people of Puerto Rico. The decision was sudden and without any form of mitigation for the dying economy. Puerto Rican citizenship - formally existed - but Puerto Rican national identity became ambiguous. The pro-independence elites rebuked the decision. The US citizenship undermined the pro-independence efforts, and to the Nationalist

186

Party, it became an existential threat to national identity.[346]

The nationalist elites promulgated the identity that was utterly inherent to the island and resistant to any existential threats. North American hegemony, whether political, economic, or cultural, should not alter the Puerto Rican identity in the given political situation. Thus, identity became the center of the debate again. In the search for an overarching [347] identity were also other circles in Puerto Rico's inside politics. Their rhetoric has drifted from the independence cause. Still, it would settle for an identity widely accepted by the people, easily recognizable, attached to the island, but not to the historical territory. Two center-debates dominated the political scene. One promoted an identity integral to the island, inclusive of all Puerto Rican people in search of national identity and a state of their own. The other identity was promoted by the pro-commonwealth elite, led by Luis Muñoz Marin. This type of identity was brilliantly engineered as an economic-cultural hybrid identity after 1954. Exploiting the underdeveloped agrarian economy and the central figure of the jibaro, Luis Muñoz Marin sought an identity solution within the class struggle. Using the jibaro for political gains, Muñoz Marin displayed communist beliefs without inhibitions of class warfare and corporate greed. [348]T he demagogy won him a few seats in the 1938 elections. The FBI declassified files revealed that Muñoz Marin had used leftist tactics in his electoral campaigns.[349] The Jibaro was no longer a hillbilly, but rather a significant political and cultural capital. He became a key player in Puerto Rican politics; having the right to vote and the power to elect. The economic packet from Washington aimed to convert the agrarian economy into an industrial production force to meet the needs of the American consumer. The Jibaro gradually left the hills and moved to the industrialized cities. Although the Jibaro converted from peasant to the new Puerto Rican proletariat, it did not embrace a left leaning ideology.

In the 1940's and 1950's, Luis Muñoz Marin created a solidified working class, the most significant contributor to the island's economic development. The surging capital was an utmost accomplishment that met the immediate needs of the Jibaro. Muñoz Marin was a strategic thinker, a demagogue, a skilled orator. He captured the moment and turned the deplorable economic situation into his party's favor. By reaching out to the poor Jibaro and contextualizing his existence within the class identity, Muñoz Marin solved his party problem by creating a solid base for the PPD. The Nationalist Party struggled to reach out to the poor farmer. The party has always been a sanctuary for intellectuals and conservatives maintaining a stronghold at the University of Puerto Rico, Rio Piedras, Santurce, and other municipalities. Nationalists were occupied with ideology and not so much with concrete political solutions. The nationalist discourse was a typical anti-colonial rhetoric. Pedro Albizu Campos promulgated a political interpretation of Puerto Rico's identity that was not class related. A W Maldonado argues that it was Albizu Campos' bitter racist experiences during the time he served in WWI, which triggered his political activism and quest for independence more so than his political aspiration for a nation-state.[350] The claim Maldonado makes is a slightly distorted interpretation of the nationalist ideology. Albizu Campos' assignment to an African American battalion did not play a role in his nationalist activism. Albizu Campos was part mestizo and part Spaniard. He finished his service and was honorably discharged as First Lieutenant from the US Army. He was very proud to have served in the army and revered it. However, it was the Sinn Fen ideology he'd embraced as a student at Harvard. It's what helped shape his views as a nationalist, rather than his racist experiences in the army. Albizu Campos saw the United States as an invader even though he admired the American government, the political system and the US institutionalism. He wanted the same institutionalism on the island, yet independently of the US. Albizu Campos' nationalism was inherent, ethnic, and with a political purpose. Albizu Campos and Muñoz Marin became mortal enemies even though they had shared Puerto Rico's historical background, collective memories, tradition, territory, and language.

The answer is simple – they did not share the same ideology or the pre-requisite for national identity and independence. Here rests the answer to the Puerto Rican contested - yet painful identity path. Split loyalties and nationalist ideologies will always clash. Scholars offer a limited number of theories explaining this particular case of political nationalism. The approaches are mainly generic and based on narratives that pertain to specific cases or nations. It would be complicated to expound the failure of political nationalism in Puerto Rico on the island due to the position of the United States as an imperial power and as the sovereign. Nationalism is new and can be an elusive concept. What happens in cases where sovereignty is transferred from one authority to the other in the treaties of war? We have to take the example of Puerto Rico as is in these specific conditions. Inherently, Puerto Rican political nationalism stemmed from dissatisfaction with the status-quo, the lack of sovereignty over the state, the territory, and the institutions. Besides, I argue that the case of nationalism in Puerto Rico is deeper and stems from the identity debate. To explain the unique case of nationalism in Puerto Rico, I have used Gellner's anecdote "Ruritians in Megalomania." How did the nation of Ruritania form?

I retake the concept of modern nationalism and as it relates to the Puerto Rican case, and I prompt that there is a case of strong political nationalism in Puerto Rico that demands specific attention. First, I scan the role of diaspora and the local elites to determine their allegiances to the Puerto Rican cause and how the split loyalties played out. Then, I recapture the populist ideology of Luis Muñoz Marin in reforming the Puerto Rican cultural nationalism to erase the Nationalist Party's project once and for all. More importantly, by evaluating Gellner's [351]paradigm – I argue that the building of nation-states – or a modern nation inside a higher political power will fail for many reasons. Inside politics and small interests in insular politics also served as a deterrant in discouraging the quest for national sovereignty. I argue that Gellener's theory overlooks the dichotomy between "peripheral cultural nationalism and economic, military and security guaranteed by the metropolis." The model questions the paradigm. The diaspora relied on the metropolis economically militarily, and politically to carry out its project; thus, it crushed all separatist and nationalist projects in the metropolis and also in mainland Puerto Rico. Lastly, I retake the figure of Pedro Albizu Campos to demonstrate that apart from the conservative view stemming from the old Spain memory, Albizu Campos managed to establish a modern version of the Puerto Rican identity, based on tradition, and what was specific to the island. It was the type of identity that promoted the idea of the nation-state to protect the continuity from existential threats. [352]

The chapter is organized into three major themes that are interrelated to one another. First, it explains the theoretical framework used to sketch the failure of modern and political nationalism in Puerto Rico. Then, I make an anectodal parallelism with the tale of Ruritanians in Megalomania, which places the events into a timeframe and context. In other words, I explore the life and work of prominent Puerto Rican politicians in the 1950's, which marked the rise of socio-economic reforms led by Luis Muñoz Marin, and the fall of the nationalist and independence movement led by Albizu Campos. I present a narrative of the life, ideology, and pragmatism of Luis Muñoz Marin. I reveal his thinking behind the choice to turn Puerto Rico into a Commonwealth of the United States. I explain what freedom meant for Luis Muñoz Marin. By using the key concepts in Gellner's theory, I conclude that the nationalist movements have their specifics. Still, identity - including here contested identities - determines the success of the building of a nation-state.

The Tale of Ruritanians

"Hence as far as individual life chances went, there was perhaps no need for a virulent Ruritanian nationalism." Gellner[353]

Ruritanians spoke one of the many intelligible dialects and lived in the land of the Empire of Megalomania[354]. It is necessary to reiterate that Puerto Rico is an unincorporated territory, politically and judicially under the United States. Starting with the vernacular, or the language of the Ruritanians spoke in Megalomania, many underlying assumptions suggest that the regional dialects of jibaro Spanish were spoken in Megalomania by people who've moved there, especially after the 1920's. This population was nonetheless farmers (the Jibaros) who moved to the United States yet had family ties with the island.[355] The jibaro Spanish was neither the vernacular nor the language of the aristocratic Puerto Rican diaspora, such as the circle of Luis Muñoz Marin. More importantly, this layer of aristocratic Puerto Rican elite in the United States spoke the language of Megalomania -English- unlike the Jibaros, who worked in many factories and lived in clustered urban communities. Of course, as Gellner argues, Ruritanians lived in the slums of Megalomania and were segregated. They enjoyed their music, culture, and even their lament popular songs sung by iconic artists. I would refer here to "Lamento Borincano," the unforgettable Iibarito's song of suffering.[356] The Ruritanians in Gellners' book often thought of their valleys, life in Ruritania, and the beauty of their country. Soon they'd developed a national conscience and sought to create their own nation-state. Gellner implies that the stages and the efforts of self-determination are not always synchronized due to divided loyalties. For example, Gellner wrote *"the oppression had produced guerrilla resistance led by a social bandit who was captured by his compatriots and that the tribunal which condemned him to a painful death had as its president another compatriot."*[357]

Ruritanians flooded Megalomania. They came to seek work. Ruritanians were rough and many were illiterate. Hence, some adopted secular and liberal ideas and became journalists, teachers, and professors. Megalomania offered many concessions for the Ruritanians, and they had developed an exquisite taste for the arts, ethnography, and foreign cultures.[358] Thus, some Ruritanians were assimilated but kept their first and last names and became citizens of Megalomania. As time went by, they deplored the neglect of their river valleys back home, the discrimination of their compatriots in Megalomania, and they spoke against these ills.[359] Here Gellner's theory becomes challenging for the Puerto Rican case. The reason why Puerto Ricans failed to start a national project and build their nation state it is the same argument Gellner insists that it is *not a pre-requisite* for the building of a nation state - and that is the economic dependence and incentives of Megalomania. When the political situation becomes favorable, Gellner explains,

Ruritanians attained independence. [360] But Gellner is convinced that the economic incentives offered by Megalomania should not be detrimental to the independence cause because Ruritanians' strong cultural nationalism prevails. Meaning, even if we trade the national sentiment for the socio-economic promotion, it would not matter, as long as Ruritanians still have a strong cultural nationalism. In fact, the case of Puerto Rico has proven what the critics deemed as a charade in Gellner's theory. Trading the reduction of national sentiment with the social economic promotion, was seen as a travesty by Gellner.[361] According to Gellner, Ruritanians took their culture for granted and loved it no matter what.

How to Account for Gellner's Modern Nationalism in the Puerto Rican Case?

Gellner's theory explains how nations are formed under the most peculiar circumstances, even inside empires with multi-ethnic and multi-cultural communities. The metaphor Gellner used to describe how Ruritanians split from Megalomania and established their nation-state remains a utopia. To this significant achievement, Gellner dedicates this one sentence: Ruritanians attained independence. Independence does not usually come easily, even by using non-violent means. It took Mahatma Gandhi over forty years to achieve it without violent means. Independence is a national project that involves a vast range of factors, actors, domestically, and internationally. The question is how to consider these factors in the Puerto Rican case. First, referring to Ruritania, it must meet all the pre-conditions for building a nation-state.[362] Among the pre-conditions is Megalomania's project to grant independence. More importantly, the diaspora must frame a national project whose objective is independence, nationality, and sovereignty. In the end, the diaspora is the only force that will impact the independence cause more so than any insurgency and contentious politics in Ruritania.

Placed in a context, the nationalist and the independence movement in Puerto Rico from 1920 to 1950 was entirely silent to the public in the mainland United States. The Gag law of 1948 meant to silence the movement on the island and especially in Rio Piedras. When four nationalists attacked the US Congress in 1954, then the movement gained national attention. By then, the Nationalist Party was already slandered, discredited, and outlawed on the island in the unforgiving battle between Munoz and Albizu Campos. Albizu Campos had spent most of his political career in jail as the leader of an organization conspiring to overthrow the insular government. His agitation and propaganda rhetoric were separatist, yet the overarching goal was independence and sovereignty at any cost.[363] *Albizu Campos' national project was pulverized once it threatened diaspora's commonwealth project.* [364]

Puerto Rican Diaspora and the Commonwealth Project

In the following narrative, I argue that the nationalist and independence movement died out for three main reasons. First, the diaspora did not have a national project to build a nation-state. Secondly, the diaspora had lost the sense of the inclusive identity – la puertorriqueñidad - and replaced it with a class identity -el jibarismo. Thus, the dichotomy of *self* and the *other* was significantly impacted by the Marxist convictions of Luis Muñoz Marin. In other words, he became the jibaro as a poor farmer, and not necessarily the Puerto Rican. To Muñoz Marin, the farmers were the exploited class, and *the other* were the "blood-sucking" corporates. El jibaro had transformed from folk and popular identity into a product of the capitalist system planted on the island by the corporate after the US takeover. This new shift toward class identity had no relevance with the Puerto Rican identity. Within the schemata *self* was no longer the Puerto Rican identity, and the North American identity was not *the other*. Thus, Munoz created an entirely new schema to eliminate two factors that damaged his rhetoric. The other - was the malevolent capitalism and the sugar corporates. Therefore, the other was no longer an existential threat. Thirdly, the diaspora maintained a relationship with the United States to secure economic incentives for the future of the island. Puerto Rico became part of the New Deal programs, which materialized in the implementation of the agrarian reforms. Lastly, as Gellner had ironically mentioned, intellectuals and politicians in the diaspora, even though they would integrate into Megalomania's politics, they had higher and better chances and opportunities to become heads of government in Ruritania.

According to Gellner, the need for a modern nation-state emerges after the pre-requisites are all met. The nation must have a territory, a collective historical past, a vernacular, a standardized language, and a high culture. But most of all, the people of the nation must have a robust ideological will and the means to institutionalize the same unifying ideology. Also, the pre-requisite that holds priority in Gellner's theory is the industrialization, and the emergence of a proletariat without which a modern nation would be a failure. Eugene Weber *argues* that rural communities cannot build a nation-state because they are driven by their own interest and small private property. But, if rural communities, move out of the countryside they'll end up in working-class clusters inside of urban areas where they'd become enlightened with modern ideas.

The island between 1920 and 1950 was predominantly a rural society willing to accept any solution to survive hunger. Frequent hurricanes and corporate greed had impoverished the farmers and expropriated them from their land.[365] The farmers moved into the industrialized cities but never became a proletariat. Yet, referring again to Gellner's allegory, we ask the question "What drove Ruritanians to seek their nation-state, and why has Gellner overlooked the process of self-determination? The above assumption represents Puerto Rico as a classic case of nation-state failure prompted by diaspora. The models of sovereign nations are bountiful, and Megalomania (the US) itself is a model of a modern nation. The relationship between Puerto Rico and the United States in the first thirty years of the takeover went from military occupation to a tutelary system. In the mid- 20th century it evolved to a corporate-owned territory, and lately to a paternalistic form of governing. The key to understanding why Gellner's Ruritanians do not always seek a state of their own has to do with two major ideas: The identity debate, the duality of self and other, and secondly is the economic dependence on Megalomania.

Luis Muñoz Rivera and His Admiration for the Puerto Rican Jíbaro

Luis Muñoz Rivera was one of the most prominent politicians in Puerto Rico in the early 1900's. He was a pro-independence politician even though the movement did not consolidate until the 1930's under the leadership of Pedro Albizu Campos and the Nationalist Party. Luis Muñoz Rivera had a clear vision of identity, independence, and sovereignty for the Island. As for class relations, he came from a conservative family, but admired the jibaro. Muñoz Rivera saw not a class identity in him, but the authentic Puerto Rican, the mirror of puertorriqueñidad. The first half of the 1900's was instead a tumultuous era not only for the United States but also for Puerto Rico's. The divisiveness and power struggle characterized the political scene. The hybrid form of the Government as a result of the lack of experience in governing. [366]The United States Congress was not entirely clear about the future of Puerto Rico as one of the territories acquired through the treaty of Paris in 1898. Governing the island was a significant concern after four hundred years of the Spanish colonial system. Judicially and politically, Puerto Rico, along with the Philippines, were US unincorporated territories, yet undetermined for how long. The political havoc between the political parties in Puerto Rico had overwhelmed the elites. Since the US invasion in 1898, the political parties had already expressed their loyalties openly. The conservatives were loyalists to the Crown; the liberals leaned in favor of statehood or annexation. On the verge of the Spanish American War, the political circles were divided fundamentally by strong ideologies and loyalties. Three dominating platforms dominated the political circles in the late 1800's - *los incondicionales (the loyalist), los autonomistas and los anexionistas.* When American troops entered Guanica, Luis Muñoz Rivera, a well-known member of the political elite whom one of the founders of the Autonomous Party in 1887 fled his family to Rios Piedra. At that time Luis Muñoz Marin was a newborn baby.[367]

In 1909, Muñoz Rivera became the Resident Commissioner in US Congress. Muñoz Rivera was a poet and a compelling one. He was a diplomatic and sophisticated politician who played with the ambiguity of his words to convey the message. He sang to the jibaro in his poems and, spoke on the floor of Congress with great eloquence and dignity.

A skilled journalist, Muñoz Rivera, promulgated the very delicate nature of Puerto Rico's political status through the printed press and what awaited ahead if people had lost their rights to liberty. In 1916, shortly before his death, he argued in Congress about Jones Act clearly stating his disagreement with the status quo

"If the Island of Puerto Rico was to sink, people would prefer US citizenship more than anything, but for as long as the island exists, people would prefer Puerto Rican citizenship."

His writing revealed anti-imperialist and anti-colonial rhetoric. Muñoz supported and defended the people he had represented, especially the *jibaros and the poor.* His core argument was self-determination and people's right to govern their own state and the right to own their economy. He died in Santurce Puerto Rico from a gallbladder infection in 1916. People flocked the streets to pay their last respects. Jibaros left their farms and work in the fields to say goodbye to one of the most beloved Puerto Rican politicians of the early 1900's. Muñoz Rivera's son, Luis Muñoz Marin will later on become one of the most prominent politicians on the island, and will win himself the name: "Father of Modern Puerto Rico," otherwise known as the architect of the commonwealth.

Luis Muñoz Marin: The Man of Many Ideologies

I will start the narrative with a verbatim statement made by Luis Muñoz Marin in an interview.

"They (the nationalists) want to force the people of Puerto Rico to wish for a form of freedom that they claim to prefer, which is independence, but the people of Puerto Rico have overwhelmingly chosen another form of freedom, and that is the Commonwealth Status in voluntary association with the United States."[368]

Muñoz Marin took freedom for an elusive concept. Ideologically, he remains an ambiguous figure in Puerto Rico's politics. He has played a significant role in the shaping of Puerto Rico's status as a Commonwealth of the United States and modernizing the island. It is paramount to interpret the figure of Luis Muñoz Marin - not as many of his foes or admirers have portrayed it - but for his philosophical thought, and his leadership in moving the island toward a political direction that he had envisioned.

Muñoz Marin was a skilled orator; he later turned a populist politician. Pedro Caban argues that Puerto Rico was nothing short of a social experiment.[369] With the ratification of the commonwealth status, Luis Muñoz Marin signed one of the most transcendental deals ever signed by any transactional leader in Puerto Rico's history.

Muñoz Marin spent part of his childhood and teenage years in the US when his father Luis Muñoz Rivera was the Commissioner for the Affairs of Puerto Rico in the US Congress. Much like Puerto Rican diaspora, he lived between two worlds.[370] He admired the United States yet lamented the suffering of the jibaros and their families, driven to starvation in the island. Like many Puerto Ricans in the US, Luis Muñoz Marin mastered both English and Spanish and preferred living in between the two worlds. He spoke and wrote with elegance and admirable eloquence in both languages. His writing mirrored the thought of a keen and elevated man.

Muñoz Marin was inspired by his late father's work as a poet, journalist, and politician. In his early years in New York, he was a traveling poet, with spiritual depth and a bohemian soul. He lived in Greenwich Village and hung out with theatrical troupes, poets, and socio-literary elites.[371] Muñoz Marin married Muna Lee – an American poetess with whom he had two children with and abandoned for months at a time. In the 1920's, the couple moved to Staten Island and suffered financially. Muñoz Marin's work as a writer and a translator was not enough to pay the bills. He embraced Marxist ideas in class relations and frequented various literary circles where class struggles and worker exploitation fueled subversive poetry.[372]   It was the socialist poet and activist Edwin Markham- whom influenced Muñoz Marin's early conceptual understanding of class stratification, and revolutionary thought. Muñoz Marin became very ambitious; he sought to expand and promulgate his views outside of the United States. He had joined syndicalist organizations, labor unions and workers' movements across the United States and Latin America.[373] He traveled to national and international conferences to diffuse red propaganda about the ills of the capitalist society and human exploitation. [374] According to A. W Maldonado, Muñoz Marin became an activist and an agitator – as he called himself in the poem *Pamfleto. "I am God's Puppeteer, God's agitator."* Shortly after, he embraced Bolshevik ideas, Josef Stalin, Red October and sought to adhere in a political structure that supported class warfare that shared his views. [375] He joined the Socialist Party in Puerto Rico founded by Santiago Iglesias and campaigned from town to town where he had witnessed the poverty-stricken island and the hungry images of the Puerto Rican jibaro. Muñoz Marin felt compelled to save the suffering agrarian class. The impoverished jibaro tapped into his ideological side and as A. W Maldonado wrote, "Muñoz Marin connected immediately with the first line of the Communist Manifesto and the class warfare[376] *The history of all hitherto existing society is the history of class struggles."* [377] In his childhood memory, the jibaro was the soul of the island, now the jibaro had become a human tragedy, oppressed by foreign investors and North American sugar cane

200

corporates. [378] Enlightened by leftist ideas, Muñoz Marin interpreted the economic crisis in Puerto Rico as a class struggle. He had urged the political parties to side with the working class. Amidst the disagreement he declared that parties cannot side with the exploiter and the exploited at the same time. He inferred to the Unionist Party, the party in power and at the same times his father's political party. [379] During the 1920's, Muñoz Marin campaigned for the Socialist Party and encouraged the sugar cane workers to continue the strike. He traveled around the island supporting sugar cane workers in their fight for justice and better working conditions. He supported their rights by demanding the improvement of working conditions for the agricultural workers and for the early emerging proletariat. [380]

His successful electoral campaign won him the majority not only in municipal elections for the cities of Guayama and Salinas, but also thanks to his electoral campaign, the Socialist Party in Guayama and Salina sent their representatives to the General Assembly. [381] In 1922, Muñoz Marin along with Salvador Iglesias traveled to Oregon to partake in the convention of the American Federation of Labor. He presented his resolution to push for an investigation on Juan Vicente Gomez, the Venezuelan dictator on repression allegations of workers' rights. He urged Samuel Gompers, leader of the American Federation of Labor to present the finding of the investigation to the US President and urged that the US must cut their diplomatic relations with Venezuela. The declassified FBI files revealed that Muñoz Marin was diffusing communist propaganda and that he had used Bolshevik rhetoric in the elections during the 1940's, but for pragmatic reasons, he had not aligned himself with the communists. [382] Thus, in the 1930's Muñoz Marin's ideas in Puerto Rico were considered revolutionary.[383] He denounced five major American sugar cane corporates that maximized the profit and took all the gains back to the US. In his newspaper, *La Democracia* he called it *"el capital ausente"* - the "missing capital." [384]

Senator Millard Tydings and the Independence Bills

Muñoz Marin changed his views about independence during the 1930's. Once promulgated in his platform, the independence rhetoric died out with the rise of his political career. It was not clear why Muñoz Marin became the number one opposition of the independence bill proposed in US Congress by Senator Milliard Tydings in the Senate Insular Affair Committee. Such reasons were puzzling, as it were his deviation from the independent cause.

During the 1930's the island was in political turmoil. In 1933, Millard Tydings, the Senator from Maryland, Chairman of the Senate Committee of the Insular Affairs stated: "If you want your independence, I will help you get it." Referring to the Puerto Rican people and political elites. [385] Senator Tydings was against the takeover of territories made of cultures that were alienated from the United States as he stated. He suggested that the United States would be better off leaving the island. In 1934, the United States appoints Blanton Winship, a retired army General to govern Puerto Rico.[386] This assignment in part was due to major strikes that had taken place that year, causing the administration to fear social unrest.[387] In 1936, to ease the tensions in the Island, Senator Tydings introduced a bill calling for the independence for Puerto Rico. Under the terms of the deal, if the people of Puerto Rico voted yes in the referendum in November 1937, then the United States will grant Puerto Rico the independence after a four-year transitional period with limited autonomy.[388] Luis Muñoz Marín, openly opposed the bill. Most of the Puerto Rican political parties supported the bill, which was modeled after

Tydings and McDuffie Act for the independence of the Philippines. Tydings also suggested that Puerto Ricans must follow the example of the Philippines. But Muñoz Marin was outraged. He was excluded from the preparation of the bill but most of all, President Roosevelt, the Secretary of the Insular Affairs and the Director of US Territories Ernest Gruening were also in favor of the bill. Muñoz Marin took his fight against the bill with Washington calling it "La ley de la fuga" – a metaphor for "release and shoot in the back." [389] He thought the bill was a devious way of backstabbing Puerto Ricans. Unlike the Philippines, Puerto Rico was given only four years of transitory –autonomy period instead of twenty. Muñoz Marin argued that independence with hunger is not the solution and killed the bill by calling it a diabolical scheme of Ernest Gruening as a revenge for the killing of appointed Insular Chief of Police Elisha Riggs by the nationalists. Tydings then withdrew the bill. [390] Muñoz Marin portrayed the bill as one of the tribulations that can ever happen to the people of Puerto Rico. Furthermore, independence meant that Puerto Rico would be excluded from the New Deal. The exclusion meant tragedy for the agrarian class, the jibaros.

In 1943, Millard Tydings submitted a new bill. Under the new proposal, Tydings offered a twenty-year tariff phase-in structure just like the Tydings–McDuffie Act, which provided independence to the Philippines. Muñoz Marin traveled to Washington again opposing the bill.[391] To Tydings' surprise the bill contained everything that Muñoz Marin had wished. Yet Muñoz Marin stated that if Congress passed the bill Puerto Rico will vanish in five years. [392] In 1945, the Senator rewrote the bill as Tydings-Piñero bill of Independence, which Marin Muñoz opposed again. By that time, Muñoz Marin had abandoned the independence cause for good. [393] After two days of debates inside his Partido Popular

Democratico, the independence faction broke off and founded the Puerto Rican Party for Independence claiming that PPD has betrayed the independence cause.

Pan Tierra y Libertad, a Matter of Class Warfare.

Pan tierra y libertad was the slogan that won the heart of the jibaro but did not bring economic sovereignty nor independence to Puerto Rico.[394] In the late 1930's and early 1940's, el Partido Popular Democratico, launched a program that aimed to help and strengthen the jibaro economically and push him out of poverty. The problem was not as easy as the solution sounded. The US sugar companies owned a total of 170,675 acres. Fajardo Sugar Company owned 37,741 acres, United Porto Rican Sugar Company 44,030 acres, the Central Aguirre Sugar Company owned 39,269 and the South Porto Rico Sugar Company owned 49,635. In total the US owned sugar companies controlled approximately 51% of the sugar production in the 1930's. Apart from the US owned companies there were other investors in the sugar industry, among other a few wealthy creoles, a few French, and Spaniards investors. The conflict between the creoles and other investors were common and triggered by unfairness in policies and price compatibility of the sugar cane. [395] With the cabotage laws enforced after the Foraker Act, the North American investments were booming while the people of Puerto Rico lived in poverty. Regardless of the mind-blowing profits, the workers' pay was close to nothing. [396] Muñoz Marin implemented a few agrarian reforms that would have never been successful without the assistance of Washington. With the help of Tugwell, the last North American Governor of Puerto Rico, and a close friend of Luiz Muñoz Marin, Washington gave the green light for the operation of economic reforms. To alleviate carrying out, a series of agencies were put in place. Among others were *la Autoridad de Tierras, la Autoridad de Transporte, la Autoridad de Comunicaciones, la Autoridad de Fuentes Fluviales, la Autoridad de Acueducto y Alcantarillado, la Junta de Planificación, and la Compañía de Fomento.* [397]

Moving toward the 1950's decade, the position of Luis Muñoz Marin strengthened and so did the PPD. The reforms gave the jibaros an economic solution to make it out of poverty, but most of all, it gave them dignity. It was a pragmatic, short lived solution, yet Muñoz Marin was able to save this class from hunger, disease and shame.

The lands appropriated by the government would be distributed among small families to promote subsistence agriculture, and on larger farms to promote commercial agriculture. Between 1941 and 1945, 1,400 parcels of land were distributed. Until 1960, 58,320 plots had been delivered, comprising a total of 35,848 acres of land. The land distribution did not end the problem of land ownership, but it did reduce it considerably. This program consolidated the PPD politically, especially in rural areas. For most of the people who benefited from the distribution of parcels, the land they received was the first they had in their lives and the proof that the people lived up to their promises. This guaranteed Muñoz Marín the support of thousands of Puerto Ricans."[398]

Under his situational leadership, Muñoz Marín mobilized the country, reaching out to the national symbol of Puerto Rico - the jibaro. As a prominent part of the diaspora, Muñoz Marin drifted from the independence rhetoric - once the driving ideology of his party. After the island became a commonwealth, Luis Muñoz' idea of freedom and dignity was always associated with the United States.[399] Muñoz Marín advocated for spiritual freedom and dignity – yet believed that a Puerto Rican nation-state would never be able to grant these freedoms. Self-determination efforts led by any political force inside Puerto Rico were simply rhetoric. Muñoz Marin had many political opponents from all political spectra. Throughout his life as a politician, he changed four political parties. Munoz's idea of freedom was a mere pragmatic solution for the people of Puerto Rico. First, the micro-economic freedom: A rearrangement of wealth distribution among agrarian workers and families. It meant for the agrarian class to receive small land as a mean of survival. Also, the tax alleviation for small businesses through the operation Manos a la Obra (operation bootstrap) would allow the people to gain economic stability. [400] Muñoz Marín had no long-term vision about the national economy or macroeconomics. In other words, Muñoz Marin sought a short-term economic solution. He lacked the understanding of how the deprivation of economic sovereignty would affect the future of the country for years to come with the attrition of the existing economies. Simply put, the economy of Puerto Rico has been sanctioned since Jones Act of 1917. Muñoz Marín changed the island drastically in a short-term period by improving the economy, urbanizing the island, and improving life conditions. The second type of freedom for Muñoz Marin was a metaphysical freedom and the right to feel free within. [401] This freedom was very personal to him, and we will discuss it in the next section.

When Ethnies do not Seek Their Own Nation-state

In fact, the metaphor goes beyond not seeking a nation state. The political elite from the diaspora, according to the course of the events crushed all independence efforts in Puerto Rico, more importantly; it eliminated the political parties in favor of independence by imprisoning leaders, activists and sympathizers of the cause. For this study, I will focus on a few ideas that played a dramatic role in the future of Puerto Rico as it was architected by Luis Muñoz Marín; his understanding of freedom, independence and sovereignty and his political aspirations. Later, I will discuss the social and economic reforms, and his economic vision for the island. In addition, the promotion of the cultural nation –instead of the nation -state have played a significant role in shaping the new Puerto Rican identity. Going back to Muñoz Marin's idiosyncratic quote about the Puerto Rican nationalists, he argued that there are two types of freedom. One is the feeling of being free within a larger system. This freedom existed within the commonwealth - *estado libre associado con los Estados Unidos* – which translates as Free State Associated with the United States. This type of freedom was in fact security whether economic or military, but mostly economic. It was the security that the United States could offer to Puerto Rico as one of the territories: Thus, in essence, freedom and security are different. Freedom is a civil liberty, and security is a privilege guaranteed by the state. The other freedom that Muñoz Marin recognized, but did not see it as necessary under the specific political status, was the sovereignty of Puerto Rico. His upbringing played a significant role in the shaping of his beliefs. However, there were major incongruences between his rhetoric and actions. Furthermore, in a discussion with his constituents, Muñoz Marin mentioned that the commonwealth status has given us the right to be free, spiritually free and live with dignity while independence is related to many ideological factors which deal with national identity.

One of the driving forces behind any independence movement is nationalism and self-determination. Freedom, on the other hand, is a very abstruse term. From a statist point of view, freedom is limited by constitutional constraints and it is regulated through constitutional provisions. In fact, under the commonwealth status, Muñoz Marín was aware that sovereignty would be out of the question and so was independence. At face value, Muñoz Marin's idea of democracy was the protection of the vote with any cost, and the respect to the voting process and democratic values. In 1946, Muñoz Marín broke up with the independence faction inside of the popular Democratic Party. Gilberto Concepción de Gracia and Fernando Milán Suárez founded the Independence Party. They felt the independence movement had been "betrayed" by the Popular Democratic Party.

The Rise of Political Nationalism

Before analyzing the rise of political nationalism in Puerto Rico, it is paramount to understand the categorization of the type of nationalism that was particular for the period from 1930 to 1950. This period marked a gradual rise of political nationalism. The case of Puerto Rico, nationalism cannot be limited to one conceptual understanding. When it comes to the principles of political nationalism, one has to understand that the state plays a primary role. Anthony Smith has underlined that autonomy (not political autonomy) is key in defining the self-determination movement. But on the other hand, one would ask what constitutes political nationalism and how a political objective translates in political nationalism. For us to understand the role of the Nationalist Party and the Independence Party we must understand the nationalist rhetoric before, and as we do so, we also answer the dilemma that nationalism as a sentiment can be present before the nation state, but the nation state is key for preserving and promoting nationalism.

Elements of political nationalism are inclusive to the idea of state but at the same time must have a solid base. In the case of Puerto Rico, the base for the political nationalism became cultural nationalism.[402] Earlier, I have defined cultural nationalism as the patrimonial heritage of a community; what makes that community unique and distinguishable; traditions, myths, symbols, costumes, the share culture etc. In this book, I argue that Albizu Campos's political nationalism was not limited to cultural nationalism only, but it had much more gradient factors. Political nationalism promulgated by the Nationalist Party and the Independence Party, apart from cultural nationalism was an anti-thesis of the North American presence in Puerto Rico. In that prism, political nationalism was not only a platform to promote the idea of a Republic of Puerto Rico, but the exclusion of everything North American from Puerto Rico's soil. [403] Limiting political nationalism to cultural nationalism disregards many factors that relate to the core identity of the Puerto Rican people. I chose the term antithesis during the discussion of this chapter to illustrate the path that the Nationalist Party chose to build an identity in total opposition with the *other* being the North American identity.

Thus far I have used a few frameworks to construct the identity in Puerto Rico in key moments and historical events, and I mentioned that the universality of Gellners' nationalism is pertinent to the case of Puerto Rico, only if we use it in the analogy of Ruritania. If Puerto Rico were to meet the prerequisites of building a nation state then, it would be inherently related to the figure of Pedro Albizu Campos and not Luis Muñoz Marin. In that case, nationalism would not be a sentiment, but it will be manifested in the political status of

Puerto Rico. In the first thirty years of North American presence in the island, a series of violent struggles and an ongoing political nationalist movement turned into insurgency. When discussing Albizu Campos, it would be necessary to consider him in a timeframe and in a multidimensional plan. Albizu Campos was a mestizo. His mother was a mestiza, and his father was a Basque merchant from Spain - a Peninsular. Thus, he identified as a typical Puerto Rican whose heritage emerged from the mixing of the three races, which he later calls *"la raza humana."* But this human race that he frequently mentions is part of the larger identity, "Spain's engineered imperial race." Albizu Campos in his speeches, unlike like Jose Luis Gonzalez, albeit, separates the two identities: La Puertorriqueñidad and the Antillean or overarching Latin American identity. To Albizu Campos these identities were tightly related to one another and considered both as the Puerto Rican *selves.* Spain – to Albizu Campos - constituted the cradle of the Puerto Rican identity - an identity with "spiritual" ties with former Madre-Patria. In his case, even though he was a Harvard educated lawyer and had spent a considerable amount of time in the United States, North American identity was still *the other,* the irreconcilably different. Cited in Francisco Matos Paoli, former nacionalista Fredo Arias de la Canal writes: [404]

> *"Those who in the US government believe in the possibility of annexing Puerto Rico to the Union, do not know the struggles of our Castilians that lasted five centuries to recover the territories that had been taken from them by Islam (Moors), the struggles against Bonaparte in the 19th century and the struggles against German and Italian fascism in the 20th century."*

With this affirmation, the Puerto Rican nationalist movement not only determined loyalties, but also

210

separated the Puerto Rican identity – as inherent from Spain- from the incompatible different Anglo-Saxon- identity of North America. Elements of the Betances' nationalism, the peninsular hidalgo mentality, the Castellan heritage, are found abundantly in the nationalist rhetoric at the time. But most profoundly and touched in this excerpt is *el espiritus de las armas* – depicted in the historical narrative. Within a few words, and parallel to Pedro Albizu Campos's political discourse, it is evident that Spain - regardless- will remain the genesis of Puerto Rico's identity. The kind of identity we have seen in the identity forming gradually in chapter one and two.[405]

How Political Nationalism Fell off the Political Discourse

There is a gap, an unexplained or more precisely a silent theory about the fall of the nationalist movement in Puerto Rico. In other words, it is not quite clear for the public how and when political nationalism fell off the political discourse. To dismiss the role of the Nationalist Party as a terrorist organization would be disingenuous. While the Nationalist Party became an insurgent organization and adapted violence as a strategic means to meet their political objective, it did in fact clarify the identity path of Puerto Rico and Puerto Ricans. It established the *self* and the *other* dichotomy more so than revealed the ills of an imperialist power and the corporate greed against whom Albizu Campos was determined to fight. United States economic deal proved to be the short-term solution for Puerto Rico to overcome the economic crisis and release the economic tensions in the island after the depression period of 1930's and 1940s. Pedro Albizu Campos was not a problem, nor was the Nationalist Party until the political discourse became arduous and reached out to the sugar cane workers – the largest agrarian and working class. It meant that Pedro Albizu Campos had entered into his political opponent Luis Muñoz Marin's territory. The fear that nationalist ideology could spread throughout the island worried the appointed insular government and pro-annexation elites. Ponce's Massacre on March 21, 1937 marked the breaking point and the irreconcilable differences between the nationalists and the United States. Later on, the insurgency became a headache for the authorities in the island and also the United States.

The following years, from 1948 until 1950, the members of the Nationalist Party were charged with sedition to overthrow the Insular Government of Puerto Rico and its subdivision in order to declare independence and establish the Puerto Rican Republic. The charges included separation from the United States by means of force in the municipalities of Ponce, Guanica, Lares, Arecibo, Utuado, Cabo Rojo, Manati, and San Juan. Pedro Albizu Campos, alone, had twelve charges pending against him by the insular government. [406] The movement was intensified and reached out to the people, without distinction of class whereas jibaros, students, intellectuals and workers.

Although the study supports the thesis that national identity and cultural nationalism are precursors of the political nationalism, based on Albizu Campos' political discourse, political nationalism had already transcended the realm of cultural nationalism. Cultural nationalism is a national unifier, yet not enough to claim political sovereignty. The discourse of the Nationalist Party evolved around imperialism and liberation from colonialism – to seek international support and pressure the insular government and United States into accepting an independent Puerto Rico. On June 10th, 1948 the Gag Law marked the damning of the nationalists out of the political discourse. The

212

law mirrored the inside politics, pragmatism and the diaspora project to annex the island to the United States but preserve a distinct Puerto Rican identity.   The speech given by Albizu Campos in Guanica on July 25, 1948 revealed that Albizu Campos and the Nationalist Party had become a threat to the system, the newly proposed political status and the deal that it entailed. [407] Pedro Albizu Campos, as a nationalist and as a politician must be analyzed separately. While politically, Albizu Campos used Sinn Fein type of measures to achieve the party goals; as an ideologue, Albizu Campos, was perhaps the only Puerto Rican voice at the time who had anticipated hurdles in the island's politics and economy under the status of commonwealth – much of what we see nowadays with Puerto Rico's unsettled economic policies and ongoing economic crisis and corruption. [408]

Criminalizing the Independence Movement

The Puerto Rican independence movement in the first twenty years after the US takeover was substantial. With three parties advocating for independence the movement has grown stronger. Among these parties were the Union Party of Puerto Rico founded in February 1904 by Luis Muñoz Rivera, the Liberal Party of Puerto Rico founded by Antonio R. Barceló; and the Puerto Rican Nationalist Party founded by José Coll y Cuchí. With Albizu Campos as the head of the Nationalist Party in 1923 the rhetoric changed. Once an elitist party made of conservatives and intellectuals, it became a revolutionary cellule, modeled after Sinn Fein. The party attracted many young Puerto Ricans. By the 1930's, the movement had entered an informal insurgency stage against the North American presence in the island.

As a result of the growing discontent with the presence of the US in the island, from 1936 until

1941, the MID (military intelligence division) was fully concentrated on the Nationalist Party activism (cited in Maria E Estades Font). In 1936, two nationalists – Hiram Rosado and Elias Beauchamp assassinated Elisha Riggs, the Chief Police of Puerto Rico assigned by the United States. They were put to death without a due process of law and were both murdered in the police headquarters. [409] From 1933-1937, the island entered into a political turmoil culminating with Ponce's Massacre. On March 21, 1937, nineteen people were ambushed and killed by the insular police and two hundred others were wounded. The victims were peacefully walking on Palm Sunday to show support for Albizu Campos while imprisoned on sedition charges. Among those murdered and wounded were young men, women and children. Congress criticized the massacre. Under pressure from the United States Commission on Civil Rights President Roosevelt let go of Blanton Winship as the governor of Puerto Rico directly responsible for the shooting of the nationalist led march.   The conflict between the nationalists and the authorities whether federal, or insular gave an account of a substantial resistance. After the 1930's the social unrest reigned the island. In 1937 Pedro Albizu Campos was sent to prison for ten years on sedition and conspiracy charges to overthrow the insular government- again. He was released in 1947. In 1948 after struggles with the independence movement, the Puerto Rican Senate presided by Luis Muñoz Marin passed the Public Law 53 or Ley de la Mordaza. The law which stayed in effect for ten years was modeled after the Smith Act. [410] Law 53 made it a felony and prohibited all activity, speech, encouraging, and displaying, voluntarily or knowingly of all independence matters. The law institutionalized Muñoz Marin's authoritarianism, and out of fear alienated the electorate that was in favor of the independence. [411] The criminalizing of the independence movement was a series of institutionalized retaliations against the nationalist activism throughout the island. Despite the civil society's opposition, the bill was signed into law in May of 1948 by Piñero. The Gag law had three main objectives according to Ivonne Acosta Lespier: First, it meant to silence the University of Puerto Rico - a strong hold of the Nationalist Party. Secondly, it intended to decrease the votes in favor of the Puerto Rican Independence Party and enable Muñoz Marin to demonstrate to Congress that the independence movement was insignificant and was contained within the island. Thirdly, it drove the nationalists to extremism until its own demise.

With nationalist activism outlawed, and the newly founded Independent Party out of the political scene, Muñoz Marin was able to win an absolute majority as the first elected Governor of Puerto Rico in 1949. In 1952 with an absolute majority, Muñoz Marin ratified the Constitution of Puerto Rico. Under his terms as a governor over 100,000 Puerto Ricans were persecuted, lost their jobs. The insular police opened files (*carpetas*)[412] where it recorded their political activities. In the next thirty years the persecution of the independentistas in public and private institutions including higher education became one of the darkest chapters in the history of Puerto Rico.[413] The PIP lost about 80,000 of its votes in the 1948's elections. The Gag Law, and the crushing of the independence movement marked the end of self-determination efforts of the 1950's. The law eclipsed all the political forces to favor the election of Muñoz Marin as the first governor of Puerto Rico chosen by the people. All the roads were clear for Muñoz Marin to carry out the experiment.

In this chapter I have covered a few concepts that in my view are important to understand why the Puerto Rican people and the nationalist movement failed to form their nation state, in other words failed to gain independence and sovereignty in the same transitory autonomy period as the Philippines. I have also discussed how the political rhetoric played out for both sides, for the independentistas and the pro-commonwealth political parties. The inside political conflict grew so hostile that it split into loyalties. The political opponents became mortal enemies. The pro-commonwealth political party used the Insular and the Federal Government to crush the independence movement not only led by Albizu Campos, but also the PIP (Puerto Rican Independence Party). The nationalists were thrown off the political debate to eliminate the nationalists from the political scene.

As the leading political figure in the fight against the independence of Puerto Rico, I have analyzed the figure of Luis Muñoz Marin in three aspects: Frist, as a proponent of the left ideology, a socialist leader, a communist agitator, and labor union organizer. Secondly, I have questioned his role in the independence movement; the political aspirations and circumstances that drove him to abandon the independence cause. Thirdly, I have examined his work as a reformer of Puerto Rico's economy under the auspices of the United States Congress to find a temporary solution to overcome one of the most difficult periods in Puerto Rico's history – the economic crisis of the first half of the 19th century. In these three crucial moments of his career, I have argued that Muñoz Marin did not see the Puerto Rican identity as fundamental until 1956 with the launching of operation Serenity and the founding of cultural institutions and preservation. After he realized that the jibaro could no longer be a social class, Luis Muñoz Marin needed to shift back to the identity rhetoric. By then, the identity had become a trope and was forged for the purpose to keep the population together under the new cultural nation. Muñoz Marin strengthened the cultural nationalism and the type of the Puerto Rican identity that was not a threat to dissolve the association. Hence, he gave people of Puerto Rico an economic stability and a cultural identity.

Luis Muñoz Marín created a set of formal and informal institutions that improved the political culture of Puerto Rico and the democratic values through the right to vote – The informal institutions were the pivotal aspects of Muñoz Marín's work. To accomplish this, Muñoz Marín undertook one of the biggest challenges in his career; tour around the island, by car, foot and sometimes by horse to reach out to the peasant and stop the selling of the vote for a few dollars – as he said. I placed Luis Muñoz Marin in Gellner's framework of modern nationalism, to explain that diaspora played a crucial role in changing the rhetoric from independence to economic dependence and political pragmatism. Since this study ends with the failure of political nationalism, it would not be ethical to analyze the economic crisis that Puerto Rico faces today.

In the field of political nationalism, I analyzed in a timely fashion why and how the local elites and the diaspora's split loyalties brought friction, violence and instituted legislature to crush all efforts for independence. I also explained that the role of Albizu Campos must not be considered for his rhetoric. That was a direct result of the persecution and the crushing of the nationalist efforts. Pedro Albizu Campos was the first Puerto Rican to understand the role of economic, political and judicial sovereignty and the impact it will have in the future of the island. Puerto Rico remains divided more than ever on the issue of its political status. The division consist between the island and the diaspora. As we see from the documents and speeches, Albizu Campos was not a politician, he was an idealist who inspired at the time, not only people who followed his lead, but also the workers, farmers and students at Rio Piedras. His legacy continues to inspire people in Puerto Rico to seek for their own independent state at least in a democratic from. He was loved by the people of Puerto Rico yet misunderstood by the diaspora. With the passing of Gag Law and the persecution of the pro- independence activist thought carpetas[414] were silenced for decades and kept his rhetoric in small enclaves, and closed circles.

CONCLUSION

The core argument of this book is the deconstruction of Puerto Rico's identity in search of various threads, such as socio genetic, cultural, national, and political. The purpose of this book is as simple as answering the question: What is your nationality? Whether answered or left hanging in the air, the book tapped into a very delicate subject - the trajectory of Puerto Rican identity. Such historical path showed us that Puerto Rico – identity- while similar to other identity-forming in the Antilles, had very distinct particularities. The book reveals that contested identities became a precursory indicator of the political future of Puerto Rico. When it all boils down to the basics, the groups that clashed were within the island's political elite and the substantial diaspora in the US. On the verge of becoming a legislative and judicial unit under the overarching political system of the United States, the ruling elites of the island became mortal enemies and existential threats for one another. The two major Puerto Rican elitist groups presented the many "selves" of the Puerto Rican identity. They fought relentlessly in very unparalleled realities. One became the governing body of the island, and the other the insurgent. While Luis Muñoz Marin promoted economic reforms downplaying the national identity, Albizu Campos had done the opposite; he downplayed the recovery from the deplorable financial state of Puerto Rico and sought a long-term solution through independence, and sovereignty.

Faced with power struggles and a loss of prestige in their effort to take hold of Puerto Rico as a sovereign territory, the local elites found no other solution but to promote the idea of the nation-state. This political objective became divisive and led to clashes between the elite competing for power. One cluster supported independence from the United

States. The other group promoted cultural nationalism seeking to obtain as many advantages from the relationship with the US. In their political discourse, for both clusters, the *United States* were the *other*. This leads to the fundamental premise of the book: The conflict between *self* and the *other* becomes essential to preserve one's identity. The corollary in this case was prompted by the diaspora, which sided with the *other* and became the existential threat to the presumed shared national Puerto Rican identity.

Jorge Duany in his work *A Nation on the Move*, highlights the schism that exists between diaspora Puerto Ricans and Puerto Ricans who live on the island.[415] As I have mentioned in previous chapters after the US takeover of the island, waves of Puerto Rican migrants flooded the major cities. Puerto Ricans came to live in exchange for economic incentives and a better life. However, nothing comes without a price. Diaspora Puerto Ricans as Duany argues were looked down upon when they returned to the island. They had no longer preserved the authenticity that made them unique to the island. As upward social mobility brought workers, the political structures were put in place to integrate the migrant workers into the mainstream way of life. By the 1960's, over two hundred associations and non-governmental agencies operated in the major cities to mobilize the Puerto Rican migrant worker into exercising their constitutional rights in the mainland USA by voting in the elections and actively participating in US politics.[416] Muñoz Marin promoted the same ideology, yet emphasized that while practicing politics in the USA, Puerto Ricans should never give up their cultural identity. By the 1950's there were clearly two identities related to Puerto Rican people.

The purpose of this research was not only to reveal the identity path but to emphasize the genetic and cultural contributors that have played a fundamental role in the shaping of Puerto Rican identities including here, the cultural identity, the political identity, the diaspora identity, the insular identity, and also the peninsular identity that is often overlooked. Occurring themes in this book are congruent with the overarching claims made by scholars in the field.

COMPLEX IDENTITIES

In this book, I traveled through a timeline, from the days the island became a Spanish dominion until the 1950's where insurgency arose to separate Puerto Rico from the United States and to start the process of nation building. This process never came to fruition due to the clashes between the local nationalist elite and the diaspora in the US. There are various theoretical threads that try to explain the identity forming and the rise of nationalism in Puerto Rico. I will summarize these strands and make room for future implication about the case of Puerto Rico.

First attempt to explain genetic identity in Puerto Rico is introduced by a cluster of sociologists that argue on the basis of mestizaje and its contributing factors. Within this cluster there are various views. We have the overarching Antillean identity introduced by Stuart Hall and Jose Luis Gonzalez whose idea of the Antillean mestizo is Afro dominant. According to this cluster, the mestizo is class related and is a heavily exploited individual whom inhabits the Caribbean Islands including here, the West Indies. Opposite mestizo is the colonial system imposed by an imperialist, and mercantilist power such as the US. This argument is a bit superficial when describing race and identity because it tends to reduce the identity hypotheses to class, economics and exploitation instead of highlighting what makes Puerto Rico culturally and nationally distinct from the other Afro mestizos.

The second identity thread rests on the debate over Taino heritage and their presence in the Puerto Rican genesis. Here as well, we see two contradicting points. The assimilation theory argued by Haslip Viera and the New Taino Survival movement whose proponents include various researchers in the US and Canada. Sherena Feliciano Santos – a researcher in the linguistic and anthropology field also supports the Taino survival beyond the legends. The converging point is that both views – although opposes ideological and political purposes - consider the Taino presence in the Puerto Rican mestizaje as a contributing factor. Yet, the diverging points between the two views exist in the survival of Taino pedigree after the Spanish conquest. While Haslip Viera calls the survival of Tainos after the Spanish conquest a fallacy, Felicano Santos argues researchers ought to look deeper in linguistic utterances and anthropological relics and artifacts. This identity debate is also propelled by Taino activist groups who claim indigeneity for political agendas. In fact, many self-claimed indigenous people have distanced themselves from the overarching Puerto Rican identity.

The third thread in Puerto Rican identity is what we call la puertorriqueñidad, the thread that emerged from the process of mestizaje as a combination of three races, but most of all as the melting of cultures in one. La puertorriqueñidad, promulgated by the nationalists and later by cultural nationalist movement was the center of the identity known as native to the Island of Puerto Rico. After the ICP's cultural revolution, the building of institutions, the PPD shifted the rhetoric from the jibaro class identity– the poor Puerto Rican farmer, to the idea of puertorriqueñidad, the

222

widely accepted identity – the pride of every Puerto Rican on the island and diaspora.

The fourth thread of the Puerto Rican Identity emerges from the trenches and the hills of Puerto Rico and is otherwise known as the jibaridad. There are some overlapping areas between the jibaridad and the Puertorriqueñidad, however, jibaro applies to the Puerto Rican country male who emerged as a widely accepted identity in the mid 1800's since the majority of the population of the island were farmers that lived in rural areas. Manuel Alonso, as we read- in chapter three, gives us another account of the jibaridad. He attributes the traits of the jibaro, to a true Puerto Rican man, but most of all, jibaro according to Alonso is witty, with a strong character. Later on, after the US takeover, jibaros became destitute and were devastated by famine, poverty and a lack of resources. As we have seen in chapter six, the jibaro becomes the central figure of the populist ideology proponed by the PPD. In agreement with Marxist view on the expropriation of farmers from their land, Muñoz Marin, initiated the Agrarian Reform of 1941. [417] Thus, the jibaro, from a cultural identity, shifted into a political and class identity, an electoral base for the PPD.

The fifth identity thread of the overarching identity probe is the Spaniard identity, or the hidalgo legacy. After 1898, we see that the thread consolidated as an ideology due to existential threats from the US takeover of the island. This ideology is mirrored in conservative beliefs, not only to those who were loyalist to the Spanish throne, but to those who also were against the rise of the United States as a world power after the Mexican American War, the purchasing of vast territories, the annexation of Puerto Rico, the Philippines and Guam. More importantly, the rationale that this identity cluster makes are the irreconcilable differences between the "Spanish Hidalgo" and the North American Gentleman." Argimiro Ruano, in his book "La Idenidad de los puertorriqueños" has treated the problem from two angles. He argues that no matter how complex the Puerto Rican identity is, it could never be compatible with the North American, or the Anglo-Saxon identity. Secondly, Ruano mentions that there are not only genetic differences, but the values, mentality and the philosophy of life are inherently different. With this strong case, Ruano builds a precedent for Puerto Rico's independence, even though he does not materialize it. "La identidad de los puertorriquenos" exhibits how two cultures refuse to melt into one. There can never be a second "criollismo" says Ruano, implying that the Puerto Rican identity is already established and rejects what is not inherent- or the other.

The last thread of the Puerto Rican identity is the most powerful political force that changed the political direction of the island. This identity includes Puerto Ricans who have moved to the US and have lived there for many generations. This cluster, whom we discussed in Gellners' framework, lives in metropolitan areas and large cities with a big Latino population. The Puerto Rican diaspora is very much involved in the economic and political life as well as American Pop culture. This cluster has embraced a form of nationalism that is strictly symbolic and cultural, based on the triad and the endless love for the island. Puerto Ricans in the US keep close ties with the island, and many of them live between the two worlds. Yet they are excluded from the island's political activism and are very quiet about the relationship between the US and Puerto Rico but have the power to vote in the US Presidential, state and local elections. Those who have close ties with the island are mainly from the countryside and make up the lower income portion of the American society. Their children are ESL or bilingual students and receive instruction in both languages. The striking evidence is that the diaspora has a powerful lobby in the Unites States and representatives in Congress. Thus, Puerto Rican diaspora is a powerful political class that has moved legislations in the US especially in the second half of the Twentieth Century. Much of the legislation has to do with social justice matters for the diasporic population and their political representation in Congress. In conclusion, a part of having a cultural identity, the diaspora in the US has a political identity.

Considering the wide range of identities, one can only think with that many claims would be extremely hard, and impossible to have a national project and claim independence over the island. The identities mentioned above fell into the political discourses promulgated by either the commonwealth proponents and the nationalists circles. These loyalties decided the political future of the island without the slightest doubt.

We have already established why and how the loyalties of every one of these groups have impacted the independent cause. The nationalist promotors remained within the islands' conservative circles of young intellectuals. Whereas the jibaros and the cultural nationalists joined the commonwealth cause and stayed within the US overarching constitution and sovereignty.

From work in the field, whereas here in the States or in Puerto Rico, I observed that the schism is very obvious. While we enjoy the Puerto Rican heritage and cultural nationalism in the States and on the Island, nationalism is quite different. The divergences are irreconcilable. While the nationalists remain ideologically faithful, those who supported the commonwealth are caught in between the anti-colonial rhetoric and the ongoing economic dependence on the US. Thus, many in the diaspora are promoting the statehood - while on the island it is the last resource for survival. Puerto Rico has a very complex political status that has worked for years and has changed the lives of many enjoying the economic abundance and the opportunities that the US has offered on every spectrum, yet Puerto Ricans are not fulfilled and satisfied. They have a citizenship but lack national identity. Of many reasons and implications, we discussed in this book that the bottom line is, Puerto Ricans cannot overcome their split loyalties to bring forward a national project. With the islanders living mainly in continental US, that project is farfetched. I will end this book with a quote by Juan Mari Bras, "Puerto Rico will become one day independent, if not now, in seven hundred years." Efforts of self-determination might come to fruition when there is a national project, and this national project can only be led by the Puerto Rican people. Until then, Puerto Rican nationalism remains a right of self-expression as guaranteed in the constitution.

Bibliography

A.,Van Middeldyk R., and Martin Grove Brumbaugh. *The History of Puerto Rico: From the Spanish Discovery to the American Occupation.* N.Y: D Appleton and Company, 1903. pg.

Abrams, Dominic, and Michael A Hogg. *Social Identity Theory□: Constructive and Critical Advances.* New York Etc., Harvester Wheatsheaf, 1990.

Acosta, Ivonne. *La Mordaza□: Puerto Rico, 1948-1957.* Río Piedras Puerto Rico, Editorial Edil, 2008.

Adams, Richard N. "Guatemalan Ladinization and History." *The Americas* 50, no. 04 (1994): 527-43

Albizu, Don. "Campos Speaks." *YouTube*, 4 June 2015, www.youtube.com/watch?v=Ab13_zIoNYQ. Accessed 17 Aug. 2020.

Amiot, Catherine E., Roxane De La Sablonnière, Deborah J. Terry, and Joanne R. Smith. "Integration of Social Identities in the Self: Toward a Cognitive-Developmental Model." Personality and Social Psychology Review 11, no. 4 (2007): 364-88.

Anderson, Benedict R. OG. *Imagined Communities: Reflections on the Origin and Spread of Nationalism.* London: Verso, 2016.

Anthropology Online. "Benedict Anderson About Nationalism (In Mijn Vaders Huis,

1994)." *YouTube*, 12 Nov. 2013, www.youtube.com/watch?v=cNJuL-Ewp-A&t=160s. Accessed 15 Aug. 2020.

Archivo Albizu Campos. "Albizu Campos Habla Sobre El Estado Libre Asociado de Puerto Rico (PARTE 1 de 3)." *YouTube*, 24 Aug. 2011, www.youtube.com/watch?v=Y9z2Uwh9rfY. Accessed 15 Aug. 2020.

Argimiro Ruano. *La Identidad de Los Puertorriqueños*. Mayagüez, P.R., Recinto Universitario De Mayagüez, 2001.

Articles of Agreement between the Lords, the Catholic Sovereigns and Cristobal Colon." *American Journeys Collection* p 248.

Ball, Kimberly (1999), "Facundo by Domingo F. Sarmiento", in Moss, Joyce; Valestuk, Lorraine, Latin American Literature and Its Times, 1, World Literature and Its Times: Profiles of Notable Literary Works and the Historical Events That Influenced Them, Detroit: Gale Group, p. 171–180.

Bauböck, Rainer, and Thomas Faist. *Diaspora and Transnationalism: Concepts, Theories and Methods*. Amsterdam University Press, 2010.

Birtle, Andrew J. "Persuasión Y Coerción En Las Guerras De Contrainsurgencia." Military Review, November/December 2008, 23-26.

Burke, Peter J., and Jan E. Stets. *Identity Theory*. New York, NY: Oxford University Press, 2009, p. 9.

Chaar-Pérez, Kahlil. "'A Revolution of Love': Ramón Emeterio Betances, Anténor Firmin, and
	Affective Communities in the Caribbean." *The Global South*, vol. 7, no. 2, 28 July 2014, p. 11–36.

Caban, Pedro. *Scholars Archive The Colonizing Mission of the U.S. in Puerto Rico.* 2002.

Calderin, Rafael. "La Catedral De San Juan Bautista Y Los Monasterios De Santo Tomás De
	Aquino Y De San Francisco De Asís." May 2016.

Carlosantonioperez. "La Música Tradicional Puertorriqueña, Las Raíces." *YouTube*, 12 May
	2011, www.youtube.com/watch?v=Ch6fSrJc11M. Accessed 15 Aug. 2020.

 Carrión, Juan Manuel. "El Imaginario Nacional Norteamericano Y El Nacionalismo
	Puertorriqueño." *Revista De Ciencias Sociales* 7 (1999): 68-85.

Carrion, Juan Manuel. "The War of the Flags: Conflicting National Loyalties in a Modern
	Colonial Situation." *Centro Journal* 18, no. 2 (2006).

 Cast, Alicia D., and Peter J. Burke. 2002. "A theory of self-esteem." *Social Forces* 80:1041–68.
	Hall, Stuart. "Cultural Identity & Cinematic Representation." Framework 36 (1989).

Castellas, Salvador E. Causas y Antecedentes Diplomáticos de la guerra Hispanoamericana,
	1895-1898. Revista de ciencias Sociales, Puerto Rico, 1965, Vol. 9, Nº 1.

Cintron, David. *The Taino Are Still Alive, Taino Cuan Yahabo: An Example Of The Social Construction of Race And Ethnicity*. University of Central Florida, 2006.

CONSTITUCIÓN DEMOCRÁTICA DE LA NACIÓN ESPAÑOLA PROMULGADA EL DÍA 6 DE JUNIO DE 1869. (n.d.). Retrieved March/April, 2019, from Gobierno de España.

Cubano, A. (1990). El café y la política colonial en Puerto Rico a fines del siglo XIX: Dominación mercantil en el Puerto de Arecibo. *Revista De Historia Económica / Jornal of Iberian and Latin American Economic History,8*(01), 95-103.

Dávila, Arlene M. *Sponsored Identities: Cultural Politics in Puerto Rico*. Philadelphia: Temple University Press, 1997

Deagan, Kathleen. "Colonial Origins and Colonial Transformations in Spanish America." *Historical Archaeology* 37, no. 4 (2003): p. 3-13.

Denis, Nelson A. *War against All Puerto Ricans: Revolution and Terror in Americas Colony*. New York: Nation Books, 2015.

Dooley, Eliza B. K. *Old San Juan*. Santurce, P.R.: Puerto Rico Almanacs, 2005.

Duany, Jorge. *The Puerto Rican Nation on the Move: Identities on the Island & in the United States*. Chapel Hill, Nc, Univ. Of North Carolina Press, 2003.

Elliott, John Huxtable. *Imperial Spain: 1469-1716*. London: Penguin Books, 2002. p. 17

"Europe, Spanish America, and the Monroe Doctrine." *The American Historical Review*, Jan. 1922.

Feliciano-Santos, Sherina, Barbra Meek, Bruce Mannheim, Judith T. Irvine, Ruth Behar, and La Fountain-Stokes Lawrence M. *An Inconceivable Indigeneity: The Historical, Cultural, and Interactional Dimensions of Puerto Rican Taino Activism.* PhD diss.

Font-Guzmán, Jacqueline. *Experiencing Puerto Rican Citizenship and Cultural Nationalism.* Basingstoke: Palgrave Macmillan, 2015. p 112.

Franqui-Rivera, Harry. *National Mythologies: U.S. Citizenship for the People of Puerto Rico and Military Service Mitología Nacional: Ciudadanía Norteamericana Para La Gente de Puerto Rico y Servicio Militar.* 17 Aug. 2020.

Garcia, Hector A. "Expresiones Culturales De Sector Criollo." Proyecto Salon Hogar.

Gellner, Ernest. *Nations and Nationalism.* Ithaca, NY: Cornell University Press, 1983.

Génnis, Carlos Fregoso. "La Identidad Criolla En Los Documentos Independentistas Del Occidente De México." *Sociocriticism* XXIII, no. 1-2 (2008).

Go, J. (2008). *American empire and the politics of meaning: Elite political cultures in the Philippines and Puerto Rico during U.S. colonialism.* Durham, NC: Duke University Press.

González, José Luis. *El País De Cuatro Pisos Y Otros Ensayos*. San Juan, P.R.: Ediciones
    Huracán, 2007 (Notas para una definición de la cultura puertorriqueña) José Luis González.

Grafe, Regina, and Alejandra Irigoin. "A Stakeholder Empire: The Political Economy of Spanish
    Imperial Rule in America1." *The Economic History Review* 65, no. 2 (2011): 609-51.

Grossberg, Lawrence. "*Identity and Cultural Studies: Is That All There Is?*" Questions of
    Cultural Identity: 87-107.

Guerra, L. (1998). *Popular expression and national identity in Puerto Rico: The struggle for self,
    community, and nation*. Gainesville: Univ. Press of Florida.

Hera, Alberto De La. "La Iglesia Y La Independencia De América Latina." *Anuario De Historia
    De La Iglesia* 17 (2008): 27-30.

Hogg, Michael A., and Dominic Abrams. 1988. *Social identifications: A social psychology of
    intergroup relations and group processes*. London: Routledge. (Cited in Burke and Stets
    p. 118).

Juan Ponce De Leon, Hombre De Empresa, Descubridor, Conquistador Y Poblador." *Boletin De
    La Academia Puertorriqueña De La Historia* 1, no. 1 (November 19, 1968): 50-51.

Keegan, William F. *National Academy of Sciences*. 2007. Benjamin Irving Rouse 1913-2006,
    Washington D.C.

Lange, Matthew, James Mahoney, and Matthias Vom Hau. "Colonialism and Development: A Comparative Analysis of Spanish and British Colonies." *American Journal of Sociology* 111, no. 5 (2006): 1412-462

MacDonald, Lauren Elaine. *"The Hieronymites in Hispaniola, 1493-1519."* 2010.

Meniketti, Marco. "Surviving Spanish Conquest: Indian Fight, Flight, and Cultural Transformation in Hispaniola and Puerto Rico." *Ethnoarchaeology* 10, no. 1 (2018): 68-70.

Monge, José Trías. *Puerto Rico: The Trials of the Oldest Colony in the World.* New Haven: Yale University Press, 1999.

Muñiz, Rafael González. *Mi Pueblo Taíno: Un Recorrido Por El Mundo De Nuestros Indios Taínos De Borikén.* Panamericana Formas e Impresas, Colombia .: 2004

O., Ayala Santiago Mario. *Orden Y Palabra En Los Discursos De Pedro Albizu Campos.* Rio Piedras (Puerto Rico): Publicaciones Gaviota, 2008.

Pedreira, Antonio S. *Obras De Antonio S. Pedreira.* San Juan De Puerto Rico: Instituto De Cultura Puertorriqueña, 1970.

Pedreira, Antonio Salvador, Nicolas Kanellos, and Aoife Rivera. Serrano. *Insularismo: An Insight into the Puerto Rican Character.* New York: Ausubo Press, 2005.

Pinto, José. "El Reformismo Fiscal Borbónico En La Nueva Granada, Balance Y

Perspectivas." *Historia Caribe* 11, no. 29 (2016): 53-82.

Puerto Rico. United States Governemnt. Instituto Nacional De Estadisiticas. *Censo De La Isla De Puerto Rico.* 1887.

Quiros, Ronald Soto, and David Diaz Arias. "Indígenas, Mestizaje E Identidad Nacional En La Centroamérica Liberal, 1870-1950." *Cuaderno De Ciencias Sociales* 143. Accessed 2007.

Rivera, Alejandro Tapia. *Biblioteca Historica De Puerto Rico. Que Contiene Varios Documentos De Los Siglos XV, XVI, XVII, Y XVIII,* Puerto Rico: Imprenta De Márquez, 1854. p 35.

Roscoe, T., René, L. S., Brady, J. H., & Alemán, M. (1881). *The life and adventures of Lazarillo de Tormes.* London: J.C. Nimmo and Bain.

Rouse, Irvin. *The Tainos: Rise & Decline of the People Who Greeted Columbus.* New Haven, CT: Yale University Press. p. 9.

Rousseau, Jean-Jacques, and Robert Chesnais. *Projet De Constitution Pour La Corse.* Paris (5 Rue Saint-Sébastien, 75011): Nautilus, 2000.

Ruano Argimiro. *La Identidad De Los Puertorriqueños.* Quebradilla, PR: Imprenta San Rafael, 2001.

Scarano, Francisco. "The Jíbaro Masquerade and the Subaltern Politics of Creole Identity

Formation in Puerto Rico, 1745–1823." *The American Historical Review*, 1996.

Sese, Lourdes Soria. "La Hidalguia Universal." *Iura Vasconiae*, no. 3 (2006): 283-316.
Universidad Del Pais Vasco.

Siegel, Peter E., Peter G. Roe, Peter E. Siegel, Joshua M. Torres, John G. Jones, Lee A.
Newsom, Deborah M. Pearsall, Jeffrey B. Walker, Susan D. DeFrance, Karen F.
Anderson-Cordova, and Anne V. Stokes. *Ancient Borinquen Archaeology and Ethnohistory of Native Puerto Rico.* Alabama: University of Alabama Press, 2009.

Smith, Anthony D. *The Ethnic Origins of Nations.* Oxford, Basil Blackwell, 1986.

Smith, Anthony D. *National Identity.* Reno: Univ. of Nevada Press, 1993.

Smith, Anthony D. *Nationalism: Theory, Ideology, History.* Oxford: Polity, 2001

Staudenmaier, M. (2009). Puerto Rican Independence Movement, 1898-present. *The International Encyclopedia of Revolution and Protest, 1-11*

The American Historical Review, vol. XXVII, no. 2, Jan. 1922, 10.1086/ahr/27.2.207. Accessed 9 June 2019.

The Gilder Lehrman Institute of American History. 2012. Columbus reports on his first voyage, 1493, New York.

1512-1513. The Laws of Burgos." Science of the Marimba - Page 4. Accessed January 24, 2019.

Trincado González, Íñigo. *Hidalgos E Infanzones En El Norte De La Península Ibérica.*
Universidad Del Pais Vasco.

Unites States. US War Department. Director Census of Porto Rico. *Census of Porto Rico 1899.*
By J. P. Sanger, Henry Gannett, and Walter Wilcox. Washington: Government Printing Office, 1900.

Vejo, Tomas Perez. "Criollos Contra Peninsulares. La Bella Leyenda." *Les Cahiers Alhim, Amerique Latine Histoire Et Memoire* 19 (2010).

Viera, Gabriel Haslip. "The "Indigenous" or "Neo-Taíno" Movement in the Spanish-speaking Caribbean and Its Diaspora and the Return of the Old Anglo Neo-Imperialist Scholarship?" *National Institute for Latino Policy* NILP. February 15, 2015.

Vizcaino, Enrique Mendoza y. *Historia De La Guerra Hispano-Americana.* Librerías "Paris-Valencia, 2003. p. 5.

Zuili, Marc. *Société Et Économie De L'Espagne Au XVIe Siècle.* Palaiseau : École Polytechnique, 2008. p.19.

---

[1] The mid-part of Vieque Island
[2] Ruben Berrios, the leader of the Independence Party and Lolita Lebron, one of the nationalists who opened fire in US Congress in 1954, were among those arrested in the protesting.

[3] Smith, Anthony D. *Nationalism: Theory, Ideology, History.* Oxford Polity, 2001 pg.28
[4] Ibid (28)
[5] Ibid Rousseau in *Projet de Constitution pour la Corse* states, "Tout peuple a, ou doit avoir, un caractère national s'il en manquait, il faudrait

236

commencer par le lui donner". (All people have or must have a national character, and if they do not, we will start by giving them one).

[6] Many anthropological studies focus on ethno genesis, cultural, identity, national identity.

[7] Segal, 1994 (Cited in Arlene Davila)

[8] Smith (8)

[9] Ruano, Argimiro. *La Identidad De Los Puertorriqueños*. Quebradilla, PR: Imprenta San Rafael, 2001.

[10] Country men

[11] Social Caste

[12] Ruano (95-97).

[13] Ruano (101)

[14] Anderson, Benedict R. OG. *Imagined Communities: Reflections on the Origin and Spread of Nationalism*. London: Verso, 2016.

[15] Carrión, Juan Manuel. "El Imaginario Nacional Norteamericano Y El Nacionalismo Puertorriqueño." *Revista De Ciencias Sociales* 7 (1999): 68-85

[16] Anderson, Benedict R. OG. *Imagined Communities: Reflections on the Origin and Spread of Nationalism*. London: Verso, 2016.

[17] Ibid

[18] Ibid

[19] Ibid

[20] In 1903, Panama seceded from Colombia with the help of the US. The two countries became independent republics.

[21] Before the Spanish American-War

[22] Vejo, Tomas Perez. "Criollos Contra Peninsulares. La Bella Leyenda." *Les Cahiers Alhim, Amerique Latine Histoire Et Memoire* 19 (2010)

[23] Ibid

[24] The nationalist movement between the 1930s and 1950s, from a legal-political standpoint was symbolic. In fact, behind closed doors the nationalists had a different agenda. According to documents, the nationalists were secretly collecting an arsenal of firearms, bombs and guns. The nationalists emulating the Sinn Fein rhetoric and movement chose not to follow Gandhi's approach on Indian nationalism. The insurgency drifted the cause from independence to an unforgiving battle between the nationalists and the diaspora.

[25] Gellner, Ernest. *Nations and Nationalism*. Ithaca, NY: Cornell University Press, 1983

[26] Ibid

[27] Carrion, Juan Manuel. "The War of the Flags: Conflicting National Loyalties in a Modern Colonial Situation." *Centro Journal* 18, no. 2 (2006) War on symbols.

[28] Hall, Stuart. "Cultural Identity & Cinematic Representation." *Framework* 36 (1989):

[29] Ibid

[30] Grossberg, Lawrence. "Identity and Cultural Studies: Is That All There

Is?" *Questions of Cultural Identity*: 87-107

[31] Font-Guzmán, Jacqueline. Experiencing Puerto Rican Citizenship and Cultural Nationalism. Basingstoke: Palgrave Macmillan, 2015. p 112

[32] Smith, Anthony D. *National Identity*. Reno: Univ. of Nevada Press, 1993. P 72

[33] José Luis González was a 20th Century Puerto Rican essayist, novelist, professor and author who lived in exile in Mexico due to his pro-independence views. He is mostly known for his essay El Pais de Cuatro Pisos, *Four-Storied Country.*

[34] González, José Luis. *El País De Cuatro Pisos Y Otros Ensayos*. San Juan, P.R.: Ediciones Huracán, 2007 (Notas para una definición de la cultura puertorriqueña) José Luis González

[35] Ibid

[36] "Las Carpetas" (the Files) is a documentary presented in 2011 at the *Festival Del Cine International* in San Juan. Directed by Maite Rivera Carbonell, the documentary reveals the surveillance by the insular government on independence activists and dissenters.

[37] Denis, Nelson A. *War against All Puerto Ricans: Revolution and Terror in Americas Colony*. New York: Nation Books, 2015.

[38] In March 17, 2017, the Nationalist Party organized a conference in Ponce's Massacre Museum. Former members of the Nationalist Party along with the Independence Party, and other political structures advocated for the independence and sovereignty of the Island from the US.

[39] Ibid

[40] Dávila, Arlene M. *Sponsored Identities: Cultural Politics in Puerto Rico.* Philadelphia: Temple University Press, 1997

[41] O., Ayala Santiago Mario. *Orden Y Palabra En Los Discursos De Pedro Albizu Campos*. Rio Piedras (Puerto Rico): Publicaciones Gaviota, 2008.

[42] The law deemed a crime to own or display a Puerto Rican flag. In violation with the freedom of expression and peaceful gathering, Public Law 53 made it a crime, to sing patriotic tunes, to mention in speaking or writing the independence cause, or hold any assembly in favor of independence. The law passed in Puerto Rican General Assembly and Senate, presided by Luis Muñoz Marín, on May 21, 1948.

[43] El mestizo as a sociobiological outcome of colonialism, but culturally is known as el Jibaro. The socio-biological characteristics of the Jibaro are also contested by many authors, essayists and academics.

[44] Carrión, Juan Manuel. "El Imaginario Nacional Norteamericano Y El Nacionalismo Puertorriqueño." *Revista De Ciencias Sociales* 7 (1999): 68-85

[45] Partido Popular Democratico (Democratic Popular Party) led by Luiz Muñoz Marin

[46] Smith, Anthony D. *Nationalism: Theory, Ideology, History*. Oxford: Polity, 2001 pg.28

[47] The Nationalist Party under the leadership of Pedro Albizu Campos

modeled the Sinn Fein ideology of self-determination.

[48] Indigenous name for Taino Indians in the island of Puerto Rico

[49] Thomas Hobbes "Social contract theory"

[50] Machiavelli, Niccolo . *The Prince.*

[51] Elliott, John Huxtable. *Imperial Spain: 1469-1716.* London Penguin Books, 2002. p. 17

[52] Zuili, Marc. *Société Et Économie De L'Espagne Au XVIe Siècle.* Palaiseau: École Polytechnique, 2008. p.19
"Ce lien personnel entre les souverains de deux immenses États de la péninsule Ibérique constitua l'une des étapes essentielles du processus qui conduisit à l'unité nationale espagnole. "

[53] Ibid., p 20

[54] Elliott, John Huxtable. *Imperial Spain: 1469-1716.* London: Penguin Books, 2002. P. 20

[55] Ibid. Ferdinand of Aragon had inherited Jewish blood from his mother's side and the Jewry was seeking for stable political and social status. They were very much invested in this union.

[56] Ibid.

[57] Ibid 20

[58] Elliott, John Huxtable. *Imperial Spain: 1469-1716.* London: Penguin Books, 2002. p. 35

[59] Ibid. In 1479, Castile was under Isabella's control. Early the same year John II of Aragon died. With Castile calmed, and with Ferdinand now succeeding to his father's crown, Ferdinand and Isabella had become joint sovereigns of Aragon and Castile. Spain – a Spain that was Castile Aragon, not Castile-Portugal – was now a fact.

[60] Zuili, Marc. *Société Et Économie De L'Espagne Au XVIe Siècle.* Palaiseau: École Polytechnique, 2008. p.19

[60] Ibid. p 20

[61] Nobility

[62] " Trincado González, Íñigo Trincado. *Hidalgos E Infanzones En El Norte De La Península Ibérica.* Universidad Del País Vasco.

[63] Ibíd. *"Para ser más exacto, la mayor parte de las teorías que intentan iluminar estas cuestiones, se remontaron a la época de las invasiones germánicas de la Hispania romana y al posterior establecimiento del reino visigodo."*

[64] Ibid.

[65] Claudio Sánchez-Alborno Madrid April 7, 1893 – Ávila July 8, 1984 was a Spanish medieval historian, public official, and President of the Spanish Republican Government in exile during the rule of Francisco Franco.

[66] Íñigo, Trincado González. *Hidalgos E Infanzones En El Norte De La Península Ibérica.*

[67] Sese, Lourdes Soria. "La Hidalguia Universal." *Iura Vasconiae,* no. 3 (2006): 283-316. Universidad Del Pais Vasco.
"En el caso del reino de Castilla y en el ámbito de su derecho, el cambio de estado, de plebeyo a noble, se operó sobre todo por la vía de la

milicia mientras existió la necesidad de fomentar la repoblación en zonas difíciles, de frontera de moros, lo que requería un ejército de caballería fuerte, del que se pudiese disponer con rapidez

68 Elliott, John Huxtable. *Imperial Spain: 1469-1716*. London: Penguin Books, 2002.

69 Ruano, Argimiro. *La Idenitidad De Los Puertorriqueños*. Quebradilla, PR: Imprenta San Rafael, 2001. p. 99
"La sociedad española del siglo XVI con seiscientos mil nobles entre once millones de habitantes está presidida por esa nobleza que tramposa o auténticamente vive la hidalguía como filosofía de vida."

70 Refers to the population who refused to convert into the catholic religion.

71 Rivera, Alejandro Tapia. *Biblioteca Historica De Puerto Rico. Que Contiene Varios Documentos De Los Siglos XV , XVI , XV I 1 Y XVIII ,.* Puerto Rico: Imprenta De Marquez, 1854. P. 35

72 Ruano, Argimiro. *La Idenitidad De Los Puertorriqueños*. Quebradilla, PR: Imprenta San Rafael, 2001

73 Juan Ponce De Leon, Hombre De Empresa, Descubridor, Conquistador Y Poblador." *Boletin De La Academia Puertorriqueña De La Historia* 1, no. 1 (November 19, 1968): 50-51

74 A.,Van Middeldyk R., and Martin Grove Brumbaugh. The History of Puerto Rico: From the Spanish Discovery to the American Occupation. N.Y: D Appleton and Company, 1903. pg. 34

75 Elliott, John Huxtable. *Imperial Spain: 1469-1716*. London: Penguin Books, 2002

76 *"Hasta hace muy pocos años, todas las historias de América lo hacían aparecer tal como lo describió el cronista Gonzalo Fernández de Oviedo, «un escudero pobre cuando aca paso», pero en realidad era ya todo un veterano de las guerras moras, habiendo participado en la toma de Granada."*

77 Governor of the Hispaniola 1501-1502. Known for cruelty toward Taino Indians

78 Conqueror of Jamaica. Founder of Salvaleon de Higuey (Dominican Republic)

79 A.,Van Middeldyk R., and Martin Grove Brumbaugh. The History of Puerto Rico: From the Spanish Discovery to the American Occupation. N.Y: D Appleton and Company, 1903. pg. 23

80 Rivera, Alejandro Tapia. *Biblioteca Historica De Puerto Rico. Que Contiene Varios Documentos De Los Siglos XV , XVI , XV I 1 Y XVIII ,.* Puerto Rico: Imprenta De Marquez, 1854. Pg.18
" Después que el comendador mayor» D. Frey Nicolás de ¡Ovando vino por gobernador a.la Isla Española, e ovo conquistado en olla é pacificado la provincia de Higüey, que es á la parte mas oriental de toda la isla y más vecina á la isla de Borinquén ó de. Sanct Johan, de quien aqui se tracta, puso por su teniente en aquella villa de Higüey, á un capitán hombre de bien é hidalgo llamado Johan Ponçe de León. El qual yo conosçí muy bien, é es uno de los que passaron á estas partes con el almirante primero D.

Chripstóbal Colon, en el segundo viaje que hizo á estas Indias: é como se avia hallado en las guerras passadas, teníase experiencia de su esfuerço y persona y era tenido por hombre de confiança y de buena habilidad"
[81] A.,Van Middeldyk R., and Martin Grove Brumbaugh. The History of Puerto Rico: From the Spanish Discovery to the American Occupation. N.Y: D Appleton and Company, 1903. pg.23
[82] Juan Ponce De Leon, Hombre De Empresa, Descubridor, Conquistador Y Poblador." *Boletin De La Academia Puertorriqueña De La Historia* 1, no. 1 (November 19, 1968): 49-61.
"Se deduce por estos hechos, que Ponce de León poseía conocimientos que hoy denominamos de ingeniería militar, magnífica para su época. Fue un organizador sin par, y así vemos como en su primera expedición a Puerto Rico, trazó pueblos, constituyó gobiernos, sondeó los nuevos puertos, levantó mapas y tenía conocimientos de metalurgia, lo que le permitió descubrir minas en las nuevas tierras.
."
[83] "Official Definitions of Indigeneity." Caribbean Indigenous Legacies Project. http://www.tainolegacies.com
[84] Cintron, David. *The Taino Are Still Alive, Taino Cuan Yahabo: An Example Of The Social Construction Of Race And Ethnicity*. University of Central Florida, 2006.
[85] Feliciano-Santos, Sherina, Barbra Meek, Bruce Mannheim, Judith T. Irvine, Ruth Behar, and La Fountain-Stokes Lawrence M. *An Inconceivable Indigeneity: The Historical, Cultural, and Interactional Dimensions of Puerto Rican Taino Activism*. PhD diss.
[86]Cintron, David. *The Taino Are Still Alive, Taino Cuan Yahabo: An Example of The Social Construction of Race and Ethnicity*. University of Central Florida, 2006.
[87]Cintron, David. The Taino Are Still Alive, Taino Cuan Yahabo: An Example of The Social Construction of Race and Ethnicity. University of Central Florida, 2006.
[88] Cintron, David. The Taino Are Still Alive, Taino Cuan Yahabo: An Example of The Social Construction of Race And Ethnicity. University of Central Florida, 2006.
[89] Ibid.
[90] Feliciano-Santos, Sherena, Barbra Meek, Bruce Mannheim, Judith T. Irvine, Ruth Behar, and La Fountain-Stokes Lawrence M. An Inconceivable Indigeneity: *The Historical, Cultural, and Interactional Dimensions of Puerto Rican Taino Activism*. PhD diss. Sherena Feliciano Santos has defended a thesis where she sustains that Tainos never disappeared, they are present in Puerto Rico, not only as culture but also as identity.
[91] Erasing the colored factor and leaving only the white (creole) distorts the reality and the base of the mestizaje.
[92]Feliciano-Santos, Sherena, Barbra Meek, Bruce Mannheim, Judith T. Irvine, Ruth Behar, and La Fountain-Stokes Lawrence M. An Inconceivable Indigeneity: *The Historical, Cultural, and Interactional*

Dimensions of Puerto Rican Taino Activism. PhD diss. There has been efforts a reviving movement of Taino culture and heritage. Activists are trying to reconstruct the Taino culture through documents, language, and traditions.

[93] Cintron, David. *The Taino Are Still Alive, Taino Cuan Yahabo: An Example of The Social Construction of Race and Ethnicity*. University of Central Florida, 2006. Cited in David Cintron, Berger and Luckman 1966, Yancey et al. 1976).

[94] Viera, Gabriel Haslip. "The "Indigenous" or "Neo-Taíno" Movement in the Spanish-speaking Caribbean and Its Diaspora and the Return of the Old Anglo Neo-Imperialist Scholarship?" National Institute for Latino Policy (NiLP. February 15, 2015

[95] Via et al. 2011, Gravel et al. 2013 Cited in Haslip-Viera

[96] Ibid

[97] Via et al. 2011, Gravel et al. 2013, Haslip-Viera 2014. Cited in Haslip Viera

[98] Siegel, Peter E., Peter G. Roe, Peter E. Siegel, Joshua M. Torres, John G. Jones, Lee A. Newsom, Deborah M. Pearsall, Jeffrey B. Walker, Susan D. DeFrance, Karen F. Anderson-Cordova, and Anne V. Stokes. *Ancient Borinquen Archaeology and Ethnohistory of Native Puerto Rico*. Alabama: University of Alabama Press, 2009 p.337

[99] Keegan, William F. *National Academy of Sciences*. 2007. Benjamin Irving Rouse 1913-2006, Washington D.C.

[100] A thesis sustained by Neo Taino activists and Sherena Feliciano Santos

[101] Vanished here is used to support the declining in number of the societies of the Antilles after the Spaniards colonized the islands of Puerto Rico, Jamaica, Cuba and Hispaniola.

[102] *The Gilder Lehrman Institute of American History*. 2012. Columbus reports on his first voyage, 1493, New York

[103] A.,Van Middeldyk R., and Martin Grove Brumbaugh. *The History of Puerto Rico: From the Spanish Discovery to the American Occupation*. N.Y: D Appleton and Company, 1903. Source

[104] Rouse, Irvin. *The Tainos: Rise & Decline of the People Who Greeted Columbus*. New Haven, CT: Yale University Press. P. 48

[105] The system in which the natives were distributed among the Spaniards as slaves.

[106] Muñiz, Rafael González. *Mi Pueblo Taíno: Un Recorrido Por El Mundo De Nuestros Indios Taínos De Borikén*. Panamericana Formas e Impresas, Colombia .: 2004

[107] Rouse, Irvin. *The Tainos: Rise & Decline of the People Who Greeted Columbus*. New Haven, CT: Yale University Press. P. 9

[108] Rouse, Irvin. *The Tainos: Rise & Decline of the People who Greeted Columbus*. New Haven, CT: Yale University Press. P. 9

[109] Ball, Kimberly (1999), "Facundo by Domingo F. Sarmiento", in Moss, Joyce; Valestuk, Lorraine, Latin American Literature and Its Times, 1, World Literature and Its Times: Profiles of Notable Literary Works and

the Historical Events That Influenced Them, Detroit: Gale Group, pp. 171–180

[110] Karen Ball is the English translator of Civilizacion y Barbarie

[111] Ruano, Argimiro. *La Idenitidad De Los Puertorriqueños*. Quebradilla, PR: Imprenta San Rafael, 2001

[112] Elliott, John Huxtable. *Imperial Spain: 1469-1716*. London: Penguin Books, 2002. p. 17

[113] Ibid. p 44

A hereditary title granted by medieval Castilian kings and conferring upon its holder special military powers and the rights of government over a frontier province.

[114] Ibid 44

[115] Such as the case of Cristobal Sotomayor.

[116] Elliott, John Huxtable. *Imperial Spain: 1469-1716*. London: Penguin Books, 2002. p. 17

[117] "Articles of Agreement between the Lords, the Catholic Sovereigns and Cristobal Colon." *American Journeys Collection* p 248

[118] Ibid p 248

[119] Cristobal Colon was appointed and recognized as the lifelong Admiral of all the lands he discovered and acquired, until death. In addition, he was appointed Viceroy General Governor of all the lands, mainland that he discovered.

[120] A., Van Middeldyk R., and Martin Grove Brumbaugh. *The History of Puerto Rico: From the Spanish Discovery to the American Occupation.* Library of Puerto Rico.

[121] Meniketti, Marco. "Surviving Spanish Conquest: Indian Fight, Flight, and Cultural Transformation in Hispaniola and Puerto Rico." *Ethnoarchaeology* 10, no. 1 (2018): 68-70

[122] A., Van Middeldyk R., and Martin Grove Brumbaugh. *The History of Puerto Rico: From the Spanish Discovery to the American Occupation.* Library of Puerto Rico.

[123] *The Gilder Lehrman Institute of American History.* 2012. Columbus reports on his first voyage, 1493, New York

[124] A., Van Middeldyk R., and Martin Grove Brumbaugh. *The History of Puerto Rico: From the Spanish Discovery to the American Occupation.* Library of Puerto Rico.
Library of Congress.

[125] A., Van Middeldyk R., and Martin Grove Brumbaugh. *The History of Puerto Rico: From the Spanish Discovery to the American Occupation.* Library of Puerto Rico. P. 22

"It is rather ascertained that the mainland of these Indies is another half of the world, as large as or perhaps greater than Asia, Africa, and Europe; That is, the whole earth, the world is divided into two parts. One is what the ancients called Asia, Africa and Europe, which they divided as I have said; and that the other half of the world is the one of our Indies. And so, Pedro Martyr[125] was right to call it New World, according to the news or ration given by the ancients, and so it is now that they have noticed that

they (Indios) have been there as we see." [125] Adapted from Spanish.
"The old BORINQUEN, today San Juan de Puerto Rico, is the smallest of the great Antilles. Located to the South East of Hispaniola, it serves as a link that connects to this with the smaller islands, in the chain that leaves from Florida and ends in the confines of the Colombian sine. Crossed from east to west by a system of mountains, it has delightful valleys, laughing hills and abundant rivers; And its temperate climate and its beautiful sky and green countryside, make Puerto Rico worth a page in the wallet of the traveler and a memory in the heart of the poet." [125] Adapted from Spanish

The above descriptions of the island of Borinquen it is not much different from what Columbus saw in all of the Antilles. The letters to the Queen Isabelle revealed the beginning of the new chapter in the modern history; that of the colonization and expansionism, the search for new territories, cheap labor markets, the search for industries, and natural resources under auspices of the Crown. The unifying ideology and the belief that natives must be at the service of the European settlers, along with the monarchial policies yield a new social order that was quite different from what we see in the British settlements.

[126] A.,Van Middeldyk R., and Martin Grove Brumbaugh. *The History of Puerto Rico: From the Spanish Discovery to the American Occupation.* N.Y: D Appleton and Company, 1903. pg. 29

[127] A.,Van Middeldyk R., and Martin Grove Brumbaugh. *The History of Puerto Rico: From the Spanish Discovery to the American Occupation.* N.Y: D Appleton and Company, 1903. pg.

[128] San Juan

[129] Feliciano-Santos, Sherina, Barbra Meek, Bruce Mannheim, Judith T. Irvine, Ruth Behar, and La Fountain-Stokes Lawrence M. *An Inconceivable Indigeneity: The Historical, Cultural, and Interactional Dimensions of Puerto Rican Taino Activism.* PhD diss. P.44

[130] Columbus was awarded the Title of Admiral.

[131] A.,Van Middeldyk R., and Martin Grove Brumbaugh. *The History of Puerto Rico: From the Spanish Discovery to the American Occupation.* N.Y: D Appleton and Company, 1903.

[132] Ruano, Argimiro. *La Identidad De Los Puertorriqueños.* Quebradilla, PR: Imprenta San Rafael, 2001.

[133] Rouse, Irvin. *The Tainos: Rise & Decline of the People Who Greeted Columbus.* New Haven, CT: Yale University Press. P. 9

[134] Explorers, pioneers

[135] Deagan, Kathleen. "Colonial Origins and Colonial Transformations in Spanish America." *Historical Archaeology* 37, no. 4 (2003): 3-13. Money making trading venture in which largely self-contained European communities would establish profitable trading alliances with American natives and share the profits with the Crown.

[136] Lange, Matthew, James Mahoney, and Matthias Vom Hau. "Colonialism and Development: A Comparative Analysis of Spanish and British Colonies." American Journal of Sociology 111, no. 5 (2006): 1412-462.

[137] Lange, Matthew, James Mahoney, and Matthias Vom Hau. "Colonialism and Development: A Comparative Analysis of Spanish and British Colonies." *American Journal of Sociology* 111, no. 5 (2006): 1412-462.

[138] Color of skin in Spanish colonial determined the rank in the social order. Darker the color lower the stratum.

[139] Lange, Matthew, James Mahoney, and Matthias Vom Hau. "Colonialism and Development: A Comparative Analysis of Spanish and British Colonies." American Journal of Sociology 111, no. 5 (2006): 1422

[140] Lange, Matthew, James Mahoney, and Matthias Vom Hau. "Colonialism and Development: A Comparative Analysis of Spanish and British Colonies." American Journal of Sociology 111, no. 5 (2006): 1420

[141] A.,Van Middeldyk R., and Martin Grove Brumbaugh. *The History of Puerto Rico: From the Spanish Discovery to the American Occupation.* N.Y: D Appleton and Company, 1903

[142] Lange, Matthew, James Mahoney, and Matthias Vom Hau. "Colonialism and Development: A Comparative Analysis of Spanish and British Colonies." American Journal of Sociology 111, no. 5 (2006): refer to the table

[143] Pedreira, Antonio Salvador, Nicolas Kanellos, and Aoife Rivera. Serrano. *Insularismo: An Insight into the Puerto Rican Character*. New York: Ausubo Press, 2005.
"...en el quinto y último capítulo de los que dedica a estudiar el estado de Puerto Rico a fines del siglo xvm, trata de la hacienda pública y afirma que la isla es muy "gravosa a la Corona, que no cubre sus gastos y que el tesoro, como todo lo demás, está pidiendo a gritos una reforma. Sabido es que desde el año 1586 se nutría nuestro tesoro con el dinero que enviaba anualmente el de Méjico. "

[144] Grafe, Regina, and Alejandra Irigoin. "A Stakeholder Empire: The Political Economy of Spanish Imperial Rule in America1." *The Economic History Review* 65, no. 2 (2011): 609-51.

[145] Laws of Burgos promulgated on 27 December 1512 in Burgos, Kingdom of Castile (Spain), was the first codified set of laws governing the behavior of Spaniards in the Americas, particularly with regard to the Indigenous people of the Americas ('native Caribbean Indians'). Wiki

[146] Deagan, Kathleen. "Colonial Origins and Colonial Transformations in Spanish America." *Historical Archaeology* 37, no. 4 (2003): 3-13. doi:10.1007/bf03376619

[147] Deagan, Kathleen. "Colonial Origins and Colonial Transformations in Spanish America." *Historical Archaeology* 37, no. 4 (2003): 3-13.

[148] Fray Bartolome de las Casas

[149] Slave distribution among settlers

[150] MacDonald, Lauren Elaine. "The Hieronymites in Hispaniola, 1493-1519." 2010. P 59

[151] MacDonald, Lauren Elaine. "The Hieronymites in Hispaniola, 1493-1519." 2010.

[152] Hera, Alberto De La. "La Iglesia Y La Independencia De América Latina." *Anuario De Historia De La Iglesia* 17 (2008): 27-30

[153] MacDonald, Lauren Elaine. *"The Hieronymites in Hispaniola, 1493-1519."* 2010.

[154] A.,Van Middeldyk R., and Martin Grove Brumbaugh. *The History of Puerto Rico: From the Spanish Discovery to the American Occupation.* N.Y: D Appleton and Company, 1903. Pg 72

[155] A.,Van Middeldyk R., and Martin Grove Brumbaugh. *The History of Puerto Rico: From the Spanish Discovery to the American Occupation.* N.Y: D Appleton and Company, 1903. pg. 72

[156] Ibid 73

[157] MacDonald, Lauren Elaine. *"The Hieronymites in Hispaniola, 1493-1519."* 2010. P 63

[158] Ibid

[159] Ibid

[160] MacDonald, Lauren Elaine. *"The Hieronymites in Hispaniola, 1493-1519."* 2010. Pg. 66

[161] Ibid 66

[162] Ibid 66

[163] Deagan, Kathleen. "Colonial Origins and Colonial Transformations in Spanish America." *Historical Archaeology* 37, no. 4 (2003)

[164] Deagan, Kathleen. "Colonial Origins and Colonial Transformations in Spanish America." *Historical Archaeology* 37, no. 4 (2003): 3-13.

[165] Cited in Deagan (Morner 1967; Nash 1980; Esteva-Fabregát 1995).

[166] Benedict Anderson sustains that the creole pioneers were the class that mostly identified with the new post-colonial identities that became paramount in the wars for independence against Spain.

[167] Génnis, Carlos Fregoso. "La Identidad Criolla En Los Documentos Independentistas Del Occidente De México." *Sociocriticism* XXIII, no. 1-2 (2008)

[168] Génnis, Carlos Fregoso. "La Identidad Criolla En Los Documentos Independentistas Del Occidente De México." *Sociocriticism* XXIII, no. 1-2 (2008)

[169] Ibid

[170] Ibid

[171] Ibid

[172] Vejo, Tomas Perez. "Criollos Contra Peninsulares. La Bella Leyenda." *Les Cahiers Alhim, Amerique Latine Histoire Et Memoire* 19 (2010)

[173] Vejo, Tomás Pérez. "Criollos Contra Peninsulares: La Bella

Leyenda." *Amérique Latine Histoire et Mémoire. Les Cahiers ALHIM. Les Cahiers ALHIM*, vol. 19, no. 19, 15 Oct 2010,

[174] Ibid

[175] Ibid

[176] Y el resultado, sobre todo, de la invención de memorias separadas en el interior de un grupo humano que si se caracterizaba por algo era por su homogeneidad racial y cultural. En un mundo pre-nacional, caracterizado por la heterogeneidad, las élites de la Monarquía Católica eran extrañamente homogéneas, compartían lengua, religión, memorias de origen, etc.

[177] Pertaining to the nobility social rank.

[178] Spanish philosopher.

[179] Quiros, Ronald Soto, and David Diaz Arias. "Indígenas, Mestizaje E Identidad Nacional En La Centroamérica Liberal, 1870-1950." *Cuaderno De Ciencias Sociales* 143. 2007

[180] Ibid

[181] Definicion.de Academia Real Española

[182] Ibid

[183] Adams, Richard N. "Guatemalan Ladinization and History." *The Americas* 50, no. 04 (1994): 527-43

[184] Quiros, Ronald Soto, and David Diaz Arias. "Indígenas, Mestizaje E Identidad Nacional En La Centroamérica Liberal, 1870-1950." *Cuaderno De Ciencias Sociales* 143. 2007 pg 19

[185] Echánove, Carlo Alberto. Sociología mexicana. México: Editorial Cultura, 1948, p. 90 Cited in Cuaderno de Ciencias Sociales pg 27

[186] Martínez Peláez, La patria del criollo, pp. 2 (cited in Cuaderno de Ciencias Sociales 143)

[187] Quiros, Ronald Soto, and David Diaz Arias. "Indígenas, Mestizaje E Identidad Nacional En La Centroamérica Liberal, 1870-1950." *Cuaderno De Ciencias Sociales* 143. 2007. P 29

[188] Quiros, Ronald Soto, and David Díaz Arias. "Indígenas, Mestizaje E Identidad Nacional En La Centroamérica Liberal, 1870-1950." *Cuaderno De Ciencias Sociales* 143. 2007. pg 35

[189] Ibid

[190] Pinto, José. "El Reformismo Fiscal Borbónico En La Nueva Granada, Balance Y Perspectivas." Historia Caribe 11, no. 29 (2016): 53-82

[191] Quiros, Ronald Soto, and David Díaz Arias. "Indígenas, Mestizaje E Identidad Nacional En La Centroamérica Liberal, 1870-1950." *Cuaderno De Ciencias Sociales* 143. 2007. pg 39
"se deduce en los negros, mulatos y ladinos una vida perversa y abandona-da, sin temor de Dios, ni del rey"

[192] Blanqueamiento, branqueamento, or whitening, is a social, political, and economic practice used in many post-colonial countries to "improve the race" (mejorar la raza) towards a supposed ideal of whiteness. The term blanqueamiento is rooted in Latin America and is used more or less synonymous with racial whitening.

[193] Wade, Peter. "REPENSANDO EL MESTIZAJE." *Revista Colombiana De*

Antropología 39 (January/February 2003): 273-296
[194] Ibid
[195] Ibid
[196] Anderson, Benedict R. OG. *Imagined Communities: Reflections on the Origin and Spread of Nationalism.* London: Verso, 2016. P. 3-14

[197] Female and male,
[198] Puerto Rico. United States Government. Instituto Nacional De Estadisiticas. *Censo De La Isla De Puerto Rico.* 1887. 783
[199] Unites States. US War Department. Director Census of Porto Rico. *Census of Porto Rico 1899.* By J. P. Sanger, Henry Gannett, and Walter Wilcox. Washington: Government Printing Office, 1900.
[200] Monge, José Trías. *Puerto Rico: The Trials of the Oldest Colony in the World.* New Haven: Yale University Press, 1999.
[201] The idea of how ethno genesis has modified the social fabric of a group whether spontaneously, or by social engineering.
[202] Ruano, Argimiro. *La Identidad De Los Puertorriqueños.* Quebradilla, PR: Imprenta San Rafael, 2001.
Pg 125. "Europa funcionaba a base de una sociedad clasificada. Clases altas y clases no tan altas. La no tan altas al servicio de la que están por la encima.
[203] Ibid. pg. 126
[204] Ibid.
[205] Diaz Soler Puerto Rico XXXI (Cited in Argimiro Ruano pg. 126)
"Racial y culturalmente, la pequeña tierra antillana es un hibrido con profundas raíces indo-africana que España se encargó de aglutinar al imponer sobre sus dominios ultramarinos la cultura grecolatina junto a la experiencia de largos siglos de convivencia con otros pueblos con que se mestizaron. Esa actitud trasplantada a sus colonias de ultramar dio basa a la mestización, que en el caso de Puerto Rico ha sido más bien un largo e ininterrumpido un proceso de mulatización"
[206] *"El Mestizaje se inició al mismo año que dio principio a la colonización, o sea 1509. Según las leyes de la antropología una nueva generación comprende el espacio de treinta años que se considera como la duración media de cada generación de la raza humana. Un siglo comprende por término medio tres generaciones. De modo en 1539 ya había en el país 50% mestizos con la sangre blanca y 50% indígena. "Coll y Toste"* Cited in Argimiro Ruano pg. 132
[207] Introduced by Durkheim in Division of Labor, the term is disputed and lost in translation. Conscience Collective in French means collective awareness and not necessary morality norms and values, nor is it translated "common understanding". A common understanding translation reduces the semantics to a "cognitive ability" from the individual transferred to the society. In the case of Puerto Rico, the economic elites sought more a legal solution for Puerto Rico which did not rely on a conscience collective but rather on a relationship between the individual and the society. Thus, at this point the latifondistas and

the merchants wanted financial stability rather than a political status for Puerto Rico as a nation.

208 *CONSTITUCIÓN DEMOCRÁTICA DE LA NACIÓN ESPAÑOLA PROMULGADA EL DÍA 6 DE JUNIO DE 1869.* (n.d.). Retrieved March/April, 2019, from Gobierno de España Constitución democrática de la nación española promulgada el día 6 de junio de 1869:"Artículo 1º. Son españoles: 1º. Todas las personas nacidas en territorio español.

209 Garry Leech The FARC.

210 Refers to Luiz Marin Muños

211 Dávila, Arlene M. *Sponsored Identities: Cultural Politics in Puerto Rico.* Philadelphia: Temple Univ. Press, 1997

212 Smith, Anthony D. *Nationalism: Theory, Ideology, History.* Oxford: Polity, 2001. Pg. 37

213 Dávila, Arlene M. *Sponsored Identities: Cultural Politics in Puerto Rico.* Philadelphia: Temple Univ. Press, 1997. p 10.

214 The Institute of Puerto Rican culture 1955

215 Calderin, Rafael. "La Catedral De San Juan Bautista Y Los Monasterios De Santo Tomás De Aquino Y De San Francisco De Asís." May 2016

216 Pedreira, Antonio S. *Obras De Antonio S. Pedreira.* San Juan De Puerto Rico: Instituto De Cultura Puertorriqueña, 1970A. p27

217 Ibid 12-14

218 Scarano, Francisco. "The Jíbaro Masquerade and the Subaltern Politics of Creole Identity Formation in Puerto Rico, 1745–1823." *The American Historical Review*, 1996.

219 1512-1513. The Laws of Burgos." Science of the Marimba - Page 4. Accessed January 24, 2019.

220 Ibid

221 Ibid

222 Settlers who owned slaves.

223 Dooley, Eliza B. K. *Old San Juan.* Santurce, P.R.: Puerto Rico Almanacs, 2005.

224 Ibid

225 Monge, José Trías. *Puerto Rico: The Trials of the Oldest Colony in the World.* New Haven: Yale University Press, 1999.

226 Monge, José Trías. *Puerto Rico: The Trials of the Oldest Colony in the World.* New Haven: Yale University Press, 1999.

227 Garcia, Hector A. "Expresiones Culturales De Sector Criollo." Proyecto Salon Hogar Expresiones culturales del sector Criollo. On the verge of the Spanish American War the elites had a completely culture form the masses. Politically elites had formed their split loyalties.

228 Ibid

229 Arlene Davila argues that El Ateneo Puertorriqueño remained a strong hold of the intellectual elite pg 27

230 Desde mediados del siglo XIX, un grupo de puertorriqueños que realizaban estudios universitarios en Europa, llamaron la atención

sobre la necesidad de conocer las raíces de nuestro pueblo. En 1851, fundaron la Sociedad Recolectora de Documentos Históricos de la Isla de San Juan Bautista de Puerto Rico. Algunos de sus miembros fueron Alejandro Tapia y Rivera, Román Baldorioty de Castro, José Julián Acosta y Ramón Emeterio Betances.

[231] Benedict ANderson

[232] Scarano, Francisco. "The Jíbaro Masquerade and the Subaltern Politics of Creole Identity Formation in Puerto Rico, 1745–1823." *The American Historical Review*, 1996. pg 13.

[233] Arlene Davila distinguished sponsored cultural identities associated with the three main options for Puerto Rico political status. Statehood, Independence and Commonwealth. (p.10)

[234] Go, J. (2008). *American empire and the politics of meaning: Elite political cultures in the Philippines and Puerto Rico during U.S. colonialism.* Durham, NC: Duke University Press.

[235] Carrion, Juan Manuel. "The War of the Flags: Conflicting National Loyalties in a Modern Colonial Situation." *Centro Journal* 18, no. 2 (2006)

[236] Cubano, A. (1990). El cafe y la politica colonial en Puerto Rico a fines del siglo XIX: Dominacion mercantil en el Puerto de Arecibo. *Revista De Historia Económica / Journal of Iberian and Latin American Economic History,*8(01), 95-103.

[237] Smith, Anthony D. *Nationalism: Theory, Ideology, History*. Oxford: Polity, 2001 pg.

[238] Anderson, Benedict. Imaggined Communities. London 1982

[239] Ruano, Argimiro. *La Identidad De Los Puertorriqueños*. Quebradilla, PR: Imprenta San Rafael, 2001.

[240] Carrión, Juan Manuel. "El Imaginario Nacional Norteamericano Y El Nacionalismo Puertorriqueño." *Revista De Ciencias Sociales* 7 (1999): 68-85

[241] Smith, Anthony D. *Nationalism: Theory, Ideology, History*. Oxford: Polity, 2001 pg. 28

[242] Scarano, Francisco. "The Jíbaro Masquerade and the Subaltern Politics of Creole Identity Formation in Puerto Rico, 1745–1823." *The American Historical Review*, 1996.

[243] Staudenmaier, M. (2009). Puerto Rican Independence Movement, 1898-present. *The International Encyclopedia of Revolution and Protest,* 1-11

[244] Denis, Nelson A. 2016. *War against All Puerto Ricans: Revolution and Terror in America's Colony*. New York: Nation Books

[245] Ibid

[246] Ibid

[247] A.,Van Middeldyk R., and Martin Grove Brumbaugh. *The History of Puerto Rico: From the Spanish Discovery to the American Occupation*. N.Y: D Appleton and Company, 1903. pg.

[248] Juan Bobo translate to silly John.

[249] Roscoe, T., René, L. S., Brady, J. H., & Alemán, M. (1881). *The life and*

adventures of Lazarillo de Tormes. London: J.C. Nimmo and Bain.

250 Guerra, L. (1998). *Popular expression and national identity in Puerto Rico: The struggle for self, community, and nation*. Gainesville: Univ. Press of Florida. P 138

251 Smith, Anthony D. *The Ethnic Origins of Nations*. Oxford, Basil Blackwell, 1986.

252 Man of the hills

253 Scarano, Francisco. "The Jíbaro Masquerade and the Subaltern Politics of Creole Identity Formation in Puerto Rico, 1745–1823." *The American Historical Review*, 1996.

254 Subaltern Studies Group, a team of South Asian scholars at University of Sussex who dealt with post-colonial and postmodern studies.

255 Brown color, clear front,
 Languid look, haughty and penetrating,
the black beard, the pale face,
lean figure, nose well proportioned.
Medium size, compassed march;
the soul of longing illusions,
sharp wit, free and arrogant,
Think restless, heated mind.
Human, affable, fair, generous,
in a company of always variable love,
after the glory and always eager.
And in love to his insurmountable homeland
This is, to be sure, faithful design
to copy a good Puerto Rican

256 Manuel Alonso el Puertorriqueño

257 Although, from interviews and testimonies of Puerto Rican DNA, the presence of Taino accounts on 8-12 percent of the DNA. 18-24 percent African presence and 50 or more percent European.

258 Feliciano-Santos, Sherina, Barbra Meek, Bruce Mannheim, Judith T. Irvine, Ruth Behar, and La Fountain-Stokes Lawrence M. *An Inconceivable Indigeneity: The Historical, Cultural, and Interactional Dimensions of Puerto Rican Taino Activism*. PhD diss.

259 Anderson, Benedict R OG *Imagined Communities*. London, 1982

260 Feliciano Santos describes the 18th century Jíbaro as distinct from the elite population and city people as well. These differences consist in speech, habits and living environment. The way of speaking is marked as unsophisticated, the habits are considered rustic, and their clothing are described a consisting of a wide brimmed hat (often called a pava), a machete, and comfortable cotton Indiana. P 58

261 Quarrelsome

262 Anderson, Benedict R. O'G. *Imagined Communities*. London, 1982.

263 Go, Julian. *American Empire and the Politics of Meaning: Elite Political Cultures in the Philippines and Puerto Rico during U.S. Colonialism*. Durham: Duke University Press, 2008.

264"La Parranda Puertorriqueña: The Music Symbolism and Cultural Nationalism of Puerto Rico's Christmas Serenading Tradition.," 2003.
265 Jibaro Soy. Raphy Leavitt.
266"La Parranda Puertorriquena: The Music Symbolism and Cultural Nationalism of Puerto Rico's Christmas Serenade Tradition.," 2003.

267 Dávila Arlene M. *Sponsored Identities: Cultural Politics in Puerto Rico.* Philadelphia, Pa: Temple University Press, 1997.

268 Dávila Arlene M. *Sponsored Identities: Cultural Politics in Puerto Rico.* Philadelphia, Pa: Temple University Press, 1997.
269 Ibid
270 "Documenting a Puerto Rican Identity." Washington DC. Accessed August 2, 2020. https://www.loc.gov/collections/puerto-rico-books-and-pamphlets/articles-and-essays/nineteenth-century-puerto-rico/documenting-puerto-rican-identity
271Denis, Nelson A. 2016. *War against All Puerto Ricans: Revolution and Terror in America's Colony.* New York: Nation Books.
272 Ibid
273 Staudenmaier, M. (n.d.). *Puerto Rican independence movement, 1898–present.* Retrieved August 08, 2020, from Puerto Rican independence movement, 1898–present.
Denis, Nelson A. 2016. *War against All Puerto Ricans: Revolution and Terror in America's Colony.* New York: Nation Books.
275 Ibib
276 Ibid
277 Duany, Jorge. 2003. *The Puerto Rican Nation on the Move: Identities on the Island & in the United States.* Chapel Hill, Nc: Univ. Of North Carolina Press.
278 Ibid
279 Puerto Rican peasants were not interested building a nation-state back home. Their motives were pure economic and individual.
280 source
281 Dávila, Arlene M. *Sponsored Identities: Cultural Politics in Puerto Rico.* Philadelphia: Temple Univ. Press, 1997.p 11
282 Albizu, Don. "Campos Speaks." *YouTube*, 4 June 2015, www.youtube.com/watch?v=Ab13_zIoNYQ. Accessed 17 Aug. 2020.
283 Ibid
284 Ibid
285 Dávila, Arlene M. *Sponsored Identities: Cultural Politics in Puerto Rico.* Philadelphia: Temple Univ. Press, 1997
pg 14
286 As the jíbaro became mobilized as a national icon that embodied the essence of the islands national character—a symbol that defined the Island against the U.S. Antonio S. Pedreira (1935), a canonical Puerto Rican
intellectual, critiques the extension of Jibaridad to the whole Puerto Rican population. Cited in Sherena Feliciano-Santos p 64

287 Pedro Albizu Campos, and Ivonne Acosta. *La Palabra Como Delito: Los Discursos Por Los Que Condenaron a Pedro Albizu Campos, 1948-1950*. Río Piedras, Puerto Rico, Editorial Cultural, @ Atlanta, Georgia Talleres Gráficos Shekerow Graphics, 2000.

288 Scarano, Francisco A. "The Jibaro Masquerade and the Subaltern Politics of Creole Identity Formation in Puerto Rico, 1745-1823." *The American Historical Review*, vol. 101, no. 5, Dec. 1996, p. 1398, 10.2307/2170177. Accessed 15 Aug. 2020.

289 Carlosantonioperez. "La Música Tradicional Puertorriqueña, Las Raíces." *YouTube*, 12 May 2011, www.youtube.com/watch?v=Ch6fSrJc1lM. Accessed 15 Aug. 2020.

290 Smith, Anthony D. *Ethno-Symbolism and Nationalism: A Cultural Approach*. London; New York, Routledge, 2009. P 39

291 B Anthropology Online. "Benedict Anderson About Nationalism (In Mijn Vaders Huis, 1994)." *YouTube*, 12 Nov. 2013, www.youtube.com/watch?v=cNJuL-Ewp-A&t=160s. Accessed 15 Aug. 2020.

292 Dávila, Arlene M. *Sponsored Identities: Cultural Politics in Puerto Rico*. Philadelphia, Temple Univ. Press, 1997. Pg.39

293Bova, Russell. *How the World Works: A Brief Survey of International Relations*. Boston: Pearson, 2015.p 100.

294 Go, Julian. *American Empire and the Politics of Meaning: Elite Political Cultures in the Philippines and Puerto Rico during U.S. Colonialism*. Durham: Duke Univ. Press, 2008. P. 74

295 "El Gobierno de la Isla se compondrá de un Parlamento Insular, dividido en dos Cámaras, y de un Gobernador General, representante de la Metrópoli, que ejercerá en nombre de ésta la Autoridad Suprema."

296 "Europe, Spanish America, and the Monroe Doctrine." *The American Historical Review*, Jan. 1922, 10.1086/ahr/27.2.207.

297 Julien Go

298 Causas y antecedentes diplomáticos de la Guerra hispano americana. 1895-98. Salvador E. Castelas

299 Causas y antecedents diplomaticos de la Guerra hispano americana. 1895-98. Salvador E. Castelas

300 De Cómo La Prensa Provocó Una Guerra - CineHistoria. www.cinehistoria.com/la_prensa_provoco_una_guerra.

301 General Valeriano Weyler." General Valeriano Weyler - The World of 1898: The Spanish-American War (Hispanic Division, Library of Congress), loc.gov/rr/hispanic/1898/weyler.html.
He came to the same conclusions as his predecessors as well -- that to win Cuba back for Spain, he would have to separate the rebels from the civilians by putting the latter in safe havens, protected by loyal Spanish troops. By the end of 1897, General Weyler had relocated more than 300,000 into such "reconcentration camps," not to be confused with the use of a similar phrase by twentieth century regimes. Although he was

successful moving vast numbers of people, he failed to provide for them adequately. Consequently, these areas became cesspools of hunger, disease, and starvation where thousands died.

302 Causas y antecedents diplomaticos de la Guerra hispano americana. 1895-98. Salvador E. Castelas 58

303 Based on the class stratification in the Spanish Americas the bottom of the social ladder was made of black, (slaves), indigenous and mestizos.

Causas y antecedents diplomaticos de la Guerra hispano americana. 1895-98. Salvador E. Castelas

304 Causas y antecedentes diplomáticos de la Guerra hispano americana. 1895-98. Salvador E. Castelas

The moral question that Spain was entitled to keep and protect their dominions in the New world was based on the assumptions that the mixture of races and culture under the colonial rule was no longer a question of ethnicity. It was a philosophical question; an obligation that Spain had toward people in the colonies as part of the greater empire (Mother Land) Madre Patria. Spaniard sustain that they created a Latin race, using the Iberic heritage and the indigenous roots.

305 Vizcaino, Enrique Mendoza Y. Historia De La Guerra Hispano-americana. Valencia: Librerias "Paris-Valencia, 2003.

306 Rosario Sevilla Solerhttp://digital.csic.es/bitstream/10261/6671/3/R.Occidente.pdf pg 282

307 Rosario Sevilla pg 283

308 Castellas, Salvador E. Causas y Antecedentes Diplomaticos de la guerra Hispanoamericana,.

309 Peninsulares and Creole landowners, merchant, businessmen

310Born in the Island of Puerto Rico, whether to Spanish descent of variation of mix races.

311 Go, Julian. *American Empire and the Politics of Meaning: Elite Political Cultures in the Philippines and Puerto Rico during U.S. Colonialism. Durham*: Duke Univ. Press, 2008.

312Go, Julian. *American Empire and the Politics of Meaning: Elite Political Cultures in the Philippines and Puerto Rico during U.S. Colonialism. Durham*: Duke Univ. Press, 2008. p. 56

313 Julian Go explains that the Puerto Rican elites welcomed the American Troops and sought their political support, economic cooperation and pragmatism to fill the void the Spaniards had left on the verge of the war. There is no explanation other than pure opportunity and pragmatism based on personal interest. The island on the verge of the war had grown politically. There two political parties: "El Partido Autonomista which sought autonomy from Spain and Los Incondicionales seeking to remain under Spain's colonial rule. There were the peninsulares which Luis Muñoz Rivera an called them as a group of impudent prospering by taking all the government jobs. Luis

Muñoz Rivera calls them enemies of Puerto Rico

[314]Go, Julian. *American Empire and the Politics of Meaning: Elite Political Cultures in the Philippines and Puerto Rico during U.S. Colonialism. Durham*: Duke Univ. Press, 2008. P. 56

[315] Go, Julian. American Empire and the Politics of Meaning: Elite Political Cultures in the Philippines and Puerto Rico during U.S. Colonialism. Durham: Duke Univ. Press, 2008.

[316] Manifest Destiny was an inspiration of Darwin findings.
La creación de esta filosofía del Destino Manifiesto tuvo su origen alrededor de 1840, su renaci. miento tuvo lugar unos cuarenta años más tarde impulsado por el profundo impacto que tuvieron las teorías de Charles Darwin sobre el pensamiento y desarrollo intelectual del siglo diecinueve. La teoría evolucionaria de Darwin, basada en la supervivencia de los más aptos, fue adaptada política y económicamente por intelectuales. Salvador Casellas p.39-40

[317] Smith, Anthony D. *Ethno-Symbolism and Nationalism: A Cultural Approach.* London; New York, Routledge, 2009.

[318] Dávila, Arlene M. *Sponsored Identities: Cultural Politics in Puerto Rico.* Philadelphia, Temple Univ. Press, 1997.

[319] Smith, Anthony D. *The Ethnic Origins of Nations.* Oxford, Basil Blackwell, 1986

[320] Smith, Anthony D. *Ethno-Symbolism and Nationalism: A Cultural Approach.* London; New York, Routledge, 2009.

[321] "Loss of demographic continuity, on the other hand, either through gradual infertility or through admixture with immigrant populations in sufficient force or through partial genocide, will erode or interrupt ethnic persistence and threaten survival." ---. *The Ethnic Origins of Nations.* Oxford, Basil Blackwell, 1986.

[322] Smith, Anthony D. *Ethno-Symbolism and Nationalism: A Cultural Approach.* London; New York, Routledge, 2009.

[323]Ibid

[324] Ibid

[325] Ibid

[326] Juan Manuel. "El Imaginario Nacional Norteamericano Y El Nacionalismo Puertorriqueño." *Revista De Ciencias Sociales* 7 (1999): 68-85

[327] Smith 74 Smith, Anthony D. *Ethno-Symbolism and Nationalism: A Cultural Approach.* London; New York, Routledge, 2009.

[328] Archivo Albizu Campos. "Albizu Campos Habla Sobre El Estado Libre Asociado de Puerto Rico (PARTE 1 de 3)." *YouTube*, 24 Aug. 2011, www.youtube.com/watch?v=Y9z2Uwh9rfY. Accessed 15 Aug. 2020.

329 Chaar-Pérez, Kahlil. "'A Revolution of Love': Ramón Emeterio Betances, Anténor Firmin, and Affective Communities in the Caribbean." The Global South, vol. 7, no. 2, 28 July 2014, pp. 11–36
330 Ibid
331 Ibid
332 Staudenmaier, Michael. *Puerto Rican Independence Movement, 1898-Present International Encyclopedia of Revolution and Protest.* Blackwell Publishing, 2009.

333 A limited citizenship that was granted by Spain in 1897. It is recognized by the Constitution of Puerto Rico. US recognized the Puerto Rican citizenship starting with the Foraker Act in 1900. Then based on the immigration laws, Puerto Ricans were not allowed to enter US. In 1917, Woodrow Wilson through Jones Act granted citizenship to all Puerto Ricans born in the island.
334 As permitted by Section 349 (a) (5) of the INA, 8 USC 1481 a.
335 Ramírez De Ferrer, Miriam, et al. *Ramírez de Ferrer v. Mari Brás.* 18 Nov 1997
336 "Lozada Colon v. Department of State - Opposition." *www.justice.gov*, 21 Oct. 2014, www.justice.gov/osg/brief/lozada-colon-v-department-state-opposition. Accessed 18 Aug. 2020
337 Tajfel, Henri, and John Turner. *The Social Identity Theory of Intergroup Behavior 277 READING 16.* 2011.
338 Abrams, Dominic, and Michael A. Hogg. *Social Identity Theory: Constructive and Critical Advances.* New York Etc., Harvester Wheatsheaf, 1990
339 Argimiro Ruano. *La Identidad de Los Puertorriqueños.* Mayagüez, P.R., Recinto Universitario De Mayagüez, 2001.

340 Burke, Peter J, and Jan E Stets. *Identity Theory.* New York; Oxford, Oxford University Press, 2009.
Tajfel, Henri, and John Turner. "Social Identity Theory - Tajfel and Turner 1979." *Age-of-the-Sage.Org*, 2019.

341 Dávila, Arlene M. *Sponsored Identities: Cultural Politics in Puerto Rico.* Philadelphia, Temple Univ. Press, 1997.
342 Denis, Nelson A. *War against All Puerto Ricans: Revolution and Terror in America's Colony.* New York, Nation Books, 2016.
343 Ibid
344 Acosta, Ivonne. *La Mordaza: Puerto Rico, 1948-1957.* Río Piedras Puerto Rico, Editorial Edil, 2008.
In 1948, the Puerto Rican Senate passed a bill that restricted freedom

256

of expression related to the nationalist movement. The Senate at the time was controlled by the PPD and presided over by Luis Muionz Marin

345 Ibid

346 Ibid

347 Acceptable refers to an identity that will save the island core identity such as the jibaro, but other than national identity, it is a widely accepted cultural identity and recognizable by all.

348 Muñoz, Luis. "El Joven Muñoz - Archivo s.20 [E05]." *YouTube*, 14 Oct. 2016, www.youtube.com/watch?v=dseMc01Eg-4. Accessed 22 Aug. 2020.

349 Maldonado, A W, and Rico. *Luis Muñoz Marin: Puerto Rico's Democratic Revolution*. San Juan De Puerto Rico, Universidad De Puerto Rico, 2006.

350 Ibid

351 ---. *Nations and Nationalism [by] Ernest Gellner*. Oxford, Blackwell, 1983.

352 Ibid pg 59

353 Ibid pg 60

354 Ibid pg 59

355 Many Puerto Rican who live in the US speak the dialect which equivocally is labeled as a non-sophisticated version of Spanish, yet in reality is the jibaro version of Spanish, and not the standardized language.

356 Sale. Loco de contento con su cargamento para la ciudad
Para la ciudad
Lleva.
En su pensamiento todo un mundo lleno de felicidad
De felicidad
Piensa remediar la situacion
Del hogar que es toda su ilusion
Y alegre.
El jibarito va pensando asi, diciendo asi, cantando asi por el camino
"Si yo vendo mi carga mi Dios querido
Un traje a mi viejita voy a comprar"
Y alegre.
Tambien su yegua va al presentir que su cantar es todo un himno de alegria
En eso le sorprende la luz del dia
Y llegan al mercado de la ciudad
Pasa.
La manana entera sin que nadie pueda su carga comprar
Su carga comprar

Todo.
Todo esta desierto, el pueblo esta muerto de necesidad
De necesidad
Se oye este lamento por doquier
De mi desdichado Borinquen
Y triste.
[357] Gellner's analogy depicts a society divided by loyalties and interests. In this case it illustrates perfectly the rivalry and the lethal conflict between Albizu Campos and Muñoz Marin
[358] Refers to the life of Luis Muñoz Marin in socialists' circles and his association with prominent leftwing writers and poets in New York
[359] *Nations and Nationalism [by] Ernest Gellner.* Oxford, Blackwell, 1983. 60-61
[360] The quote is applicable in the Tydings' bill for independence. A very favorable political situation for Puerto Rico.
[361] *Nations and Nationalism [by] Ernest Gellner.* Oxford, Blackwell, 1983. P. 61

[362] Territory, tradition, culture, ethnicity or multi-ethnic with a shared political purpose and aspiration, that wishes to have a common economy and its own political institutions.
[363] Denis, Nelson A. *War against All Puerto Ricans: Revolution and Terror in America's Colony.* New York, Nation Books, 2016.
[364] José Trias Monge. *El Sistema Judicial de Puerto Rico.* Puerto Rico, Universidad, 1988.

[365] Santiago Caraballo, Josepha. "Agrarian Reform of 1941 - History | EnciclopediaPR." *Encyplopedia Pr. Org,* enciclopediapr.org/en/encyclopedia/agrarian-reform-of-1941/. Accessed 22 Aug. 2020.

[366] Caban, Pedro. *Scholars Archive The Colonizing Mission of the U.S. in Puerto Rico.* 2002.
[367] Denis, Nelson A. *War against All Puerto Ricans: Revolution and Terror in America's Colony.* New York, Nation Books, 2016.

[368] Interview given to Drew Pearson in Washington Merry Go Round after the terrorist attack carried out by Lolita Lebron, Rafael Cancel Miranda, Andres Figueroa, Irvin Flores on March 1, 1954
[369] Caban, Pedro. *Scholars Archive The Colonizing Mission of the U.S. in Puerto Rico.* 2002.
[370] Maldonado, A W, and Rico. *Luis Muñoz Marin: Puerto Rico's Democratic Revolution.* San Juan De Puerto Rico, Universidad De Puerto Rico, 2006.

371 Ibid

372 Maldonado, A W, and Rico. *Luis Muñoz Marin: Puerto Rico's Democratic Revolution*. San Juan De Puerto Rico, Universidad De Puerto Rico, 2006.

373 Muñoz, Luis. "El Joven Muñoz - Archivo s.20 [E05]." *YouTube*, 14 Oct. 2016, www.youtube.com/watch?v=dseMc01Eg-4. Accessed 22 Aug. 2020.

374 Ibid

375 Ibid

376 Maldonado, A W, and Rico. *Luis Muñoz Marin: Puerto Rico's Democratic Revolution*. San Juan De Puerto Rico, Universidad De Puerto Rico, 2006.

377 Muñoz, Luis. "El Joven Muñoz - Archivo s.20 [E05]." *YouTube*, 14 Oct. 2016, www.youtube.com/watch?v=dseMc01Eg-4. Accessed 22 Aug. 2020.

378 Maldonado, A W, and Rico. *Luis Muñoz Marin: Puerto Rico's Democratic Revolution*. San Juan De Puerto Rico, Universidad De Puerto Rico, 2006. pg 58

379Maldonado, A W, and Rico. *Luis Muñoz Marin: Puerto Rico's Democratic Revolution*. San Juan De Puerto Rico, Universidad De Puerto Rico, 2006. pg 58-62

380 Muñoz, Luis. "El Joven Muñoz - Archivo s.20 [E05]." YouTube, 14 Oct. 2016, www.youtube.com/watch?v=dseMc01Eg-4. Accessed 22 Aug. 2020.

381 Ibid

382 Ibid

383 Denis, Nelson A. *War against All Puerto Ricans: Revolution and Terror in America's Colony*. New York, Nation Books, 2016, p. 100

384 https://www.youtube.com/watch?v=dseMc01Eg-4

385 A W. Maldonado Maldonado, A W, and Rico. *Luis Muñoz Marin: Puerto Rico's Democratic Revolution*. San Juan De Puerto Rico, Universidad De Puerto Rico, 2006. pg 142

386 A. W. Maldonado, Luis Muñoz Marín: Puerto Rico's Democratic Revolution, (San Juan, PR: Editorial Universidad de Puerto Rico, 2006) p. 121.

387This was in part due to major strikes that had taken place that year, causing the administration to fear social unrest. Colonel Francis Riggs accompanied Winship as chief of police pg. 121

388 Denis, Nelson A. *War against All Puerto Ricans: Revolution and Terror in America's Colony*. New York, Nation Books, 2016. pg 103

389 Ibid

390 W Maldonado, A W, and Rico. *Luis Muñoz Marin: Puerto Rico's Democratic Revolution*. San Juan De Puerto Rico, Universidad De Puerto Rico, 2006.

391 Denis, Nelson A. *War against All Puerto Ricans: Revolution and Terror in America's Colony*. New York, Nation Books, 2016.

392 Ibid

393 Maldonado, A W, and Rico. *Luis Muñoz Marin: Puerto Rico's Democratic Revolution*. San Juan De Puerto Rico, Universidad De Puerto Rico, 2006.

394 Nelson A. *War against All Puerto Ricans: Revolution and Terror in America's Colony*. New York, Nation Books, 2016.

395 Fuente: Bailey W. Diffie y Justine W. Diffie, Porto Rico: A Broken Pledge. New York, Vanguard Press, 1931, p. 5 (cited in History of Puerto Rico lectura 18)

396 *HISTORIA DE PUERTO RICO LECTURA 18-El Reformismo Popular, Los Años 1940. "Las tierras apropiadas por el gobierno serían distribuidas entre pequeñas familias para propiciar la agricultura de subsistencia y en fincas mayores para promover una agricultura comercial. Entre 1941 y 1945, se repartieron 1,400 parcelas de terreno. Hasta 1960, se habían entregado 58,320 parcelas que comprendían un total de 35,848 cuerdas de terreno. El reparto de tierras no acabó con el problema de la propiedad de la tierra, pero sí lo redujo de forma considerable. Este programa consolidó políticamente al PPD, especialmente, en las zonas rurales. Para la mayoría de las personas que se beneficiaron del reparto de parcelas, la tierra que recibieron era la primera que poseían en su vida y la prueba de que los populares cumplían con sus promesas. Ello le garantizó a Muñoz Marín el respaldo de miles de puertorriqueños"*

397 *HISTORIA DE PUERTO RICO LECTURA 19-El Reformismo Popular, Los Años 1940.*

398 Santiago Caraballo, Josepha. "Agrarian Reform of 1941 - History | EnciclopediaPR." *Encyplopedia Pr. Org*, enciclopediapr.org/en/encyclopedia/agrarian-reform-of-1941/. Accessed 22 Aug. 2020.

399 Muñoz, Luis. "El Joven Muñoz - Archivo s.20 [E05]." *YouTube*, 14 Oct. 2016, www.youtube.com/watch?v=dseMc01Eg-4. Accessed 22 Aug. 2020.

400 Ibid

401 Muñoz, Luis. "El Joven Muñoz - Archivo s.20 [E05]." *YouTube*, 14 Oct. 2016, www.youtube.com/watch?v=dseMc01Eg-4. Accessed 22 Aug. 2020.

402 Staudenmaier, Michael. *Puerto Rican Independence Movement, 1898-Present International Encyclopedia of Revolution and Protest*. Blackwell Publishing, 2009.

403 Marino, John. "Puerto Rican Activist Sentenced." *Www.Washingtonpost.com*, 14 June 2000, www.washingtonpost.com/wp-srv/WPcap/2000-06/14/076r-061400-idx.html. Accessed 22 Aug. 2020.

404 Paoli, Francisco, et al. *PEDRO ALBIZU CAMPOS PIEDRA DE PUERTO RICO*. 2001.

Fredo Arias de la Canal cited in Matos Paoli "Quienes en el gobierno estadounidense crean en la posibilidad de anexar Puerto Rico a la Unión, no conocen las luchas de nuestros castellanos que duraron cinco siglos para recuperar los territorios que les había arrebatado el Islam las luchas contra Bonaparte en el siglo XIX y las luchas contra el fascismo alemán e italiano en el siglo XX

[405]Ibid

[406] Acosta, Ivonne. *La Mordaza: Puerto Rico, 1948-1957*. Río Piedras Puerto Rico, Editorial Edil, 2008.

pg 24

[407] Law 53 of 1948 known as the Gag Law, (Spanish: Ley de La Mordaza) passed by the Puerto Rico legislature of 1948. The law suppressed the freedom of speech and expression as it related to the independence cause. In other words, it was a crime to own or display a Puerto Rican flag, to sing a patriotic tune, to speak or write of independence, or to meet with anyone or hold any assembly in favor of Puerto Rico's independence.

[408] Acosta, Ivonne. *La Mordaza: Puerto Rico, 1948-1957*. Río Piedras Puerto Rico, Editorial Edil, 2008.

[409] Pedro Albizu Campos, and Ivonne Acosta. *La Palabra Como Delito: Los Discursos Por Los Que Condenaron a Pedro Albizu Campos, 1948-1950*. Río Piedras, Puerto Rico, Editorial Cultural, @ Atlanta, Georgia Talleres Gráficos Shekerow Graphics, 2000.

[410] The law was a direct translation of Smith Act, a law that was meant to prohibit the spread of communism in US

[411] Acosta, Ivonne. *La Mordaza: Puerto Rico, 1948-1957*. Río Piedras Puerto Rico, Editorial Edil, 2008.

[412412412412] *Las Carpetas*. Directed by Maite Rivera Carbonell, 2010.

[413413] Ibid

[414] Police files

[415]Jorge. *The Puerto Rican Nation on the Move: Identities on the Island & in the United States*. Chapel Hill, NC, Univ. Of North Carolina Press, 2003. 174-179

[416] Ibid

[417] Marx, the Capital, chapter 26, Expropriation of agriculture fares from their land.

Agrarian Reform of 1941 Puerto Rico.